DECEPTION

DECEPTION

Counterdeception and Counterintelligence

Robert M. Clark

William L. Mitchell

Los Angeles | London | New Delhi
Singapore | Washington DC | Melbourne

FOR INFORMATION:

CQ Press

An Imprint of SAGE Publications, Inc.

2455 Teller Road

Thousand Oaks, California 91320

E-mail: order@sagepub.com

SAGE Publications Ltd.

1 Oliver's Yard

55 City Road

London, EC1Y 1SP

United Kingdom

SAGE Publications India Pvt. Ltd.

B 1/I 1 Mohan Cooperative Industrial Area

Mathura Road, New Delhi 110 044

India

SAGE Publications Asia-Pacific Pte. Ltd.

3 Church Street

#10-04 Samsung Hub

Singapore 049483

Library of Congress Cataloging-in-Publication Data

Names: Clark, Robert M., author. | Mitchell, William L. (William Leslie), author.

Title: Deception : counterdeception and counterintelligence / Robert M. Clark and William L. Mitchell.

Description: First edition. | Washington, DC : CQ Press, [2019] | Includes bibliographical references and index.

Identifiers: LCCN 2017036696 | ISBN 9781506375236 (pbk.)

Subjects: LCSH: Deception (Military science) | Deception. | Intelligence service. | Military intelligence. | Deception (Military science)–Case studies.

Classification: LCC U167.5.D37 C53 2019 | DDC 355.3/432–dc23 LC record available at https://lccn.loc.gov/2017036696

Acquisitions Editor: Scott Greenan

Editorial Assistant: Sarah Christensen

Production Editor: Tracy Buyan

Copy Editor: Amy Marks

Typesetter: Hurix Digital

Proofreader: Annie Lubinsky

Indexer: Amy Murphy

Cover Designer: Scott Van Atta

Marketing Manager: Jennifer Jones

18 19 20 21 22 10 9 8 7 6 5 4 3 2 1

BRIEF CONTENTS

PART I: FUNDAMENTALS OF DECEPTION AND COUNTERDECEPTION

PART II: EXERCISES

DETAILED CONTENTS

PART II: EXERCISES

LIST OF TABLES, FIGURES, AND BOXES

Chapter 4. The Target

Chapter 5. The Story

Chapter 6. The Channels

Chapter 7. The Traditional Intelligence Channels

Chapter 8. The Cyberspace Channel

Chapter 9. Planning and Executing Deception

Chapter 10. Preparing to Counter Deception

Chapter 11. Identifying Deception

PART II: EXERCISES

Chapter 12. Sensor Mapping and Channel Tracking Exercises

PREFACE

All warfare is based on deception.

Sun Tzu

This book is about deception: Specifically, it addresses deception as an instrument for gaining advantage in conflict. So we explain and discuss the principles and practice of deception across all levels of government and non-government activity, especially as it is practiced to support military operations, national security, and law enforcement.

Although deception is the dominant theme, the book explores the commonality of deception, counterintelligence (CI), and psychological operations (PSYOPS). These have long been treated as separate and independent disciplines, because they tend to be separated organizationally. But to teach them as separate is a mistake; they have too many common features. This book takes a different perspective, highlighting the shared principles and methodology that underlie all three. All have the same end objective: to shape the perceptions and subsequent actions of a target (an individual or group) in such a way as to produce a favorable outcome for your side in conflicts among organizations and governments.

The core principles and methodology of deception underlie successful counterintelligence, so the book concerns CI in the most general sense of the term. Most books on "counterintelligence" focus on counterespionage—or the detecting and defeating of spies. But counterintelligence is much more than that. All counterespionage is counterintelligence, but not all counterintelligence is counterespionage. So, many of the examples in the book are about counterintelligence writ large; that is, attacking an opponent's intelligence service and inducing it to reach an erroneous conclusion through deception.

The same core principles and methodology underlie successful PSYOPS. As is the case with counterespionage, the book does not cover the subject in depth. It instead focuses on the application of deception in PSYOPS, and especially in one form of the discipline. PSYOPS comes in three forms: white (source of the message is acknowledged), gray (source is concealed), and black (purports to come from another source, usually an opponent). White and gray PSYOPS occasionally make use of deception. Black PSYOPS, often conducted as a covert operation, inevitably relies on deception. For that reason, it is the primary context for considering the topic in this book.

Although a number of books and journal articles deal with the historical and theoretical aspects of deception, the focus tends toward Soviet-era disinformation disciplines, which are now dated. This book includes many historical examples because the principles are still relevant, but also highlighted are more current illustrations. And deception is typically presented almost as an afterthought in intelligence and operations courses. But deception is deserving of its own educational and training infrastructure that fits into today's strategic context. Since the Russian deception that supported its annexation of Crimea in 2014, increasing attention is being given to the concept of deception. This text is designed to elevate the level of education in intelligence and operations courses in terms of deception planning as well as detecting and countering deception.

The basic principles of deception have not changed, and we'll cover them in some detail. But information technology, and specifically social media, constitutes a new collection asset (and new channels for deception). In that role, it adds a new dynamic to both the conduct and detection of deception activities, both in their traditional roles and as a part of counterintelligence or psychological operations. For example, the cyber domain provides a powerful channel for conducting deception. Accordingly, it receives special attention.

The book provides a main framework for a deception planning course for the civilian academic community, the intelligence community, and the military. It bridges the divide between theory and practice concerning deception that sometimes separates these communities. The target audience includes intelligence analysts and operational planners, and the book addresses both perspectives. Operations professionals have few chances during an entire career to observe the successful execution of a deception operation. A book that illustrates deception theory using historical and modern-day cases and provides opportunities to practice with hypothetical case studies will especially benefit them.

Part I of the book presents organizing frameworks (concepts) for thinking about deception. It extends the existing concepts and theory, applying a systems approach and a focus on outcome scenario thinking. Deception has to be related to the operational planner's end objective, a concept that hasn't been well understood or practiced in the past. A section on theory is followed by a discussion of the methodology for conducting deception and detecting it when it is used by an opponent. The book bridges both the historical and the theoretical aspects of deception with guidance on the practical execution of deception planning. It therefore is unique in providing step-by-step training for intelligence analysts and operational planners (practitioners of deception) to learn how to prepare for and execute deception operations, as well as how to identify an opponent's deceptions.

Part II of the book presents a series of exercises on deception and counterdeception set in current time. Although the basic concepts of deception endure, new means of conducting deception are available because of advances in information technology.

DISCLAIMER

This does not constitute an official release of CIA information. All statements of fact, opinion, or analysis expressed herein are those of the authors and do not reflect the official positions or view of the Central Intelligence Agency (CIA) or any other US government agency, the Royal Danish Defence College (RDDC), or any other Danish government agency. Nothing in the contents should be construed as asserting or implying US government authentication of information or agency endorsement of the authors' views. This material has been reviewed solely for classification.

ACKNOWLEDGMENTS

Many people throughout the US and European intelligence communities, military services, and academia have provided wisdom that we have incorporated; we cannot name them all, but we appreciate their help. We are especially grateful to reviewers Anthony Bishop, University of Massachusetts Lowell; Gary Chase, University of South Florida Sarasota-Manatee; Kathy Hogan, University of Maryland University College; Frank Plantan, University of Pennsylvania; Mark Stout, Johns Hopkins University; Ronald W. Vardy, University of Houston; and Carl Anthony Wege, College of Coastal Georgia and several anonymous reviewers who have contributed their time to improving the text. We also wish to thank Scott Greenan, Duncan Marchbank, Scott Van Atta, and Tracy Buyan at CQ Press, with special thanks to copy editor Amy Marks for a superb job in shaping the finished product.

Above all, we are thankful for the efforts of Dr. Clark's wife and partner in this effort, Abigail, whose extensive revisions made this a better book.

Robert M. Clark
Wilmington, North Carolina

William L. Mitchell
Copenhagen, Denmark

ABOUT THE AUTHORS

Robert M. Clark currently is an independent consultant performing threat analyses for the US intelligence community. He is also a faculty member of the Intelligence and Security Academy and adjunct professor of intelligence studies at the Johns Hopkins University. He previously was a faculty member of the Director of National Intelligence (DNI) Intelligence Community Officers' course and course director of the DNI introduction to the intelligence community course. Dr. Clark served as a US Air Force electronics warfare officer and intelligence officer, reaching the rank of lieutenant colonel. At the Central Intelligence Agency (CIA), he was a senior analyst and group chief responsible for managing analytic methodologies. Clark holds an SB from MIT, a PhD in electrical engineering from the University of Illinois, and a JD from George Washington University. He has previously authored three books: *Intelligence Analysis: A Target-Centric Approach* (5th edition, 2016), *The Technical Collection of Intelligence* (2010), and *Intelligence Collection* (2014). He was co-editor, with Dr. Mark Lowenthal, of *The Five Disciplines of Intelligence Collection* (2016). He co-authored *Target-Centric Network Modeling* (2016) with Dr. William L. Mitchell.

William L. Mitchell's military and intelligence career spans three decades, including operations in Afghanistan, the Balkans, Iraq, Africa, and French Guiana. Dr. Mitchell is currently an active member of Danish Defence as an advisor, instructor, and lecturer. While at the Royal Danish Defence College (RDDC), he was responsible for the synchronization of theory, practice, and education regarding intelligence, joint, and special operations. He served as a member of the RDDC Research Board and continues to support NATO and US Department of Defense research, education, and doctrine development programs. He co-authored *Target-Centric Network Modeling* (2016) with Robert M. Clark, has several publications on military intelligence and battlespace agility, and was awarded the 2014 NATO Scientific Achievement Award for his contributions to NATO research. Dr. Mitchell has a BA, an MA with distinction from Kent University, and a PhD in political science from Aarhus University. He is a decorated war veteran of two countries, with one citation and several medals, including the French Croix de Combatant and the Danish Defence medal.

FUNDAMENTALS OF DECEPTION AND COUNTERDECEPTION

PART ONE

DECEPTION

The Basics

Oh what a tangled web we weave
When first we practise to deceive!

Marmion: A Tale of Flodden Field, Sir Walter Scott

This chapter introduces the basics of deception and the role of intelligence in both supporting and defeating deception. It sets the stage, with definitions and a set of basic principles, for the following chapters that explain how to conduct deception and to identify an opponent's use of it. But first, let's look at the case of a *perfect* deception—something that happens only in the movies, of course.

THE STING

The popular media have given us many great stories about well-conducted deceptions. The staged "sinking" of a Soviet ballistic missile submarine in *The Hunt for Red October* (1990) and the elaborate scam to steal $160 million from a casino owner in *Ocean's Eleven* (2001) come to mind. But few if any Hollywood movies can offer the beautifully executed deception operation set forth in the 1973 film *The Sting*.

The film is set in 1936, in the depths of the Great Depression. In it, a small-time con man Johnny Hooker (Robert Redford) has helped pull off a minor street scam with his friend Luther. Unfortunately for them, it turns out that the mark was a courier of crime boss Doyle Lonnegan (Robert Shaw) and Luther is quickly tracked and killed. Hooker must run for his life from Lonnegan's revenge. (Lonnegan does not know what Hooker looks like, which turns out to be a key part of the story.) Hooker gets advice that perhaps Luther's old friend, the legendary con

(Continued)

(Continued)

master Henry Gondorff (Paul Newman) can help him start anew, and tracks down Gondorff, who is hiding in Chicago from the FBI. Hooker subsequently persuades Gondorff to undertake an elaborate con operation, partially to honor Luther, targeting Lonnegan.

The scam begins when Gondorff, posing as a Chicago bookie, joins Lonnegan's high-stakes poker game on a train, and outsmarts and out-cheats Lonnegan to the tune of $15,000. In the process he earns Lonnegan's enmity by behaving boorishly, gloating over his winnings, and repeatedly mispronouncing Lonnegan's name. Hooker, posing as Gondorff's employee, visits Lonnegan's berth, supposedly to collect the winnings. He instead convinces Lonnegan that he wants to betray boorish Gondorff and take over the bookie operation with the help of a partner who works in the Chicago Western Union office. The scheme involves giving the wire results of horse races to Lonnegan, who then bets on the winning horses *before* the results arrive at Gondorff's betting parlor. After winning a race in this fashion, Lonnegan decides to bet $500,000 (about $10 million at today's prices) on the next race to wipe out Gondorff's operation and exact revenge.

At the same time, an unexpected visitor arrives: a corrupt police officer named Snyder, who is searching for Hooker in Chicago after being victimized by a counterfeit money payoff. He is intercepted by undercover FBI agents led by Agent Polk and is ordered to help them arrest Gondorff with Hooker's aid. Snyder subsequently captures Hooker and brings him to Polk. Polk then pressures Hooker into betraying Gondorff.

The next day, at the designated time, Lonnegan receives the tip to "place it on Lucky Dan," and makes his $500,000 bet at Gondorff's parlor. The race description is another part of the scam—broadcast by an announcer in a back room of the parlor. As the race begins, the tipster arrives, and when told that Lonnegan had bet on Lucky Dan to win, explains that when he said "place it" he meant, literally, that Lucky Dan would "place." The panicked Lonnegan rushes to the teller window and demands his money back, but the teller says he is too late. At this moment, Agent Polk, Snyder, and a half-dozen FBI officers break into the parlor. Agent Polk tells Gondorff that he is under arrest and informs Hooker that he is free to go. In reaction to the apparent treachery, Gondorff shoots down Hooker; Agent Polk guns down Gondorff and tells Snyder to get Lonnegan out of there and away from the crime scene.

Once Lonnegan and Snyder are gone, Gondorff and Hooker get up, unhurt—their deception is complete. "Agent Polk" and his fellow "agents" are, of course, part of the con.

Aside from its entertainment value, the movie illustrates many features of a deception operation that are covered in this book:

- It has an objective, or desired outcome scenario for the perpetrators: relieving the target—Lonnegan—of $500,000 and escaping before he finds out that he has been duped.

- It presents a story—a false picture of reality—for Lonnegan to believe, in order to get him to make the $500,000 bet.

- It has several channels for presenting the story: the poker game set-up, Hooker's representations about replacing Gondorff, the fake betting parlor, a fake race announcer in the parlor back room, a staged meeting with the tipster at the Western Union office, the intrusion of "Agent Polk," and Gondorff's and Polk's shootings.

- It demonstrates the importance of a good understanding of the opponent. In this case, Lonnegan's greed is a factor, of course. But also important is his overwhelming need to "pay back" for insults or injuries suffered, in this case from a loss in a poker game to a man he despised. And, a contributing factor to the deception's success is Lonnegan's desire for respectability that causes him to depart the scene of a shooting, leaving behind his money.

- It sets up Lonnegan for the desired decision or action steps by presenting him with the opportunity to "pay back" Gondorff for humiliating him in the poker game.

- It shows a fine sense of timing that is often critical in the execution of a deception—the Western Union tipster arriving at the right moment to send Lonnegan into a panic, and "Agent Polk's" immediate arrival to force the end game before Lonnegan could recover his wits.

The movie also illustrates some other points. Most deceptions require good showmanship, and Hollywood understands how to put on a good show—a talent that the US government occasionally calls on, as we'll see in a later case study. In every deception, curveballs will present themselves. Success demands constant observing, orienting, and reacting as events unfold. The sudden appearance of the corrupt local cop, Snyder, looking for Hooker had to be dealt with. The deception plan was changed to include him as a target. It also creates an outcome that most often is the ideal—the "mark" or opponent, Lonnegan, never realized that he had been deceived (nor did Snyder). On some occasions, though, you prefer for an opponent to know he's been deceived because of the subsequent bad decisions that he makes.

Deception itself is a word that has been used in a great many contexts, from deliberate acts within wars between nations to the deliberate acts in personal relationships as exemplified in *The Sting*. In this sense deception is a process. As it is used in this book, it also refers to a deliberate and rational process executed by an actor, in order to benefit that actor within a subjective context. The spectrum of contexts in this book is focused on actions promoting governmental rather than private interests. That includes, for example, the intelligence and operational planning processes of military, police, and/or civilian organizations.

Before expounding on the specific principles stemming from this definition, context, and framework for deception, it is worth spending a little time answering the question: Why should deception be useful to antagonists in a conflict situation?

WHY DECEPTION?

There is no better place to start than by explaining why deception is important, even essential, in the conduct of national and domestic security affairs. Countries with a substantial edge in the instruments of national power often perceive deception as something that benefits a weak power but is generally a less worthy effort for the powerful. Statistics—in military conflicts, at least—don't support that assumption, as we'll show in a moment.

One does not conduct deception for the sake of deception itself. It is always conducted as a part of a conflict or in a competitive context, intended to support some overarching plan or objectives of a participant. In a military and civilian intelligence context, the overarching plan or strategy is usually stated clearly. So in this context, the most direct answer is the following axiom: The more successful the deception in support of a plan, the greater the chance the plan will be successful. In dealing with war and security issues, measures of success are usually characterized by precious resources that include material and people. Though by no means exhaustive on the issue, one of the most accessible studies as to the effects of employing deception in operational- and strategic-level military planning is Barton Whaley's 1969 book *Stratagem, Deception and Surprise in War*.[1] By drawing on the comparative analysis of 122 historical cases, Whaley shows a clear relationship between deception, surprise, and the ratio of adversary to friendly casualty results from engagements. Figure 1-1 illustrates his results. The bottom axis is the ratio of adversary to friendly casualties—higher numbers are better. As one succeeds in either deception or surprise, casualty ratios become more favorable. The ratio improves dramatically when deception is used *and* surprise is achieved.

Favorable casualty ratios are important; however, winning in a conflict must take precedence, and that requires successful operations. In Figure 1-2, the comparative study results illustrate one clear principle: As the intensity of your adversary's surprise increases, so does your chance for a successful operation. (Low surprise equates to a 1 or 2 on a scale of 0 to 5, where 0 equals no surprise; high surprise equates to a 3, 4, or 5 on that scale.)

So one answer to "Why deception?" is embedded in the dynamics of the conflict itself. Successful deception increases the intensity of surprise; the higher the intensity of surprise, the higher the chance of operational success. And in terms of armed conflict, high intensity of surprise means higher enemy casualties and lower friendly casualties. On this final dynamic, if minimizing

FIGURE 1-1 ■ Effect of Deception and Surprise on Casualties

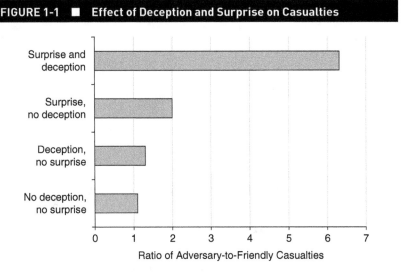

Source: Drawn by authors from statistics in Barton Whaley, *Stratagem, Deception and Surprise in War* [reprint of 1969 edition] (Norwood, MA: Artech House Publishing, 2007), 104, tables 5.19 and 5.20.

casualties and loss of material is important, then one should attempt to use deception to increase the intensity of surprise. In fact, many observers would argue that commanders responsible for the overarching plan owe as much to their troops.

Surprise clearly is an important factor in any conflict outcome, along with deception; and the two are almost always related, since surprise often is the result of deception. The two in combination are highly effective, as Figure 1-1 indicates. Intensity of surprise is also a significant factor, as Figure 1-2 shows. The percentage of defeat for the attacker in conflicts drops most dramatically as one goes from no surprise (60 percent defeats) to high surprise (2 percent defeats).

The scope of operations for militaries has widened significantly from twentieth-century state-centric interactions. Conflicts are generally more complex, with constellations of actors having diverse functions and organizational cultures becoming involved in transnational conflicts. The importance of fundamental deception skills with relation to intelligence and operational planning cannot be overstated. Deception, possibly more than ever, is an essential dynamic of conflict; therefore, how to conduct and detect it is an essential part of a twenty-first-century military's preparation of the battlespace.

Furthermore, deception has a substantial role to play in all conflicts, not just military ones. Governments must be able to apply deception activity in conflicts across the political, military, economic, social, infrastructure, and

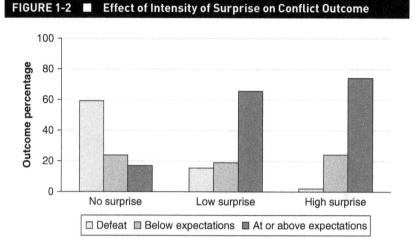

FIGURE 1-2   ■   Effect of Intensity of Surprise on Conflict Outcome

□ Defeat   ▨ Below expectations   ■ At or above expectations

Source: Drawn by authors from statistics in Barton Whaley, *Stratagem, Deception and Surprise in War* [reprint of 1969 edition] (Norwood, MA: Artech House Publishing, 2007), 115, merged tables 5.30 and 5.31.

information (PMESII) domains. Nonstate actors such as terrorists, criminal groups, and other militants directly engage governments through social and economic lines of operation. The insurgents in Afghanistan offer "shadow" governance. Hezbollah militancy in Lebanon has a strong social and economic engagement, as did Daesh (also known as ISIS, ISIL, or IS) in Syria, Libya, and Iraq. However, "shadow governance" in Afghanistan is also a cover for narcotics cartels. The social and economic engagement of Hezbollah conceals ideological activities that support a militant agenda and Iranian foreign policy. Daesh did the reverse, using a radical religious ideological screen to hide the fragile economic and social connections to the Sunni tribes that form their support base on the strategic level. On the operational level they disguise their intelligence organization as an organization of tribal engagement offices in major communities. They hide military command and control (C2) within the social domain of the population they control.

The statistics shown in Figure 1-1 and Figure 1-2 are generally available for the outcomes of military conflict. No similar statistics have been found that deal with the many deceptions in the political, economic, and social realms, in part because outcomes of "victory" or "defeat" are harder to establish in those arenas. But it is likely that similar ratios of success for both deception and surprise apply in all the fields of conflict covered in this book. Comparable statistics do not exist for the counterintelligence or psychological operations (PSYOPS) disciplines for good reason. The statistics are almost binary: Failure of the deception almost always means failure of the operation. The series of deceptions executed by Soviet and later Russian intelligence to protect two major US sources for almost twenty years, Aldrich Ames and Robert Hanssen, are described in Chapter 6. Those two were able to operate long after they should have been caught because the deceptions were so successful. The World War II *Black Boomerang* PSYOPS described in Chapter 3 succeeded because its listeners continued to believe that they were hearing a German Wehrmacht radio broadcast.

With that introduction, the following section provides a deeper dive into the definitions of deception, counterdeception, counterintelligence, and PSYOPS as they are used in the remainder of the book.

DEFINITIONS

Deception

There are a number of definitions of deception in a variety of contexts, some of which overlap. The eminent author on deception, Barton Whaley, defines deception as

> Information (conveyed by statement, action, or object) intended to manipulate the behavior of others by inducing them to accept a false or distorted perception of reality—their physical, social, or political environment.[2]

Another prominent writer on the topic, J. Boyer Bell, defines deception very simply:

> Deception is the process of advantageously imposing the false on a target's perception of reality.[3]

Both definitions are accurate in the sense of defining an end result, in terms of the belief and/or behavior of others. Both also correctly describe deception as a process of deliberately inducing misperception in a target person or group of people. Deception is therefore not an accidental or unintended outcome.

Whaley explicitly takes the definition one step further, and it is an important step. His focus is on *manipulating behavior based on a false picture*. That's the widely accepted view: that belief is not enough; action (or refraining from an action that otherwise would be taken) is required for it to be deception.

However, Bell's definition explicitly recognizes that manipulating the behavior of others may not result in a good outcome, from the deceiver's perspective. In Whaley's definition, one could succeed with deception and have an unfavorable outcome, something that has happened many times in history, a few examples of which appear in this book. Bell's definition takes this into account by using the word *advantageously*; but in doing so, he excludes unfavorable outcomes. Whether it succeeds or fails, a deception is still a deception.

In this book, we simply add a word to Bell's formulation to encompass all of the cases discussed:

> Deception is a process intended to advantageously impose the false on a target's perception of reality.

This concise definition includes three basic concepts that we'll revisit frequently:

1. It emphasizes the idea that deception must have a *target.* In the next section, we'll introduce a structured approach to thinking about the targets. The section following that discusses the means, in the form of basic principles of deception.

2. It promotes the idea of using deception to gain an *advantage.* The key to deception planning is being able to envision a future situation that is more advantageous to the pursuit of the deceiver's objectives than if he or she did not conduct a deception. That future situation takes the form of a "desired" scenario to be achieved through deception, as later chapters will discuss.

3. It highlights the concept of imposing the *false* on the target's perception of reality. This false perception takes the form of a *story,* which will be discussed in Chapter 5.

Deception generally comes in two basic forms: misleading and ambiguity-increasing.

- *Misleading deceptions* reduce ambiguity by increasing the attractiveness of a wrong alternative.[4] These have the objective of getting an opponent to believe a false picture of the situation. Known in the literature as "M" type deception, it is designed to mislead an adversary toward a specific and preconceived direction.

- *Ambiguity-increasing deceptions,* by contrast, increase uncertainty or confusion so that the target is unsure as to what to believe. They are often referred to as "A" type deceptions. Such deceptions often seek to ensure that the level of ambiguity always remains high enough to protect the secret of the actual operation. Ambiguity-increasing deceptions seek to conceal critical elements of the truth to lead the opponent away from the truth, not necessarily to a specific alternative, but simply to increase the range of incorrect alternatives that the opponent must take into account.

Counterdeception

Much like the definition of deception, the term *counterdeception* is often differentiated by context and organizational mission. For example, the US Department of Defense definition follows:

Efforts to negate, neutralize, diminish the effects of, or gain advantage from a foreign deception operation. Counterdeception does not include the intelligence function of identifying foreign deception operations.[5]

This doctrinal distinction of counterdeception illustrates the prevailing view of a clear dividing line between intelligence (identifying and assessing deception) and the operational response employed to counter deception.

Intelligence organizations and many textbook authors on the subject use a definition similar to this one below, also isolating intelligence analysis from operations in countering deception:

Counterdeception is an analytic process of identifying and assessing an opponent's deception operations. It usually is an intelligence function.[6]

This text is primarily focused on the intelligence component of counterdeception. In fact, Chapter 11, titled "Identifying Deception," is addressed to the intelligence team tasked with identification. This emphasis is a matter of priorities: One cannot deal with deception operationally until the deception has been identified and assessed.

But it is counterproductive and intellectually artificial to chop into parts what is, in reality, an interactive process involving both intelligence and operations. Therefore, counterdeception in this book refers to the collaborative practice of both identification and operational response to deception.

Counterintelligence

The US government defines counterintelligence as follows:

Counterintelligence (CI) refers to information gathered and activities conducted to protect against espionage, other intelligence activities, sabotage, or assassinations conducted for or on behalf of foreign powers, organizations or persons or international terrorist activities.[7]

The focus of this definition is on counterespionage. But counterintelligence today is more than counterespionage, and a broader perspective is needed in courses that focus on teaching the counterintelligence discipline. Most intelligence collection today relies on what the definition refers to as "other intelligence activities": open source (OSINT) and technical means—imagery intelligence (IMINT), signals intelligence (SIGINT), cyber intelligence (CYBER), and measurements and signatures intelligence (MASINT). Counterintelligence in general and deception in particular must consider all of these "INTs," or what we refer to in this book as *channels* of communication, adversarial collection, and adversarial analytical processes.

Operations

Operations is often thought of in a military context, and many of the examples in this book describe deception to support military operations. But law enforcement conducts operations to deter crime and capture criminals; and CI, as the previous definition indicates, includes "activities"—that is, operations. And nongovernmental organizations such as criminal and terrorist groups conduct operations. So the term is used in its most general sense throughout the book, in two ways: to describe an action taken, and to refer to an organization that executes political, informational, or economic as well as military actions.

Psychological Operations

Finally, before going further into the subject of deception, it's important to define psychological operations. The US military definition is as follows:

> *Psychological operations* (PSYOPS) are planned operations to convey selected information and indicators to audiences to influence their emotions, motives, and objective reasoning, and ultimately the behavior of governments, organizations, groups, and individuals.[8]

Note that this definition is somewhat broader than the definitions of deception conveyed at the beginning of this section, but it includes them all. The distinction between deception and psychological operations is often confusing to both outsiders and practitioners. One difference is the emphasis on results: PSYOPS stresses the resulting *perception* in the expectation that a desired behavior will follow. Deception emphasizes the opponent's *behavior* that produces a favorable outcome. Another difference is that PSYOPS includes conveying true information, sometimes without any falsehood. Deception, in contrast, requires conveying false information.

THE DECEPTION TARGET

All deceptions are aimed at a target. The principles, methodology, and examples in this book are concerned with three classes of targets: a decision maker, usually a military or national leader; an opposing intelligence service; or a defined group (other than an intelligence service). The target is different in each instance. But all three targets have things in common: Deception against them has a desired outcome scenario, and against all, one can make use of either misleading or ambiguity-increasing deception.

The Decision Maker

Most of the literature on deception is about targeting the decision maker for misleading deception, with good reason. In military operations where the most deceptions are conducted, misleading the opposing commander usually results in success on the battlefield. Former deputy undersecretary of the US Army Thaddeus Holt has written the definitive account of Allied deception operations during World War II. In his book *The Deceivers* he enumerates the key commandments of misleading deception that were developed during that war. They fit well with the Whaley definition of deception:

- Your goal is not to make the opponent *think* something; it is to make the opponent *do* something.

- You want your opponent not only to do something—but do something specific.

- It is not always necessary to make the decision maker in your target network believe in the false state of affairs that you want to project; but it is enough to make him so concerned over its likelihood that he feels that he must provide for it.

- Non-action is a form of action; the decision to do nothing is still a decision.

- The decision maker(s) are the targets of deception, the intelligence services are the customers of deception.[9]

In Holt's portrayal, deception is a planned process, intentionally designed and executed to make the target of deception do, or not do, something specific. It is not intended to describe stand-alone disinformation or psychological operations, though both of these could definitely be supporting activities to a deception plan.

Sometimes it is enough to leave the opponent confused and uncertain. But a confused and uncertain opponent is likely to act unpredictably, and the deceiver cannot control the opponent's actions. The outcome may not be what was intended. Furthermore, an opponent can correct for confusion and uncertainty as the situation becomes clearer.

In targeting decision makers, misleading deception usually produces better results than ambiguity-increasing deception. The best outcomes usually happen when the opponent is certain—and wrong. And one should never underestimate the demoralizing effect of an opponent's discovering that he or she has been deceived when it is too late to recover.

The Intelligence Service

An opponent's intelligence service is usually thought of as a channel for deception. The last of Holt's commandments—that intelligence services are customers, not targets—sums up that idea. But an intelligence organization also can be the target. In counterintelligence, a frequent purpose of deception is to mislead an adversary's intelligence service about the deceivers' intelligence capabilities—what are known as "sources and methods."

So deception to support counterintelligence usually is intended to mislead. It is well known that if a deceiver can get an intelligence unit to reach a certain conclusion, it will stick with that conclusion until evidence to the contrary becomes overwhelming. The case studies about the Ames and Hanssen deceptions in Chapter 6 illustrate this. Ambiguity-increasing deceptions, by contrast, can have an opposite and generally undesired effect in counterintelligence; they can focus the opposing service on resolving the ambiguity. Of course, time is a relevant factor here. If it will take the opposing service a month to resolve the ambiguity, that may be all the time we need for the deception to be successful.

A Defined Group

Both misleading and ambiguity-increasing deceptions have important roles to play in the newer types of conflict encountered in international affairs. As these nontraditional conflicts continue to develop and as new channels open for sending a deception message to large groups, there is a need for long-term deception that is not tied to specific events or not intended to produce a specific decision. The outcome can be simply a favorable situation or state of affairs. Such deceptions typically target a defined group—an organization or even an entire population.

Deception usually targets a defined group to support psychological operations. In this role, it often overlaps with both misleading and ambiguity-increasing deception. It includes deception that does not result in a decision and action by an individual and does not fall into the realm of counterintelligence. What it shares with both of those is that it does produce an outcome.

We previously noted that an intelligence service will stick with a conclusion until the evidence against it becomes overwhelming. That's even more true for many defined groups that are targets of deception. Boston Globe Media Group science writer Sharon Begley has referred to this phenomenon as the "stickiness of misinformation." Begley notes that the more familiar we are with a claim or rumor, the more likely we are to believe it—even if the familiarity comes from attempts to debunk the claim or rumor.[10]

The view of the deception target as a defined group was developed in China nearly two millennia ago. It is recorded in a book called *Thirty-Six Stratagems* that originated in both oral and written Chinese history, with many different versions compiled by different authors over time. The book was rediscovered during World War II and popularized after the Communists came to power in China. Most of the thirty-six stratagems—which use colorful metaphors to convey the concepts— are about either deception or the use of deception as an enabler.

The perspective presented in the *Thirty-Six Stratagems* fits both non-Western views of deception and those of some nongovernmental organizations, especially terrorists and criminal groups. This perspective stresses the value of ambiguity-increasing deception, or deception in which the main objective might be none other than to create uncertainty or even chaos.

One subset of the stratagems is foreign to current Western thinking about the opponent as a deception target—though Niccolò Machiavelli would undoubtedly recognize them, since he argued for the same stratagems in the sixteenth century. This subset emphasizes the use of deception against neutrals or even allies instead of opponents. Some examples follow:

- *Kill with a borrowed sword.* Attack an opponent using the strength of a third party. Use deception to persuade an ally to attack, for example.

- *Watch the fires burning across the river.* Avoid engaging in a multiforce conflict until all the others—opponents, neutrals, and allies—have exhausted themselves. Then enter the conflict with your forces intact. The form of deception implied by this stratagem is to use deceit to conceal your real intent from the others.

- *Borrow the road to conquer the State of Guo.* Borrow from an ally the means to attack a common enemy. After defeating the enemy, use those same means to attack the ally that lent them to you.[11]

The second set of stratagems (below) violates Holt's maxim for misleading deception against decision makers cited earlier: that the goal is to make the opponent *do* something. These mostly fall into the PSYOPS realm. The objective here is to use all means, including deception, to create chaos and to destabilize the opponent, thereby creating a favorable outcome scenario. There are several of these in the thirty-six stratagems, suggesting that they play an important role in Chinese thinking about conflict. Some examples follow:

- *Remove the firewood from under the pot.* This argues for an indirect approach, rather than directly confronting an opponent. Operations are aimed instead at the opponent's ability to wage a conflict.

- *Trouble the water to catch a fish.* Create confusion in the opponent's organization and use it to promote your objectives.

- *Feign madness but keep your balance.* Pretend to be a fool or a madman. Create confusion about your motives and intent. Encourage an opponent to underestimate your ability and make him overconfident.

- *Hit the grass to startle the snake.* Do something spectacular but apparently purposeless, strange, or unexpected to confuse the opponent or provoke a response that furthers your goals.

- *Replace the beams with rotten timbers.* Disrupt the opponent's organization or standard processes. The idea is to tear apart the opponent's cohesiveness.

- *Let the enemy's own spy sow discord in the enemy camp.* Undermine your enemy's ability to fight by secretly causing discord between her and her friends, allies, advisors, family, commanders, soldiers, and population. While she is preoccupied settling internal disputes, her ability to attack or defend is compromised.

Once the stage has been set using one or more of these stratagems, then it is time to apply the execution or follow-up stratagem:

- *Loot a burning house.* When an organization is racked with internal conflicts, disorganized, and confused; when the environment is plagued by outside elements such as crime and corruption; then the opponent will be weak and unable to prevail in conflict. Then you attack it without mercy and totally destroy it.[12]

An example of this approach is contained in a 2000 book called *Proteus*, sponsored by the US National Reconnaissance Office. The book has a hypothetical future scenario called "Militant Shangri-La."[13] In that scenario, an alliance of Asian and African nations executes a strategy supported by deception with the simple objective of keeping the United States and its allies on the edge of chaos—nothing more. Viewed from a Western perspective, the scenario posed an unclear threat.[14] Viewed from many Asian cultural perspectives, the strategy was both elegant and clear: Leave the opponent confused and uncertain, plagued with internal disagreements, unable to think or act effectively.

The deception approaches and objectives presented in the *Thirty-Six Stratagems* are worth noting as a different perspective for thinking about deception, for two reasons. First, it may be useful in some conflicts to make use of deception for no other purpose than to create uncertainty and confusion, even chaos. Second, it is important in countering deception to recognize that such deceptions may be used against your side.

The use of deception to destabilize has often been applied against criminal and terrorist groups and in international economic matters. The British have demonstrated some skill in this area, as the next case illustrates.

THE IRA EMBEZZLEMENT STING

In the early 1970s, the British were engaged in a bitter conflict with the Irish Republican Army (IRA) in Northern Ireland. The two sides conducted several deceptive operations against each other. One British operation was designed to aggravate an emerging split between older IRA leadership and a younger faction of leaders. The veteran leaders were willing to consider a cease-fire with the British; the younger faction opposed any cease-fire.

Called the Embezzlement Sting, the deception was carried out largely by a British unit called the Mobile Reconnaissance Force. It relied primarily on allegations made to the press by a British double agent named Louis Hammond, a Belfast Catholic who had joined the British Army's Royal Irish Rangers in 1970.

The Embezzlement Sting began when Hammond contacted two *Sunday Times* reporters claiming to be an IRA agent who had infiltrated the Mobile Reconnaissance Force on IRA orders. Hammond provided the reporters with what he identified as an internal IRA memorandum alleging that the IRA leadership was embezzling funds. The bogus document was purportedly written by a senior IRA leader in Long Kesh Prison. It alleged that seven leaders of an IRA battalion had embezzled £150,000 of IRA funds. Hammond told the reporters that he had contacted them because the leaders of the battalion had betrayed the faith and he wanted to see them punished. To bolster his claim to be a double agent working against the British, he gave the journalists basic organizational information about the Mobile Reconnaissance Force—information that the British government later confirmed in a press conference.

Convinced that Hammond's story was genuine, the journalists published a series of articles in the *Sunday Times* describing IRA corruption. The first article was titled "IRA Provo Chiefs Milk £150,000 from Funds," and cited as its source a former intelligence officer of an IRA company.

Unfortunately for Hammond, the press article pointed directly to him. The IRA enforcement arm seized him and conducted an intense interrogation. Hammond confessed to working for the British and was then shot three times in the head and once in the stomach. The IRA gunmen then dropped Hammond's apparently dead body in a deserted alleyway. Hammond somehow survived, partially paralyzed and with the loss of one eye.[15]

The deception was facilitated by information provided through a separate channel. Whenever the IRA robbed a bank to fund its operations, the British made a press announcement claiming that an amount somewhat higher than the actual loss was taken. British television reporter Desmond Hamill wrote that frequently the effects of this deception could be seen immediately, "Very often the Army found that soon afterwards, sometimes even the next day, there would be a number of kneecappings. It was not good for IRA recruiting."[16]

Let's look at the basics of what makes a deception work.

BASIC PRINCIPLES

Four fundamental principles have been identified as essential to deception. They are truth, denial, deceit, and misdirection.[17] The first three principles allow the deceiver to present the target with desirable data while reducing or eliminating signals that the opponent needs to form accurate perceptions. The last principle leads the opponent to an attractive alternative that commands his or her attention—a plausible cover story. Let's look at each of them.

Truth

All deception works within the context of what is true. Truth establishes a foundation of perceptions and beliefs; these are then accepted by an opponent and can be exploited in deception. Often, supplying the opponent with real data establishes the credibility of future communications that the opponent then relies on.

Truth can be presented to an opponent or an ally without the intent to deceive. For example, an opponent might already misperceive reality, and truth is presented to correct that misperception. Such use of truth is especially relevant when an ally or opponent plans an undesired action based on misperception. In 1940 Josef Stalin refused to believe that Nazi Germany was preparing to invade the USSR. The British, aware of this, tried to provide the truth. Stalin, suspecting a British plot to draw the USSR into the conflict, dismissed the British effort as a deception. As described in the next section, Saddam Hussein missed an opportunity to correct the US-led coalition's misperception of reality prior to Desert Storm. The coalition believed that Iraq had weapons of mass destruction (WMD). Saddam knew better, but maintaining ambiguity about his weaponry helped him both internally and in dealings with neighboring states. In retrospect, the truth might have served him better.

In the Stalin example, truth was provided with no intent to deceive. But it is possible to correct an opponent's misperception as part of a deception plan. Historically it has been applied to establishing the credibility of double agents who can be used with greater effect later. For example, one of the most famous channels used by the United Kingdom during World War II was a double agent named Juan Pujol Garcia, known as *Garbo* to the MI5 and as *Arabel* to the German Abwehr. By the end of the war MI5 had provided Garbo with enough truth to relay to the Germans that he had managed to receive an Iron Cross from them. Truth in this case was used to ensure there was no German misperception about his credibility, so that when it came time to use him for D-Day and the supporting deception, Operation Quicksilver (described in Chapter 2), the Germans were conditioned to Garbo's reporting being credible.

Truth is often presented as part of *conditioning*: repeating a pattern of operations (signals, force movements, or similar activities). The idea is to deliberately condition the target to a pattern of friendly or reliably accurate behavior, with the objective of desensitizing opponents to indications of a planned action. One of the best examples of conditioning was applied by the Egyptians against the Israelis in 1973.

CONDITIONING: THE YOM KIPPUR WAR

In the third Arab-Israeli war of 1967, Egypt had lost the entire Sinai Peninsula to Israel. The Israelis had occupied the eastern bank of the Suez Canal and built defensive works that included a 60-foot-high sand wall along the canal. Egyptian president Anwar Sadat was determined to retake the Sinai, but he needed a way to overcome the Israeli defenses, and he desperately needed the advantage of surprise.

A key element in breaching the defenses was getting through the sand wall quickly. After trying conventional methods (explosives and bulldozers), Egyptian engineers found that a sand wall could be flattened quickly by a high-pressure stream of water. Egypt subsequently purchased several high-pressure water cannons from the United Kingdom and East Germany.

The Egyptians conducted an effective conditioning campaign to achieve surprise. They projected the image of an incompetent Egyptian military in the press. President Anwar Sadat openly criticized the performance of Soviet military advisors and of the military equipment that the Soviets were providing. The Soviets responded with press releases blaming Egypt's military for poorly maintaining the missile equipment. Israeli Defense Forces (IDF) regularly observed Egyptian soldiers fishing and walking along the banks of the Suez out of uniform. The Soviets leaked false reports to the foreign press that the Egyptian missile force was negligent in its maintenance of Soviet-supplied equipment.

The success of the attack ultimately depended on the intentional conditioning. Prior to the attack, Egyptian forces staged an extensive series of conditioning operations to desensitize Israeli intelligence. During the first nine months of 1973, the Egyptian army did the following:

- Conducted twenty separate mobilizations followed by demobilization, so that the pattern became routine.

- Practiced canal-crossing operations that were easily observed by the IDF. The Egyptians moved troops to the canal, built tank ramps, and created openings in the canal ramparts, followed each time by a subsequent withdrawal.

- Just prior to October 1973, moved successive brigades to the canal to train, then moved part of each unit back to its point of origin at night with headlights on, leaving the impression that the entire brigade had withdrawn.

At first, the Israelis responded to the conditioning efforts by putting their forces on alert. By October, they had accepted the Egyptian activities as routine rather than as an invasion threat. They were caught by surprise when, on October 6, the Egyptians crossed the canal, breached the Israeli defensive wall with their water cannons, and scored major offensive gains in the opening hours of the Yom Kippur War.

Denial

In many texts and training courses, deception is coupled with denial, and the two concepts are labeled denial and deception, or D&D. There are advantages to treating them separately. One can practice denial without conducting active deception. Denial often is used when no deception is intended; that is, the end objective is simply to deny knowledge. Intelligence collectors routinely must deal with this type of denial:

- Terrorist organizations and drug cartels routinely practice operational security to deny information about their activities to human intelligence (HUMINT) sources.

- Military test ranges schedule their activity to avoid imagery collection by satellites, aircraft, and unmanned aerial vehicles (UAVs).

- Diplomats and military commanders protect their important communications by encrypting them.

- Military units in the field conceal vehicles and artillery using camouflage.

- Governments developing chemical, biological, or nuclear weaponry conceal their operations by putting them in underground facilities.

- Aircraft and ship designers work to suppress the signatures of their platforms using stealth technologies.

This book does not deal with these types of denial, unless they are a part of deception. All deception involves some form of denial. One can deny without intent to deceive, but not the converse. You cannot practice deception without also practicing denial of some aspects of the truth that you want the opponent to be unaware of or disbelieve. Operational security (OPSEC) is just as important to a deception operation as it is to the real operation, if not more, depending on how much success is hinged on the deception plan.

In fact, all deception requires that you deny the opponent access to some parts of the truth. Denial conceals aspects of what is true, such as your real intentions and capabilities.

When used as a part of deception, denial is often part of *manipulation*, which requires mixing true and false information. You can, for example, use manipulation to create a perception of strength where you are in fact weak, or the opposite. The Iraqi government, under Saddam Hussein, did exactly that in a denial effort about WMD that extended over several decades.

IRAQI WMD PROGRAMS

During the 1980s, Iraq developed chemical weapons that they used against Iranian troops and civilians during the Iran-Iraq war, and against Iraqi Kurds after the war. The chemical weapons production plants were built with the assistance of several German firms, and German companies provided Iraq with over 1,000 tons of precursor chemicals that were subsequently used to produce mustard gas, tabun, and sarin.

In the same time frame, the Iraqis pursued a biological weapons program, drawing heavily on German expertise for facility construction and on the US Centers for Disease Control and Prevention for biological samples such as anthrax, botulism toxin, and West Nile virus. The Iraqis claimed that they needed the samples for medical research. By the time of the first Gulf War (1991; codenamed by the United States as Operation Desert Storm), Iraq had weaponized (placed into munitions) thousands of liters of botulism toxin, anthrax, and aflatoxin.

Finally, Iraq pursued a nuclear weapons development program during the 1980s, relying on Italian assistance to develop several laboratories and the technologies needed for weapons production. No weapon had been produced by the time of Operation Desert Storm.

All three WMD programs relied heavily on denial—specifically, denying information about the purpose of acquiring plants, technology, materials, and know-how. In the aftermath of the first Gulf War, the Iraqis had to contend with UN-mandated inspection teams, but continued their programs at a reduced level. Their efforts were aimed at maintaining the capability to resume weapons development in the future, rather than to produce weapons—which the inspection teams would have detected.

To conceal the programs, the Iraqis relied on a detailed knowledge of the UN inspection teams' processes. Using that knowledge, they developed a plan to deceive the inspectors about their WMD efforts. The plan relied heavily on denial of imagery and specialized technical collection.[18] Specifically, they concealed WMD facilities inside existing buildings or placed them underground. Buildings designed for the same purpose were deliberately made to appear different from the exterior. They suppressed telltale emissions and hid power lines and water feeds to conceal the purpose of facilities. They moved WMD-related equipment at night.[19]

The Iraqi denial effort was unusual in that it was an attempt to project two diametrically opposite perceptions to two different targets. Against the UN, the United States, and its allies, the objective was to portray an image of weakness—the lack of WMD and WMD programs. Against Saddam Hussein's opponents in the Middle East—Iran and Israel in particular—the objective was to portray an image of strength: that Iraq possessed WMD and was prepared to use them.

Deceit

Successful deception normally requires the practice of deceit. Without deceit the target is only the victim of misperceptions due to denial, misinformation, and/ or self-deception, which is not the same as deliberate deception.

Deceit, in turn, requires *fabrication*—presentation of the false as truth. One might disguise a chemical weapons plant as a pesticide producer, as Iraq did. One can disguise friendly forces as neutrals or even as members of the enemy's force,[20] a practice commonly known as a pseudo operation.

Pseudo operations (also known as "false flag" operations) are frequently employed to combat insurgencies. They make use of organized teams disguised as insurgents, employed to penetrate insurgent camps. Their mission may be to collect intelligence or to capture or kill insurgent leadership. The team members usually are drawn from existing paramilitary or military units, though they sometimes make use of captured insurgents who have been "turned."[21]

Pseudo operations teams have proved so successful over many decades that they are considered to be an essential component of any counterinsurgency campaign:

- One of the earliest reported pseudo operations was conducted in the Philippines from 1946 to 1955. This was the time of the Huk rebellion. Originally formed to fight the Japanese, the Huks subsequently began an insurrection against the Philippine government. In response, the Philippine Constabulary created a small unit called Force X. The basic idea was to make this specially trained force look and act like a Huk unit that could infiltrate into Huk territory, gather intelligence, and kill or capture Huk leaders. Force X members were dressed and equipped like Huks. They were trained to talk and act like Huks by four guerrillas who had been captured and "turned" to work for the government.[22]

- From 1948 to 1955, at about the same time as the Huk campaign, the British ran a pseudo operation against the Malayan Races Liberation Army, a predominately Chinese Communist insurgent group. The operation was so successful that counterinsurgency experts regard it as a model for such operations.

- From 1952 to 1960, the British fought a counterinsurgency campaign against a tribally based insurgent group called the Mau Mau in Kenya. The Special Branch used pseudo gangs to infiltrate and then kill or capture roving bands of terrorists. Initially, these pseudo gangs had been formed to gain intelligence but they subsequently evolved into combat groups. Led by European officers in black face makeup, they were able to get close enough to the enemy to kill or capture them. Such pseudo groups were composed of loyal Kikuyu, sometimes drawn from tribal police or regular constables, white officers, and "turned" Mau Mau. The latter were most important for lending credibility, since they knew the latest secret signs, finger snaps, and oaths that would convince the Mau Mau of their authenticity.

- Portugal ran a number of pseudo operations in its African colonies during the 1960s and 1970s. The units were organized in small bands of African troops, often including insurgents who had been captured and turned. Their primary role was to gather intelligence.

- During Rhodesia's war against insurgents (1964–1979), military authorities within the Rhodesian Security Forces realized the need for accurate and timely intelligence. A secret unit therefore was created in 1973 to acquire this intelligence. The unit was the Selous Scouts, comprising intelligence experts from the police and military, soldiers, and turned guerrillas. Eventually this small unit expanded to a formidable counterinsurgency force of close to 1,000. The Scout operations put heavy psychological pressure on insurgents; the insurgents began to constantly fear deception, betrayal, and surprise attacks. Scouts would often stage elaborate scenarios in which black members of the unit would pretend to be guerrillas leading captured white soldiers into a guerrilla camp. At the last moment all weaponry would be returned to the apparent captives, allowing the Scouts to catch the entire camp by surprise.

- Since the 1990s, the Turkish government has relied on Special Teams, operated by the gendarmerie, and Special Action Teams, operated by the police, to counter a Kurdish Partiya Karkeren Kurdistan (PKK) insurgency. The teams were assigned to conduct high-risk "counterterrorist" actions against PKK cadres. In practice, the teams functioned as "death squads," identifying and killing PKK leaders.

- During the coalition operations in Afghanistan that started in 2001, special military task forces and police units were designed to collect human terrain intelligence in insurgent-held territories of Kandahar and Helmand. This included infiltrating hostile territories for shuras (meetings) with the locals to assess the extent of insurgent activity, as well as to generate a picture of the social networks of importance in the areas to contribute to the planning of future operations.

- In the fight against Daesh, Iraqis employed special force units to conduct long-range disruption operations against Daesh lines of communication, on some occasions using pseudo operations to infiltrate within striking range, or to draw the Daesh into striking range.

Pseudo operations teams have been successful for decades in collecting intelligence that could not otherwise be acquired. They have also had a record of success in offensive operations—disrupting insurgent leadership. The key to their success is disguise—that is, deceit.

In today's information age, pseudo operations have broadened to include the Internet and all its forms of communication. What began as simple deceit about identity in chat rooms and blogs has expanded with the rapid expansion of digital social networking possibilities. Social media such as Facebook, Twitter, and Instagram have become vibrant battlespaces for pseudo operations. Fake profiles, groups, and avatars operated relatively unhindered until several of the larger firms began applying policies that are more restrictive. However, social media today is an acknowledged battlespace domain that is inherently permissive for pseudo operations.

Misdirection

Misdirection requires manipulating the opponent's perceptions in a specific direction. You want to redirect the opponent away from the truth and toward a false perception. In operations, a feint—often called a *diversion*—is used to redirect the adversary's attention away from where the real operation will occur. The idea is to draw the adversary away from an area or activity; to divert the target's attention from friendly assets; or to draw the target's attention to a particular time and place.

Misdirection incorporates the other three principles of deception. It includes truth, an essential part of all deception. Denial is necessary to protect information about the real situation. Deceit creates the false perception.

Misdirection depends on having a good understanding of an opponent's intelligence sources and processes. The Indian government used such knowledge in developing a strategic deception plan to cover its nuclear device test on May 11, 1998. On that date, the Indians conducted three underground nuclear tests at their Pokhran nuclear test site in the country's northwestern desert. The test came as a complete surprise to the US government. This operation has a number of features that illustrate superb use of the channels for providing deception, so it will be highlighted again in Chapter 6.

THE INDIAN NUCLEAR TEST

The nuclear test deception plan succeeded because the Indian government had an excellent understanding of the keys that US imagery analysts used to detect test preparations. The US government had succeeded in deterring an earlier plan by India to stage the tests. In December 1995, US reconnaissance satellites had observed test preparations at the Pokhran site, including the movement of vehicles and the deployment of testing equipment. The US ambassador to India showed the imagery to top Indian officials in a successful demarche[23] to persuade them not to test.[24]

Using the knowledge they gained from the demarche, the Indians were able to plan an elaborate deception campaign to conceal preparations for the 1998 tests. The campaign was many faceted, aimed at protecting the operation from HUMINT and IMINT.[25] The deception campaign had several elements, making it an excellent example of multi-INT deception. And it is a prime example of all four characteristics of a deception:

Truth. Their test location was known. Indians had to work within that truth, knowing that the United States was going to monitor that facility using imagery. Also, the deception was helped along by the US government's knowledge that India wanted to improve trade relations. US officials were therefore predisposed to believe that India would not provoke a crisis by testing a nuclear weapon.[26]

Denial. The effort was protected by extensive secrecy measures within the Indian government. Few knew of the plan; the decision to test was not disclosed even to senior cabinet ministers. Work was done at night, and heavy equipment was always returned to the same parking spot at dawn with no evidence that it had been moved. The shafts were dug under a netting of camouflage. When cables for sensors were laid, they were carefully covered with sand and native vegetation was replaced to conceal the digging.

Deceit. Piles of dug-out sand were shaped to mimic the natural wind-aligned and shaped dune forms in the desert area. All technical staff at the range wore military fatigues, so that in satellite images they would appear as military personnel charged with maintenance of the test range. The Indian government issued a number of public statements just prior to the test, designed to reassure Washington that no nuclear test was contemplated. Indian diplomats also categorically told their US counterparts that "there would be no surprise testings." All scientists involved in the operation left in groups of two or three on the pretext of attending a seminar or a conference. Tickets were bought for some location other than Pokhran under false names, and after arriving at their destination the group would secretly leave for Pokhran. After finishing their part of the work, the group would go back, retracing their path. Then another group would leave for the range, employing similar means to do their part of the work on the bombs.

Misdirection. Just prior to the test, Indian leaders began an effort to focus US attention elsewhere. They were aware that the United States monitored ballistic missile tests at their Chandipur missile test range, more than a thousand miles from the Pokhran site. They consequently started preparations for what appeared to be a ballistic missile test at Chandipur. The Indians actually tested a Trishul surface-to-air missile (which was of relatively low intelligence interest to the United States), but they moved additional equipment into the test range so that the preparations appeared to be for a test of the Agni intermediate-range ballistic missile (which was of high intelligence interest).[27] As a result, US reconnaissance satellites reportedly were focused on the Chandipur site, with only minimal coverage of the nuclear test site at the time of the test.[28]

The following chapters of this book lay out the methodology for organizing a deception campaign. But first, it's worth taking a moment to understand the roles of operations and intelligence in conducting deception.

ROLES OF OPERATIONS AND INTELLIGENCE

Holt's commandments of deception described earlier were generated by lessons learned from World War II and were shaped by the organizational environment in which military deceptions were carried out by the Allies. It then should come as no surprise that those tenets are based on deceptions that required both an intelligence element and an operations element. The relationship between the two elements has often determined the success or failure of deception operations.

Deceptions are planned and carried out under the guidance of a decision maker to support a policy or military objective that can be strategic, operational, or tactical. In military terms, the decision maker is the commander; and his or her organization for attaining the overall objective, referring back to our definition, is called *operations*.

All deception should be operations led and intelligence driven. It is a simple edict; but because of the contrasting organizational cultures of operations and intelligence, it has not always been employed effectively. However, the logic that operations should be driven by the best situational understanding possible is hard to deny, and is also the overarching principle behind deception operations. As stated earlier, deception operations are not carried out for the sake of deceiving. Rather, they are carried out in order to increase the chances of success for the real operation. With this in mind, the role of intelligence becomes no different from nondeception operations; intelligence must drive the deception operation by providing the best situational understanding possible.

Deceptions are usually planned by the operations component of an organization. And experience with conducting deceptions, dating back at least to World War II, have repeatedly demonstrated that the operations unit is best equipped to handle the deception mission. PSYOPS, in particular, is an operations function. Which leaves open the question: What then is the role of intelligence?

- Operations and policy bureaucracies—especially US bureaucracies—are sometimes criticized as being reluctant to incorporate deception in their planning. So an upfront role of intelligence is to provide opportunity analysis: identifying the potential for applying deception in planned operations.

- Once a decision is made to engage in deception, intelligence has several roles in ensuring that the deception succeeds. It must identify the types of deception that are most likely to succeed. It must identify likely reactions of the target for both successful and unsuccessful deception. It must select the channels for providing the deceptive information.

- In the context of driving deception operations, the intelligence element of the organization applies a *reflexive* methodology to understanding the adversary's process for obtaining and using intelligence—that is, in counterintelligence. It is reflexive in the sense that the intelligence arm observes and assesses *how the adversary observes and assesses,* and this information is used to create a situational understanding specifically for use with designing and executing supporting deception operations.

Also, in a few cases, the intelligence organization handles both the operations and intelligence roles. These cases include several types of covert actions and those missions in which the primary objective of the operation is intelligence collection.

Finally, on the subject covered in Chapters 10 and 11—detecting and defeating deception—the answer is different. There, intelligence must take the lead. Deceptions inevitably are conducted against the sensory channels of an organization—primarily, but not exclusively, against intelligence channels. So the intelligence unit is the first line of defense in countering deception. Intelligence has the job of being aware of possible deception and ensuring that its customers are aware of it.

This focuses on two categories that both government and military leaders often don't consider: the opportunity to conduct deception against opponents, and the threat of deception operations conducted against them. It is an important capability as not only does it increase the chances of success for your operations, but it also decreases the chance of success of adversarial operations against your side.

Deception, counterintelligence, and psychological operations, as this chapter discusses, overlap each other. The traditional Venn diagram shown in Figure 1-3 illustrates that point. It also illustrates the point that operations and intelligence have specific roles to play in each area. Military organizations often have separate units responsible for deception and psychological operations, and there is a history of confusion and friction between the two.[29]

The next several chapters of this book lay out the methodology for organizing and managing deception and counterdeception. Chapters 2–9 cover how intelligence analysis should support deception operations, while Chapters 10 and 11 illustrate how intelligence analysis should drive counterdeception efforts.

FIGURE 1-3 ■ Venn Diagram of Overlapping Functions

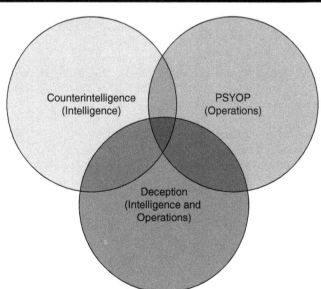

Counterintelligence
(Intelligence)

PSYOP
(Operations)

Deception
(Intelligence and
Operations)

NOTES

1. Barton Whaley, *Stratagem, Deception and Surprise in War* [reprint of 1969 edition] (Norwood, MA: Artech House Publishing, 2007), 104, tables 5.19 and 5.20.

2. Barton Whaley, "The Prevalence of Guile: Deception through Time and across Cultures and Disciplines," essay prepared for the Foreign Denial and Deception Committee, DNI, Washington, DC, February 2, 2007, https://cryptome.org/2014/08/prevalence-of-guile.pdf.

3. J. Bowyer Bell, "Toward a Theory of Deception," *International Journal of Intelligence and Counter-Intelligence* 16, no. 2 (2003): 244–79, doi:10.1080/08850600390198742.

4. D.C. Daniel and K. L. Herbig (Eds.), *Strategic Military Deception* (Elmsford, NY: Pergamon Press, 1982), 5, 6.

5. "Counterdeception," http://www.militaryfactory.com/dictionary/military-terms-defined.asp?term_id=1334.

6. Frank Stech and Kristin Heckman, "Cyber Counterdeception: How to Detect Denial and Deception (D&D)," conference paper, MITRE Corporation, March 2014.

7. US Executive Order 12333, December 4, 1981. United States Intelligence Activities, Section 3.4(a). EO provisions found in 46 FR 59941, 3 CFR, 1981 Comp., p. 1.

8. Joint Publication (JP) 1-02, "Department of Defense Dictionary of Military and Associated Terms," November 8, 2010 (amended through February 15, 2016), http://www.dtic.mil/doctrine/new_pubs/jp1_02.pdf.

9. Thaddeus Holt, *The Deceivers: Allied Military Deception in the Second World War* (New York: Skyhorse Publishing, 2007), 54–61.

10. Sharon Begley, "The Stickiness of Misinformation," *Mindful*, October 5, 2015, https://www.mindful.org/the-stickiness-of-misinformation/.

11. Stefan H. Verstappen, *The Thirty-Six Strategies of Ancient China* (San Francisco: China Books & Periodicals, Inc., 1999).

12. Ibid.

13. Pamela H. Krause, *Proteus: Insights from 2020* (Washington, DC: The Copernicus Institute Press, 2000), D-i–D-xx.

14. Ibid., 83.

15. Mark L. Bowlin, "British Intelligence and the IRA: The Secret War in Northern Ireland, 1969–1988," US Naval Postgraduate School, September 1999, pp. 80–83, https://archive.org/stream/britishintellige00bowlpdf/britishintellige00bowl_djvu.txt.

16. Ibid.

17. Edward Waltz and Michael Bennett, *Counterdeception Principles and Applications for National Security* (Boston: Artech House, 2007).

18. Director of Central Intelligence George J. Tenet, speech at Georgetown University, February 5, 2004.

19. David Kay, "Denial and Deception: The Lessons of Iraq," in *U.S. Intelligence at the Crossroads: Agendas for Reform*, ed. Roy Godson, Ernest R. May, and Gary Schmitt (Washington, DC: Brassey's, 1995), 120.

20. Scott Gerwehr and Russell W. Glenn, *The Art of Darkness: Deception and Urban Operations* (Santa Monica, CA: RAND, 1999), 21, http://www.rand.org/publications/MR/MR1132.

21. Lawrence E. Cline, "Pseudo Operations and Counterinsurgency: Lessons from Other Countries," US Army War College, June 2005, http://www.strategicstudiesinstitute.army.mil/pdffiles/pub607.pdf.

22. Ibid.

23. A demarche is a political or diplomatic step, such as a protest or diplomatic representation made to a foreign government.

24. Tim Weiner and James Risen, "Policy Makers, Diplomats, Intelligence Officers All Missed India's Intentions," *New York Times,* May 25, 1998.

25. Ibid.

26. Ibid.

27. "Strategic Deception at Pokhran Reported," *Delhi Indian Express* in English, May 15, 1998, 1.

28. Weiner and Risen, "Policy Makers, Diplomats, Intelligence Officers."

29. Holt, *The Deceivers: Allied Military Deception in the Second World War,* 54.

2

THE METHODOLOGY

The methodology discussed in this book focuses on shaping an opponent's decisions and actions. In terms of the definitions in Chapter 1, our emphasis is on misleading deceptions instead of ambiguity-increasing deceptions. The remaining chapters of the book, with a few exceptions, center on misleading an opponent into making decisions and taking actions that result in favorable outcomes for your side. Nevertheless, the basic methodology applies for all types of deception, including parts of counterintelligence or psychological operations.

Roy Godson and James Wirtz, in their journal article "Strategic Denial and Deception," provide some detailed guidance for planning and implementing the misleading type of deception. They observe that

> a successful deception campaign requires strategic coherence. The deceiver nation must have an overall plan in mind for the achievement of its objectives; it must determine in advance how the target should behave and how deception will contribute to that outcome. The deceiver also must predict how the target will react in the wake of both successful and unsuccessful deception. This is no small task. Those contemplating deception may engage in wishful thinking when predicting the consequences of their deception campaign. Additionally, the deceiver must integrate its actions with (a) efforts to deny an opponent accurate information and (b) deceptive cover stories. Again, this is no small task. D&D campaigns require coherent, if not coordinated, action from many departments, agencies, or ministries. Public statements, press articles, and Internet communications must be shaped to support the goals of the nation intent on deception. As this corrupt information is disseminated, steps must be taken to prevent accurate information from reaching the target.[1]

To summarize, all deception has four essential components. First, there must be a desired *objective*. Second, there has to be a *target,* some person or group of people who are to be deceived. Third, a *story* is presented—a false picture of reality. And fourth, one or more *channels* are selected through which the story is to be transmitted.

Deception can be successful or unsuccessful only relative to an actor's decision-making. Therefore, the underpinning to the four elements is a decision-making model that can be applied throughout the process. Determining the drivers of the decision-making of both the deceiver and the intended deceived is the foundation for bridging theory and practice. Additionally, the methodology chosen for this foundation must be capable of engaging both the intelligence and operational facets of an organization, as it will be the combined inputs of those that will make, break, or detect a deception.

Put simply, the methodology that underlies deception planning involves answering these questions:

1. What *outcome* do we want to see as a result of the deception?

2. What must the opponent *do* in order for that outcome to happen?

3. What *story* must the opponent believe in order to make the decision and take the action?

4. How can we feed the opponent the information to make him or her believe the story?

The best model to implement this methodology is a variant of John Boyd's Observe-Orient-Decide-Act (OODA) loop, but placed within the operational planning context depicted in Clark and Mitchell's *Target-Centric Network Modeling*.[2] Before delving into the methodology, let's briefly review Boyd's OODA loop.

THE OODA LOOP

The idea of an OODA decision cycle was developed by US Air Force Colonel John Boyd, originally to help train fighter pilots. Boyd later extended the concept to address all operational and strategic levels of military operations and, in fact, of all large organizations, including governments. This concept is particularly useful in thinking about deception. The OODA loop is illustrated in Figure 2-1.

Boyd's assertion is that decision-making occurs in a recurring cycle of observe-orient-decide-act. Both your opponent and you therefore operate within OODA loops. The advantage in conflict goes to a person or organization that can traverse this cycle more quickly than the opponent can—observing and reacting to unfolding events more rapidly than the opponent. To do this, your side conceals its intentions, or misleads the opponent about them, while ascertaining the opponent's intentions and level of knowledge—which of course is at the core of deception.

FIGURE 2-1   ■   John Boyd's OODA Loop

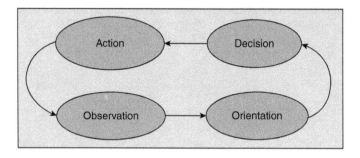

Source: Work by Patrick Edward Moran, GNU Free Documentation license, original at https://commons.wikimedia.org/wiki/File:OODA.Boyd.svg.

So deception, as it is presented within this book, must be understood within the context of competing OODA loops. Deception is a process, executed in a manner specifically intended to undermine and disrupt an adversary's OODA loop. How that is done is the subject of this chapter.

The OODA loop clearly is a useful way to think about deception, and has previously been applied to deception problems. In his work on deception methodology, Rob Dussault uses an identical framework to describe his interacting-agent model of deception. Dussault applies slightly different names; the terms in his loop are sense-interpret-plan-act[3]—reflecting the longer time frame involved in a deception operation as compared with the combat time frame of a fighter pilot. Since the Boyd OODA loop is more familiar to most readers, we have adopted it for this text.

Three perspectives regarding OODA loops are used for perpetrating deception and for detecting an opponent's deception.

OODA LOOP PERSPECTIVES

In battlespaces or highly competitive environments,[4] OODA loops constitute the interactive identity of the antagonists or competitors vis-à-vis each other. We use the term *identity* here in the same fashion that Ted Hopf describes it in his 1998 discussion of world politics. Identity tells

1. you who you are;

2. you who others are;

3. others who you are.[5]

Understanding the dynamics of deception, to the degree where practical activities can be pursued to support it, requires a grasp of three OODA perspectives that mirror Hopf's description of identity. In deception, the three distinct views of OODA loops are as follows:

1. How you see your own OODA

2. How you see your adversary's OODA

3. How you believe your adversary sees your OODA

Let's examine the three perspectives to understand why it is important to understand each, both in deception and in counterdeception.

Perspective 1—Understand Your Own OODA Loop

This perspective is the most commonly understood application of the OODA loop. It entails looking at your own organization and understanding how the structures and processes belonging to that organization affect the way it observes, orients, decides, and acts in a given situation. Understanding one's own OODA loop is not only necessary for deception planning, but it should be a must for operational planning in general. Following the loop in Figure 2-2, this entails the following:

- Knowing how your organization observes in the operational environment. Doing this requires what we call *sensor mapping*.

- Having an intimate knowledge of how your organization orients and processes the information it collects, and the challenges within the organization with regard to speed and precision. You must understand how the organization's observation function handles the trade-offs between accuracy and timeliness, for example.

- Understanding how the development and exploitation of information affects the decisions made and actions taken.

FIGURE 2-2 ■ Your OODA Loop

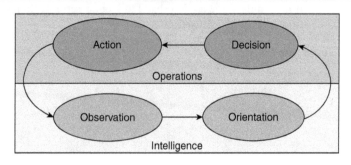

In planning deception, this perspective is employed to think about how your organization will monitor the results of a deception and make needed adjustments within its own OODA loop. As we'll see, the goal is for this loop to operate faster than the opponent's OODA loop—also known as getting inside the opponent's OODA loop.

Both your intelligence and operations components need a good understanding of your organization's OODA loop in order to plan a deception. Each has unique expertise to contribute, as Figure 2-2 indicates. Operations decides what should be done and carries out the decision. Intelligence observes, analyzes, and feeds the intelligence to operations.

Perspective 2—Understand the Adversary's OODA Loop

Planning how to get inside the adversary's OODA loop and conduct deception requires a good understanding of how your opponent observes in its operational environment. Therefore, sensor mapping the adversary is the key to understanding how to build up a deception operation. How do they collect information? What classified (such as IMINT) and unclassified (such as OSINT) platforms might they have access to? All of the adversary's lawful and unlawful collection sources and sensors need to be identified.

Just as important is knowledge of how the adversary orients information that they collect. Primarily, the goal is to consider what they want to collect on and how they collate it. In short, your organization must track the adversary's intelligence collection efforts and how they make use of the product of collection. With this information comes an understanding of how they will use intelligence to make decisions and execute actions.

As Figure 2-3 indicates, understanding the adversary's OODA loop relies heavily on intelligence. But your side's operations component inevitably has a unique understanding of the opponent's decision and action process, especially if they have long experience in dealing with the opponent. For example, the deception that Egypt carried out at the beginning of the Yom Kippur War (see Chapter 1) was well planned because the Egyptians had years of experience in dealing with the Israeli military. And the Israelis have executed many successful

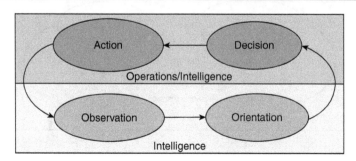

FIGURE 2-3 ■ The Adversary's OODA Loop

deceptions against the Arabs by dint of their long experience—predating, in fact, the 1948 conflict between the Arabs and Israelis that helped create the state of Israel.

Perspective 3—Understand How the Adversary Views Your OODA Loop

Gaining this point of view requires that the first two OODA perspectives are established. Knowledge of those produces sufficient grounds to estimate how the adversary understands your side's observation capability, orienting process, and the resulting decisions and actions. Perspective 3 is your side's estimate of the adversary's estimate of your own OODA loop, illustrated in Figure 2-4.

Establishing this perspective to any level of usefulness is important to both deception planning and deception detection. Its primary contribution to deception planning (if the estimate is accurate) is that it allows your side to increase its operational security surrounding the deception—knowing what indicators to avoid that might trigger the adversary's curiosity as to what the real plan is.

Where it concerns deception detection, understanding this perspective facilitates a search for incongruences and congruences in the information your side's sensors collect that might indicate that you are in fact being deceived. In particular, a comparison of your understanding of your side's OODA loop with the opponent's understanding provides an opportunity to identify both how the opponent might attempt to deceive you and the channels that your side has that would detect such a deception.

Armed with these three perspectives of OODA loops and one explicit additional step, we can plan and execute a deception operation. Boyd *assumed* an outcome, or result of his actions in every cycle around the loop—a feedback step between action and observation, based on the result of each action. This result includes the unfolding circumstances, interaction with the environment, and the opponent's actions in response to your actions. The opponent, after all, is running his or her own OODA loop while you are running yours. But it is important

FIGURE 2-4 ■ The Adversary's View of Your OODA Loop

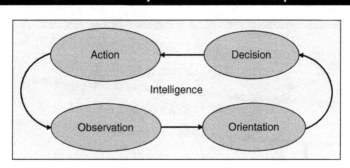

FIGURE 2-5 ■ The OODA Loop with an Explicit Outcome

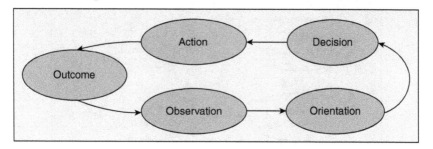

to make the outcome of the action explicit in deception planning. So for this book's purposes, an additional step is required—inserting the outcome—into Boyd's loop. The loop now looks like Figure 2-5. This is the loop for the planning process—with a slight change; a reversal of the arrows to create what is called an inverse loop.

PLANNING DECEPTION: THE INVERSE OODA LOOP

RAND researcher Scott Gerwehr has defined a process for planning deception that proceeds chronologically as if going backward in the OODA loop or, as he puts it, "planning backwards."[6] It's rather like reverse engineering the problem. That is, it starts with the desired end result: the *objective* in mind for conducting a deception. Next, choose the *target*—the person(s) who make the decision—and determine the action that you want the person(s) to take that will lead to the desired objective. Then create the *story* that leads to the decision, shaping the way the opponent orients, or analyzes the sensed information. Finally, develop the means, which focuses on the opponent's *channels* of observation and orientation.[7]

To restate, the inverse OODA loop methodology comprises these steps, as shown in Figure 2-6:

1. *The desired outcome scenario.* This is the *objective.* Envision a future—a desired end-state target—that is more favorable than the likely one if nothing were done. Both target futures take the form of scenarios—an expected one (if no deception were planned) and a desired one.

2. *Decision/action.* Identify the key branch points that lead to the desired end state (as opposed to the expected end state absent deception).

FIGURE 2-6   ■   Planning Deception

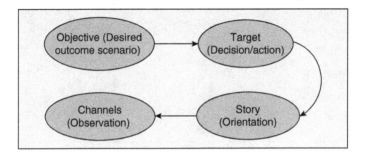

The key branch points are ones where the opponent (the *target*) must make decisions and take specific actions—or refrain from acting.

3. *Orientation.* At the key branch points where the opponent must take specific actions, create a *story*—a fictional scenario—that the opponent must believe in order to take the desired actions.

4. *Observables.* Continue working backward through the OODA loop to identify the set of observables and associated *channels* that would lead to the opponent believing the story, and thence to the opponent's desired decisions and actions.

In the following chapters, we'll discuss each of these steps. But first, let's examine an example from World War II that is a classic in deception, and see how the inverse loop worked in that case.

OPERATION MINCEMEAT

In 1943, during World War II, the Allies were developing plans for the invasion of Sicily, codenamed Operation Husky.

Desired Outcome Scenario

Absent deception, the Allies expected to face fierce resistance from German forces stationed on the island. Their objective was to create a more favorable invasion scenario that would result in facing fewer opposing troops in Sicily.

Decision and Action

Some type of deception, therefore, was called for. To get to their objective, the Allies needed to persuade the Germans to deploy troops elsewhere in the theater, away from Sicily. Decisions such as this were being handled by Adolf Hitler, so he was the target of the deception. He would likely make such a decision only if convinced that the invasion would occur in another part of southern Europe. The British orchestrated an elaborate deception operation, codenamed Operation Barclay, to convince Hitler that such was the case.

Observation and Orientation

The "story" to be used was that the invasion would hit either the Balkans or Sardinia rather than Sicily. Several channels were used to convey the "story." Radio communications; bogus troop movements; currency transactions; preparing maps of Greece and Sardinia—all accomplished in such a fashion that German and Italian intelligence would observe them—were designed to give the impression of a landing in either Greece or Sardinia.

The most interesting part of Operation Barclay had the unappetizing name Operation Mincemeat; it was first revealed in Ewen Montagu's book (later a motion picture) entitled *The Man Who Never Was*.[8] The British planned and executed this part of the deception during early 1943. Because Operation Mincemeat proved to be a critical part of the deception, the observation/orientation part of the OODA loop (Figure 2-6) is worth looking at step by step.

Observation: The British had a good understanding of how German intelligence operated. They had an especially good grasp of the German operations in Spain and the observation channel that resulted from close linkages between German and Spanish intelligence. Armed with this knowledge, they were able to plant on the Spanish coastline the body of an apparently drowned British staff officer carrying documents that indicated the targets of the next Allied invasion. This involved dressing a corpse as a British Royal Marines officer. To the corpse was attached a briefcase with documents indicating where the upcoming Allied invasion of southern Europe would take place. The corpse and briefcase were then released from a submarine near the coast of Spain, where it was expected that the body would be found and the briefcase's contents shared with German intelligence.

Orientation: The deception succeeded because the British had an excellent model of how the German and Spanish services worked together, and they knew what form of information the Germans were likely to believe. A fake operations plan probably would have aroused German suspicions. Instead, the key document was a masterpiece of subtlety, in the form of a personal letter hinting that the next invasions would hit Sardinia and Greece, and that Sicily (the actual invasion target) was a feint.

The Outcome

The deception was unquestionably successful. Hitler relied on the Mincemeat documents in ordering a redeployment of his forces to counter the expected invasion. The Germans reinforced their defenses of Sardinia and Greece, pulling units out of both Sicily and Russia. When the Allied forces came ashore on July 10, 1943, only two German divisions remained in Sicily. By July 17, Sicily was in Allied hands.

In later chapters, we will return to Operation Mincemeat. It made good use of British intelligence channels to determine that the deception was being accepted by the Germans (Chapter 9). It also provides some examples of how an astute opponent can identify a deception (Chapter 11), though the Germans failed to identify the Mincemeat deception.

EXECUTING DECEPTION: THE FORWARD OODA LOOP

When you have completed the observation step, you're not finished. The next step is to finish planning and then to execute the deception—a topic we'll visit in detail in Chapter 9. An astute reader has probably noted that Figure 2-6 does not describe a loop. To complete the loop (and the methodology), you have to go through an execution process as shown in Figure 2-7—creating the OODA loop that you desire your opponent to follow.

That process involves selecting the channels for conducting the deception and then identifying and dealing with possible undesired end states resulting from adding deception to the OODA loop. As part of this, you conduct a deconfliction analysis (see Chapter 9) and then execute the deception. The process completes a loop as shown in Figure 2-7. Finally, you monitor subsequent indicators to determine whether they are pointing to the desired outcome scenario.

These steps are listed in the logical order, but in practice they create an iterative process. That is, you might start with an *inverse* OODA loop based on the belief that a certain action by an opponent will result in a favorable outcome; then go *forward* through the loop and find that the opponent's possible actions lead to undesired outcomes—making it necessary to go back into the loop at some point and revise it. In some cases, it may become apparent that the desired outcome scenario is unachievable or too risky to attempt, given the opponent's sensory channels or decision process. In that case, you must start over with a different desired outcome.

FIGURE 2-7 ▪ Executing Deception

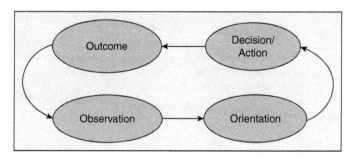

The planning phase also has to consider what is likely to happen once the deception has been executed and the outcome is apparent. Often, the opponent will recognize from the outcome that he or she has been deceived. Sometimes, the outcome will not be what was expected. In any case, you also often have to plan for multiple OODA loops as part of a deception, and for multiple circuits of a single OODA loop. That idea leads us to a second classic case from World War II—the elaborate deception that supported the Normandy invasion.

OPERATION FORTITUDE

During the spring of 1944, the Allies were busy planning for the invasion of Nazi-occupied Europe. The decision had been made for the invasion to hit the French beaches at Normandy. The problem for the Allies was that the invading forces would be highly vulnerable to counterattack during and in the days after the landing. It was likely, in fact, that the German Wehrmacht would defeat the invasion by hitting it during the landing phase, *if* they were positioned to attack soon after the invasion began. To avoid that outcome, the Allies developed an elaborate deception known as Operation Fortitude. We'll revisit this deception in later chapters to illustrate a number of points. For now, let's focus on using the inverse OODA loop.

Desired Outcome Scenario

The desired outcome had two phases (and consequently required taking the Germans through two circuits of an OODA loop). Prior to D-Day, the objective (loop one) was for as many German forces as possible to be concentrated in areas other than Normandy, and preferably far from Normandy. After D-Day, the objective (loop two) was to delay as long as possible the redeployment of German forces to the Normandy beachhead.

Loop One Decision and Action—Pre D-Day

For German units to be deployed as far from Normandy as possible, the German leadership—and specifically Adolf Hitler—needed to be convinced that an attack was coming elsewhere. This led to two separate deception operations: Fortitude North, designed to convey the threat of an invasion of Norway; and Fortitude South, an apparent invasion of the continent at Pas-de-Calais, directly across the English Channel from Dover.

Loop One Observation and Orientation—Pre D-Day

For Fortitude North, the Allies provided the Germans with evidence of a buildup of military forces in Scotland, the logical departure point for a Norway invasion. They had previously created a fictional British Fourth Army, headquartered in Edinburgh Castle. The deception was conveyed through several channels:

- Radio units based in Scotland transmitted false radio traffic, purportedly coming from Fourth Army units.

(Continued)

(Continued)

- British media broadcast fictional news about Fourth Army troop activities such as football scores and wedding announcements.

- Two double agents in Scotland codenamed Mutt and Jeff transmitted to their German handlers false information about the arrival of troops in the area.

- In early spring of 1944, British commandos attacked targets in Norway to simulate preparations for invasion. They destroyed industrial targets, such as shipping and power infrastructure, as well as military outposts.

- At the same time, British naval activity off Norway increased markedly.

- The British applied political pressure on neutral Sweden in such a fashion as to lead German observers there to conclude it was intended to facilitate an invasion of Norway.

Fortitude South was designed to reinforce Hitler's predisposition to believe that an invasion would come via the shortest route into Europe, at Pas-de-Calais. The Allies consequently created several deception operations to support that predisposition. One of these, called Operation Quicksilver, involved a fictional invasion force in the region around Dover, publicly identified as General Patton's First US Army Group (FUSAG). The Allies employed deceit in several channels by

- Transmitting radio messages simulating units of General Patton's FUSAG in the Dover area

- Leaking false information through diplomatic channels that were accessible to the Germans

- Using doubled German agents (Garbo and Brutus) to supply false reports to their handlers in Germany

- Displaying dummy landing craft in the Dover port areas

- Turning on lights to simulate activity at night where the dummy landing craft were located

- Heavily bombing the Pas-de-Calais beach area and railways in the area immediately before D-Day

Some histories have reported that Quicksilver also used large numbers of dummy tanks, military vehicles, and other equipment that appeared to be assembling for an invasion across the Channel. The dummy equipment supposedly made use of inflatables that were highly detailed and were designed to look real when photographed by overflying German reconnaissance aircraft. Though dummy equipment was used in a number of deceptive operations in Europe, it appears that Quicksilver only made use of dummy landing craft that could be observed from the English Channel; by 1944, German reconnaissance aircraft couldn't survive for long over England.

Of equal importance was denial of other channels: The Allies denied the Germans intelligence about the preparations for invasion in the ports of southern England—which would have pointed to the actual invasion target. Reports from southwestern England through doubled agents indicated few troop sightings there.

Loop One Outcome

Operation Fortitude was a success. Fortitude North was so successful that by late spring 1944, Hitler had thirteen army divisions in Norway. In response to Fortitude South, the Germans allocated much of their defenses to Pas-de-Calais, well away from the real invasion site.[9] The deception cycle then proceeded into loop two.

Loop Two Decision and Action—Post D-Day

After D-Day, the Normandy landing was an established fact readily observed by the Germans, and the Allies engaged the second round of the Fortitude South OODA loop, now with the objective of delaying the move of Wehrmacht reinforcements to Normandy. The "story" to be conveyed was that Normandy was a feint; the real invasion was to take place at Pas-de-Calais after Wehrmacht troops had withdrawn from that area to deal with the Normandy invasion.

Loop Two Observation and Orientation—Post D-Day

The key observable here came from two doubled German agents, nicknamed Garbo and Brutus, who had previously provided fictitious reporting on the activities of FUSAG. Both reported in the days after June 6 that FUSAG was still positioned near Dover, ready to invade at Pas-de-Calais.

Loop Two Outcome

On Hitler's orders, the Wehrmacht kept the 15th Army of 150,000 troops near Pas-de-Calais until August 1944. By that time, the Normandy beachhead was secure.

With this background on the methodology of deception, Chapters 3–6 delve step-by-step into the four elements that comprise it, beginning from Figure 2-6.

NOTES

1. Roy Godson and James J. Wirtz, "Strategic Denial and Deception," *International Journal of Intelligence and Counterlntelligence* 13 (2000): 426.

2. Robert P. Clark and William L. Mitchell, *Target-Centric Network Modeling* (Newbury Park, CA: SAGE, 2015).

3. Rob Dussault, "Denial and Deception in a Nutshell," *Defense Intelligence Journal* 15, no. 2 (2006): 83.

4. William L. Mitchell, "Operationalizing Battlespace Agility," *Militaert Tidsskrift* 141, no. 4 (2013): 78–95.

5. Ted Hopf, "The Promise of Constructivism in International Relations Theory," *International Security* 23, no. 1: 171–200.

6. Scott Gerwehr, "Cross-Cultural Variation in Denial and Deception," *Defense Intelligence Journal* 15, no. 2 (2006): 52.

7. Ibid.

8. Ewen Montagu, *The Man Who Never Was* (Annapolis, MD: Naval Institute Press, 1953).

9. Huw Hopkins, "D-Day 70–Pt.17–Operation FORTITUDE: Allied Deception Tactics," June 4, 2014, http://www.globalaviationresource.com/v2/2014/06/04/d-day-70-pt-17-operation-fortitude-allied-deception-tactics/.

THE OUTCOME SCENARIO

A desired outcome is best represented by a scenario. All scenarios are in essence specially constructed stories about the future, each one modeling a distinct potential outcome. Presumably, we begin with some idea of a likely outcome scenario that, absent any deception effort, is undesirable. We then identify a desired scenario, one that might be achieved via a deception effort.

Up front, the desired scenario is used to plan deception—the subject of Chapters 4–6. During execution of the deception, the desired scenario is used to search for the indicators that would tell whether it, or another scenario, is actually developing. The indicators help identify which alternative outcomes should be prepared for, so that the operations team can respond.

There are several formal methodologies for identifying likely outcome scenarios. CIA's tradecraft manual describes one such methodology, called *alternative futures analysis*.[1] Because the objective of deception is to shape the future, not simply estimate it, we take a somewhat different approach in this book.

The outcome scenario can be strategic, operational, or tactical. But an outcome scenario can be viewed from at least six different perspectives, and in considering outcomes, it is worth thinking about all six.

OUTCOME SCENARIOS: THE PMESII VIEW

When thinking about scenarios, we are concerned about how deception affects the outcome scenario. Barton Whaley's definition of deception, from Chapter 1, refers to three scenarios of deception when he says that it is "Information . . . intended to manipulate the behavior of others by inducing them to accept a false or distorted perception of reality [in] their physical, social, or political environment."[2]

Whaley's definition is a start. But to take a more complete perspective, six broad classes of outcome scenarios should be considered: political, military, economic, social, infrastructure, and information, abbreviated *PMESII*.[3] Any desired outcome scenario will be some combination of these classes. The PMESII construct stimulates original thinking about the results of a deception (both good and bad outcomes) and can be helpful in detecting and countering deception. Following is a summary of what each class of scenario might encompass with regard to deception.

- *Political.* Describes the distribution of responsibility and power at all levels of governance—formally constituted authorities, as well as informal or covert political powers. Examples of political outcome scenarios might include encouraging regime change; strengthening allies or weakening political opponents; inducing government repression of a minority population; or creating a coalition or standing alliance to oppose an opponent's expansion—NATO (the North Atlantic Treaty Organisation) is a premier example of such a coalition, though not one created by deception.

- *Military.* Explores the military and/or paramilitary capabilities or other ability to exercise force of all relevant actors (enemy, friendly, and neutral) in a given region or for a given issue. Examples of military outcome scenarios might include achieving surprise in an attack; strengthening military allies; or inducing opponents to build the wrong force structure or spend money on the wrong defenses.

- *Economic.* Encompasses individual and group behaviors related to producing, distributing, and consuming resources. Examples of economic outcome scenarios might include inducing other countries to place a trade embargo on a country; encouraging others to crack down on the narcotics trade; or disrupting existing trade agreements.

- *Social.* Describes the cultural, religious, and ethnic makeup within an area and the beliefs, values, customs, and behaviors of society members. Examples of social outcome scenarios might include introducing a contentious issue that destroys unity in a population; or its opposite, inducing popular opposition to a divisive movement. The Chinese government, for example, has conducted a number of deceptions as part of its campaign to develop domestic opposition to the Falun Gong movement.

- *Infrastructure.* Details the composition of the basic facilities, services, and installations needed for the functioning of a community in an area. Examples of infrastructure outcome scenarios might include inducing a government to abandon nuclear power, to its disadvantage; or causing a government to neglect, or overspend on, its transportation, communication, or food needs.

- *Information.* Explains the nature, scope, characteristics, and effects of individuals, organizations, and systems that collect, process, disseminate, or act on information. Many outcome scenarios in this category involve deceptions intended to disrupt or discredit an opponent's intelligence service.

An outcome scenario seldom must deal with only one of these factors. Complex scenarios are likely to involve them all. The events of the Arab Spring in 2011, the Syrian uprising that began that year, and the Ukrainian crisis of 2014 involved all of the PMESII factors.

Although no outcome scenario is likely to have only one PMESII perspective, there often is a dominant one, as illustrated in the examples that follow.

POLITICAL

Political deception is often referred to by the elegant euphemism "perception management," though all deceptions seek to manage perceptions in some fashion. It usually involves targeting national or regional leaders.

Former US Defense Intelligence Agency senior analyst Cynthia Grabo notes a number of examples of political deception where a government offered to negotiate an issue with the intent to mislead its opponent's leadership about an impending attack. She cites, for example, the negotiations or proposals that preceded the Soviet attack on Hungary in 1956 and the proposal by North Korea prior to invading the South in 1950.[4] The deception that preceded the Cuban missile crisis is another example that had military aspects but the targets of which were primarily political.

THE CUBAN MISSILE CRISIS

In early 1962 the Soviets decided to emplace nuclear-equipped SS-4 and SS-5 ballistic missiles in Cuba to counter the increasing US edge in ballistic missiles aimed at the Soviet Union. For the Soviets, the desired outcome scenario was that the US government would do nothing about the deployment—which they expected would be the case if the United States failed to recognize the deployment until the missiles were in Cuba and on combat-ready status. They envisioned a *fait accompli*—presenting the United States with a strategic missile threat from Cuba when it was too late for a US response.

The deployment was to be hidden from US intelligence by an elaborate D&D program that combined HUMINT, IMINT, OSINT, and diplomatic deception. It applied all four of the fundamental principles of deception described in Chapter 1:

Truth. En route, the ships carried agricultural equipment—tractors and harvesters—in plain sight. On reaching Cuba, anything that resembled agricultural equipment was unloaded in the daytime. Radio Moscow regularly reported that the Soviet Union was supplying Cuba with "machine tools, wheat, and agricultural

(Continued)

(Continued)

machinery . . . and fertilizer." In what proved to be a brilliant move, the Soviets leaked accurate information about the deployment to mask it. They funneled accurate details through counterrevolutionary Cuban organizations in the United States. The CIA discounted the information because they did not regard the groups as credible, and dismissed the subsequent stream of reporting from Cubans, tourists, and foreign diplomats in Cuba—some of which were valid—as simply more of the same.

Denial. Missiles were shipped from eight Soviet ports to hide the size of the effort; the missiles were loaded under cover of darkness. On reaching Cuba, weaponry was unloaded only at night, and moved directly to the missile bases along back roads at night. If visible on the decks, the missile crates and launchers were shielded with metal sheets to defeat infrared photography.

Deceit. Soviet military units designated for the Cuban assignment were told that they were going to a cold region. They were outfitted with skis, felt boots, fleece-lined parkas, and other winter equipment. Officers and missile specialists traveled to Cuba as machine operators, irrigation specialists, and agricultural specialists. The ships' captains made false declarations when exiting the Black Sea and the Bosporus. They altered the cargo records and declared tonnage well below what was being carried. They often listed Conakry, Guinea, as their destination. During September, Soviet diplomats gave repeated assurances to top US officials (including President John Kennedy) that they had no intention of putting offensive weaponry in Cuba.[5]

Misdirection. As noted earlier, a view of the top decks conveyed the impression that the ships were carrying only agricultural equipment. The Soviets and Cubans used Cuban counterrevolutionaries as a channel for reporting on missile deployments, knowing that CIA analysts would dismiss the reporting (and subsequent valid reports) as fabrications.

The political deception was a remarkably well-crafted multi-INT D&D effort that succeeded for a long time because the Soviets had a very good understanding of US intelligence capabilities and predispositions. But for a few mistakes discussed later, it might have succeeded.

MILITARY

Military deception has been practiced for several millennia. Sun Tzu's quote on deception in the preface illustrates its antiquity. Many of the best examples of military deception date from World War II. Deception was used frequently in that war to influence military leaders at the strategic, operational, and tactical levels. Much of the writings on deception since then have drawn on those examples because they illustrate the basic concepts and principles so well. Cases such as Operation Mincemeat and Operation Quicksilver have become exemplars of how to apply these concepts and principles.

However, plenty of military deceptions have been executed in more recent times. Deception can support both offensive and defensive military operations; and it can support tactical and strategic or operational actions. The desired outcome scenario in offensive operations almost always is to prevail in conflict—Egypt's objective in the Yom Kippur War was a notable exception to the rule, since the Egyptians did not expect to win but rather were setting the stage for a political settlement. In defensive deceptions, there can be a wider range of objectives. The following case illustrates a defensive and tactical deception that had the objective of simply avoiding defeat. In Chapter 4 we'll look at the deception that supported the 1990 Operation Desert Storm, which was operational and offensive and, of course, had the objective to prevail in the conflict.

TACTICAL DEFENSIVE DECEPTION IN KOSOVO

From February 1998 to June 1999, Kosovo—a former part of Yugoslavia—was the scene of bitter conflict. On one side was the Federal Republic of Yugoslavia (at that time, comprising the Republics of Montenegro and Serbia), which claimed Kosovo as its territory. On the other side was an Albanian rebel group called the Kosovo Liberation Army (KLA). After the failure of negotiations for a diplomatic solution, and responding to reports of Serbian atrocities, NATO began a campaign of airstrikes against the Serbian forces in March 1999. The Serbs responded with a deception effort that achieved some measure of success in defending against a force of 1,000 NATO aircraft during some ten weeks of airstrikes. Though the deceptions were well executed, eventually Serbia was forced to withdraw from Kosovo in the face of a threatened NATO ground forces invasion.

The war in Kosovo highlighted a Serbian military that was well versed in deception means and techniques. The Serbs drew heavily on Soviet *Maskirovka* doctrine in their deceptions. Maskirovka is defined in the 1978 Soviet Military Encyclopedia as

> A means of securing the combat operations and daily activity of forces; a complex of measures designed to mislead the enemy as to the presence and disposition of forces and various military objects, their condition, combat readiness and operations and also the plans of the commander. . . . Maskirovka contributes to the achievement of surprise for the actions of forces, the preservation of combat readiness and the increased survivability of objects.[6]

The Serbs applied Maskirovka extensively in Kosovo:

- They built decoy bridges out of plastic tarp and logs, and placed them near camouflaged real bridges—combining denial with deceit.[7]

- They painted bridges with infrared-sensitive material to break up their distinguishing shape in order to mislead US intelligence sensors.

- Serbian forces employed numerous decoy tanks throughout Kosovo. Some tanks were quite crudely built of wood and plastic; at close ranges, they were obvious decoys, but they were effective in deceiving Allied pilots flying at high altitudes.

- To add more realism to their deception, they created heat sources by burning trash, tires, and cooking oil near the decoy tanks to create an infrared signature.[8]

(Continued)

(Continued)

- Serbian forces disguised the results of Allied bombing in order to deny US intelligence an accurate battle damage assessment. Besides removing and hiding military wreckage, they created dummy bomb craters on roads and runways to portray damage and thereby avoid NATO targeting.

ECONOMIC

Deception has long been practiced by private persons and companies for economic gain. Techniques such as Ponzi schemes and deceptive corporate accounting are daily occurrences. These all are basically fraud and are not treated in this book; they typically fall in the purview of law enforcement.

Deception about trade also is common, especially in the case of illicit trade and gray arms trade. Godson and Wirtz note that "global financial markets and commerce form a new and profitable venue for D&D operations."[9] At the strategic level, deception is a tool for concealing or exaggerating economic strength or weakness to gain economic or other advantages. Deception in currency or commodities markets or products is practiced at the tactical level, as the following case illustrates.

THE 1972 SOVIET WHEAT CROP DECEPTION

In 1971 the USSR was facing a major wheat crop shortage that had to be covered by very large imports of wheat. Had that fact been generally known, it would have caused a major surge in the price of wheat worldwide—and, of course, would have resulted in the Soviets having to cover the shortfall at substantially higher prices than the existing market offered.

The Soviets perpetrated an elaborate deception to avoid that outcome scenario. They contacted major US grain exporters and arranged secret meetings to purchase the wheat without revealing the buyer. They entered into negotiations with US officials for an agricultural trade deal, meanwhile concealing their impending shortfall and their negotiations with exporters.

In July and August 1972, the USSR purchased 440 million bushels of wheat for approximately $700 million. At about the same time, the Soviets negotiated a trade deal under which the United States agreed to provide them with a credit of $750 million for the purchase of grain over a three-year period.[10]

The primary risk to the deception involved agricultural attachés from the US Department of Agriculture's Foreign Agricultural Service. These attachés had the job of monitoring crop developments worldwide and routinely reported on expected Soviet crop yields. Their estimates at the time were based on visual observations—requiring frequent visits to crop-producing areas. This part of the deception involved the Soviets steering their visitors to a few selected fields that were producing high yields—ensuring that the attachés had no chance to view other fields en route.[11] The US attachés suspected that they were being deceived but couldn't prove it.

Had the US government been aware of the Soviet shortfall, it certainly would not have extended the $750 million credit for grain purchases. It would have forced the Soviets to accept substantially higher prices for the grain that it did purchase. And it would have avoided the later political and economic consequences: The Soviets had acquired their wheat at bargain prices; the US government had funded the purchase; and US consumers had to deal with sharply higher food prices. The result was a political embarrassment for the US government.

SOCIAL

Deception is most often defined as influencing a decision maker to do something. But it is also used in information operations generally—and especially in PSYOPS—to shape public opinion, often about atrocities or, for example, adverse results of airstrikes.

- During the Kosovo conflict, the Serbs brought in news reporters to show them the results of a NATO airstrike that featured many bodies. A blood-stained baby doll was prominent in one photo and garnered such international attention that the same doll subsequently appeared in staged photographs of the results of other alleged air attacks.[12]

- During Operation Desert Storm, the Iraqis sheared off the dome of the al-Basrah mosque, then brought foreign news media to the location and falsely accused the coalition and the United States of destroying religious shrines. The deception was crude—no bomb could cleanly cut the top off of a mosque and leave the surrounding building undamaged, and the nearest bomb crater was some distance from the mosque. But many people accepted the incident as true.

- During 2015, a widespread belief developed among Iraqis that the United States was secretly supporting Daesh. Iraqi fighters reported viewing videos of US helicopters delivering supplies and weapons to Daesh. The widely believed (among Iraqis) rationale for such an unlikely collusion was a US goal to regain control over Iraq and its oil reserves.[13] Although the source of the belief (and the videos) could not be established, a PSYOP operated by Iran or its Iraqi supporters is a possibility.

Unlike most deceptions, the end objective of social deception may not be to cause specific actions by the target population, but rather to shape attitudes. Psychological operations are most commonly associated with these deceptions. But one social deception during WWII also was aimed at encouraging specific actions, as the next case—which we will return to later on—illustrates.

BLACK BOOMERANG

The British Secret Service set up a novel and very successful "black" psychological operation[14] that made use of BBC monitoring of German radio broadcasts during World War II. A black radio station in the United Kingdom was staffed with native German speakers, including anti-Nazi prisoner of war (POW) volunteers. Purporting to be a German Wehrmacht station called *Atlantiksender*, it broadcast news for the troops. Interspersed with actual news items were tidbits of distortions and gossip designed to drive a wedge between the Wehrmacht and the Nazi party. The full story is told in Sefton Delmer's book, *Black Boomerang*.[15]

The stories in the news broadcasts typically hit themes such as the inequality of sacrifice between the common soldier and the "privileged" Nazi party functionaries and, therefore, were intended to promote no more serious actions than malingering and desertions. But some broadcasts were carefully tailored to encourage sabotage. In "news items," the broadcasters criticized U-boat crew members who had, due to a "selfish desire for self-preservation," delayed the departure of their submarines by conducting unattributable acts of sabotage. The unattributable acts were, of course, carefully described in the broadcast.

Black propaganda can be a highly effective deception tool, and it is especially useful in conjunction with other types of deception, applied to achieve synergy.

INFORMATION

As noted earlier, intelligence is usually thought of as a channel for deception—the information channel. A major feature of the Indian nuclear test (see Chapter 1) was the elaborate intelligence deception the Indians conducted to defeat US imagery assets. In that case, the target was political (with a goal of having the US leadership take no action), and the information channel was simply the means.

There are a number of cases, though, where the information channel (the intelligence organization) is the target. These usually fall into the realm of counterintelligence. The Soviet and later the Russian government conducted an elaborate series of deceptions between 1985 and 2001 to protect two of its most valuable intelligence assets—Aldrich Ames and Robert Hanssen. Those cases are discussed later, in Chapter 6. Some of the earliest and most effective information deceptive operations were set up to protect the Ultra collection program.

THE ULTRA DECEPTION

During World War II, British cryptanalysts (with help from the Polish Secret Service) managed to break the German Enigma encryption system—a story that has been told in books (*The Ultra Secret and Codebreakers: The Inside Story of Bletchley Park*) and a 2014 film (*The Imitation Game*). This breakthrough allowed the British to read sizeable portions of the German military's top-secret messages to its army and navy commanders in the field. Ultra subsequently became a major factor in Allied military successes during the war. We'll revisit the Ultra case in later chapters, because it illustrates several features of a successful deception.

Soon after they successfully broke the encryption, the British recognized the dangers of aggressively using the intelligence they were getting. The messages revealed, for example, German U-boat deployments to intercept convoys and the locations of Axis supply ships bound for North Africa. If the British were to warn the convoys, or intercept the U-boats and supply ships, Germany would likely suspect a communications compromise.

The solution was a deception requiring the use of a credible alternate channel. Where action had to be taken that might appear suspicious—mostly sinking German or Italian ships and submarines based on Ultra intercepts—some action had to be taken that would point to an alternate channel. Spotter aircraft and submarines typically would be sent to identify the target, which was then attacked.[16] Axis forces monitoring the aircraft and submarine radio transmissions believed that the attacks were the result of normal reconnaissance. To avoid raising suspicions about the consistent "lucky" finds by a single aircraft, the British would send out several search missions to cover different areas, including the one where they knew that the ships would be found. As Sir Harry Hinsley describes the protocol,

> Every one of those ships before it was attacked and sunk had to be sighted by a British aeroplane or submarine which had been put in a position in which it would sight it without it [the ship] knowing that it [the British aircraft or submarine] had been put in that position, and had made a sighting signal which the Germans and the Italians had intercepted. That was the standard procedure. As a consequence of that the Germans and the Italians assumed that we had 400 submarines whereas we had 25. And they assumed that we had a huge reconnaissance Air Force on Malta, whereas we had three aeroplanes![17]

In some cases, this standard protocol wasn't feasible, and some additional deception was necessary. During 1941, a convoy of five ships left Naples carrying supplies that were critically needed by Axis forces in North Africa. Normally a reconnaissance mission would be sent out to observe the ships, and strike aircraft would take off after the sighting was reported. In this case, the ships would arrive at their North African port before the strike aircraft could catch them. British prime minister Winston Churchill ordered an attack based solely on Ultra intelligence. Fearing that the Germans would suspect that their communications had been compromised, the British conducted a special deception operation. They sent a radio message congratulating a nonexistent spy in Naples for warning them of the ships' departure. The message was sent using a cipher system that the Germans could decode, and it apparently succeeded.[18]

(Continued)

(Continued)

Sir Hinsley notes that the problem in the North Atlantic required additional deception approaches:

> Similar precautions were taken in the Atlantic, but there the problem was different. That is why the Germans got most suspicious about the Atlantic. The great feature there was that the Enigma was used in the first instance not to fight the U-Boats but to evade them. And the problem was how could you evade them without their noticing. You have a situation . . . in which the number of U-Boats at sea in the Atlantic is going up, and the number of convoys they see is going down![19]
>
> How do you cover that? We did cover it but it was done by a different system from what I have just described in the Mediterranean. We let captured Germans, people we had captured from U-Boats write home from prison camp and we instructed our people when interrogated by Germans—our pilots for example—to propagate the view that we had absolutely miraculous radar which could detect a U-Boat even if it was submerged from hundreds of miles. And the Germans believed it.[20]

This particular technique—a deception that relies on some novel source of intelligence (usually based on a technology breakthrough) is particularly effective. Intelligence services worldwide are especially vulnerable to paranoia about an opponent's "novel" sources.

INFRASTRUCTURE

An outcome scenario can sometimes include a country's infrastructure. Such was the case in the covert action associated with the Farewell Dossier.

THE FAREWELL DOSSIER

Covert operations usually depend on deception for success, as the Farewell operation shows. In 1980 the French internal security service *Direction de la Surveillance du Territoire* (DST) recruited a KGB lieutenant colonel, Vladimir I. Vetrov, codenamed Farewell. Vetrov gave the French some 4,000 documents, detailing an extensive KGB effort to clandestinely acquire technical know-how from the West, primarily from the United States. In 1981 French president François Mitterrand shared the source and the documents (which DST named the Farewell Dossier) with US president Ronald Reagan.

The documents revealed a far-reaching and successful intelligence operation that had already acquired highly sensitive military technology information about radars, computers, machine tools, nuclear weaponry, and manufacturing techniques. But the specific targets remaining on the list provided the needed guidance for an effective covert operation based on deception.

In early 1982 the US Department of Defense, the Federal Bureau of Investigation, and the CIA began developing a counterattack. Instead of simply improving US defenses against the KGB efforts, the US team used the KGB shopping list to feed back, through CIA-controlled channels, the items on the list—augmented with "improvements" that were designed to pass acceptance testing but would fail randomly in service. Flawed computer chips, turbines, and factory plans found their way into Soviet military and civilian factories and equipment. Misleading information on US stealth technology and space defense flowed into the Soviet intelligence reporting. The resulting failures were a severe setback for major segments of Soviet industry. The most dramatic single event resulted when the United States provided gas pipeline management software that was installed in the trans-Siberian gas pipeline. The software had a feature that would, at some time, cause the pipeline pressure to build up to a level far above its fracture pressure. The result was the Soviet gas pipeline explosion of 1982, described as the "most monumental non-nuclear explosion and fire ever seen from space."[21]

Mounting a deception campaign often requires extensive effort, but sometimes it is worth the payoff. The Farewell operation was expensive to run but produced many benefits in terms of damage to the Soviet infrastructure; it may have hastened the end of the Cold War.

In many ways, the Farewell operation was the perfect covert operation. Even its subsequent exposure did not reduce the effectiveness of the operation, since the exposure called into question all of the successful KGB technology acquisitions and discredited the KGB's technology collection effort within the Soviet Union.[22] Whether or not intended, the operation damaged KGB credibility and its effectiveness. The operation would not have been possible without the detailed knowledge that Vetrov provided about the KGB's intelligence channels. It allowed the United States to create detailed models of the KGB targets; the nature of the KGB operations; and the linkages—that is, the use of other Warsaw Pact country intelligence services in the technology acquisition effort.

NOTES

1. CIA, *A Tradecraft Primer: Structured Analytic Techniques for Improving Intelligence Analysis* (Washington, DC: Author, 2009), 34.

2. Barton Whaley, "The Prevalence of Guile: Deception through Time and across Cultures and Disciplines," essay prepared for the Foreign Denial and Deception Committee, DNI, Washington, DC, February 2, 2007, https://cryptome.org/2014/08/prevalence-of-guile.pdf.

3. R. Hillson, "The DIME/PMESII Model Suite Requirements Project," *NRL Review* (2009): 23539, www.dtic.mil/cgi-bin/GetTRDoc?AD=ADA525056.

4. Cynthia M. Grabo, *Anticipating Surprise: Analysis for Strategic Warning* (Washington, DC: Joint Military Intelligence College, Center for Strategic Intelligence Research, 2002), 119–28.

5. James H. Hansen, "Soviet Deception in the Cuban Missile Crisis," *CIA: Studies in Intelligence*, 46, no. 1 (2002), http://www.cia.gov/csi/studies/vol46no1/article06.html.

6. C. J. Dick, "Maskirovka in Yugoslav Military Thinking," Conflict Studies Research Centre, July 1999, http://www.da.mod.uk/Research-Publications/category/68/a100-maskirovka-in-yugoslav-military-thinking-1528.

7. Peter Martin, "The Sky's the Limit: A Critical Analysis of the Kosovo Airwar," November 1, 1999, http://www.infowar.com/iwftp/cloaks/99/CD_1999-214.txt/.

8. Ibid.; see also Steven Lee Myers, "Damage to Serb Military Less Than Expected," *New York Times,* June 28, 1999, http://www.nytimes.com/library/world/europe/062899kosovo-bombdamage.html, and Tim Ripley, "Kosovo: A Bomb Damage Assessment," *Jane's Intelligence Review* (September 1999): 10–13.

9. Roy Godson and James J. Wirtz, "Strategic Denial and Deception," *International Journal of Intelligence and Counterlntelligence* 13 (2000): 430

10. US Department of Agriculture, "Exporter's Profits on Sales of Wheat to Russia," February 12, 1974, http://archive.gao.gov/f0302/096760.pdf.

11. Bob Porter, *Have Clearance, Will Travel* (Bloomington, IN: iUniverse, 2008), 34.

12. US Department of Defense, "Background Briefing on Enemy Denial and Deception," October 24, 2001, http://www.au.af.mil/au/awc/awcgate/dod/t10242001_t1024dd.htm.

13. Liz Sly, "Iraqis Think the U.S. Is in Cahoots with the Islamic State, and It Is Hurting the War," *Washington Post*, December 1, 2015, https://www.washingtonpost.com/world/middle_east/iraqis-think-the-us-is-in-cahoots-with-isis-and-it-is-hurting-the-war/2015/12/01/d00968ec-9243-11e5-befa-99ceebcbb272_story.html.

14. Black PSYOPS messages purport to come from a source other than the actual one.

15. Sefton Delmer, *Black Boomerang* (New York: Viking Press, January 1962).

16. F. W. Winterbotham, *The Ultra Secret* (New York: Dell, 1974), 133.

17. Sir Harry Hinsley, "The Influence of ULTRA in the Second World War," lecture at Cambridge University, October 19, 1993, http://www.cix.co.uk/~klockstone/hinsley.htm.

18. Mark Simmons, *The Battle of Matapan 1941: The Trafalgar of the Mediterranean* (Stroud, Gloucestershire, UK: The History Press, 1941), 31.

19. Hinsley, "The Influence of ULTRA in the Second World War."

20. Ibid.

21. Thomas C. Reed, *At the Abyss: An Insider's History of the Cold War* (Novato, CA: Presidio Press, 2004).

22. Gus W. Weiss, "The Farewell Dossier," *CIA: Studies in Intelligence* 39, no. 5 (1996), http://www.cia.gov/csi/studies/96unclass.

THE TARGET

Once the desired outcome scenario has been established, attention is focused on the target(s) of deception. For most outcome scenarios, the objective is for the target (individual or group) to make decisions and take actions that lead to the chosen scenario. The decision and action steps are discussed together in this chapter, with a focus on the decision step; once the target makes a decision, then presumably the action will follow. The two steps are closely interrelated. Recognize, though, that they are still separate steps.

INDIVIDUAL DECISION MODELING[1]

Deception usually depends on assessing the likely behavior of political, military, or nonstate organization leaders, specifically to determine what decisions they tend to make under given conditions. Many factors have to be taken into account in making this assessment. The target's background and decision-making process have to be assessed. For example,

- To what extent does the target misperceive reality? Some opponents have a tendency to believe their own propaganda. Is the target prone to loss aversion? Some people strongly prefer avoiding losses over acquiring gains. Studies indicate that losses are up to twice as psychologically powerful as gains, and they consistently shape likely decisions.

- What preconceptions and biases does the target have? These can be cultural, political, or doctrinal in nature. What preconceptions may the target have about the deceiver's intentions and capabilities?

- Is the target prone to *inductive thinking*, that is, a tendency to draw general conclusions from past experiences? If so, what have those experiences been? The Yom Kippur deception and some cases presented in this chapter illustrate the importance of past experiences on a target's willingness to accept (and act on) a deception.

The purpose of decision analysis is always predictive: How will the target react to a given situation? The identification of key decision makers, their backgrounds, and psychological profiles are all critical components. The end state is to know what the target believes, what he wishes to believe, and what he is prepared to believe.

To do this sort of predictive analysis, simulation models of leadership decision-making have been developed and tested. Typically, they simulate the personality, problem-solving styles, values, goals, and environments of individual leaders. One example is Athena's Prism, developed by the University of Pennsylvania. Athena's Prism can be configured to identify likely decisions by real-world leaders in different conflict situations, relying on human behavior models from the social sciences.[2]

In all behavioral analysis, but especially in decision prediction, four perspectives of the decision process have to be considered: rational, administrative, emotional, and cultural.[3] The first three are highlighted in this section. Cultural models are described later in the chapter, after we look at how the decision-making process may be played out in groups.

Rational Models

Targets of deception rarely are rational, in the sense that your own culture defines rationality. That is especially true of terrorist and criminal group leadership, but it is also true of many national leaders. And even leaders regarded as rational can have "hot buttons"—issues or situations where the leader is emotionally involved and departs from a rational path, as we'll discuss later in this chapter.

Rational decision-making is broadly defined as a logical and occasionally quantitative procedure for thinking about difficult problems. Stated formally, rational decision-making requires the systematic evaluation of costs or benefits accruing to courses of action that might be taken. It entails identifying the choices involved, assigning values (costs and benefits) for possible outcomes, and expressing the probability of those outcomes being realized.

A rational model of decision making is based on the idea of optimal choice: Decision makers will make the choice that will have the best outcome for themselves or their organizations. It assumes that decision makers are objective and well informed, and will therefore select the most effective alternative. This approach is based on the assumption that decisions are made on an explicit or implicit cost-benefit analysis, also known as *expected utility theory*.[4] The theory views decision-making as behavior that maximizes utility. Individuals faced with a decision will, consciously or subconsciously, identify the available options, the possible outcomes associated with each option, the utility of each option-outcome combination, and the probability that each option-outcome combination will occur. Decision makers will then choose an option that is likely to yield, in their own terms, the highest overall utility. The following assumptions are embedded in a rational model:

- The decision maker has a number of known alternative courses of action.

- Each alternative has consequences that are known and are quantified.

- The decision maker has a set of preferences that allows for assessment of the consequences and selection of an alternative.[5]

Using these assumptions, rational decision simulations attempt to identify the most likely option that decision makers will select in a given situation.

We don't encounter many truly rational actors on the world stage, which is a good thing when you're trying to pull off a deception because they can be difficult to deceive. Even when the mechanics of a deception succeed, as happened in the following case, there may be a number of rational responses to the deception, and the decision maker may not choose the expected one.

THE ETHIOPIAN CAMPAIGN DECEPTION

In 1940 the British were preparing to reclaim British Somaliland—which the Italians had taken earlier that year—and to expel the Italians from Ethiopia. The British operations plan was to attack from the North, out of the Sudan. The British deception plan was to make the Italians expect the attack to come from the East, across the Red Sea into British Somaliland. The deception involved extensive dummy message traffic and military activity in Aden, indicating a large force assembling at the notional source of the invasion. The troops preparing for the invasion were issued maps and pamphlets about Somaliland. The Japanese counsel in Port Said, Egypt, received false information about an invasion originating in Aden.[6]

The deception succeeded, in that the duke of Aosta—the Italian leader in Ethiopia—believed that the invasion would come from Aden into Somaliland. However, it failed in its primary goal, which was to pull Italian forces away from the North and put them in Somaliland—which is what the British would have done in the same circumstances, and what most Italian generals would have done. The duke instead pulled his forces out of Somaliland and moved them into the mountains—where they were well positioned to resist the British attack from the North.

Occasionally, one encounters an opponent whose decisions fit the rational model. Such was the case with the duke of Aosta.

Prince Amedeo, third duke of Aosta, was educated at Eton College and Oxford University in England. He was, in some ways, more British than the British—in

(Continued)

(Continued)

behavior, mannerisms, and sports such as fox hunting and polo. When World War I broke out, he was offered a commission in the Italian Royal Army. Recognizing that the commission was offered only because of his connections with the royal house of Italy, he refused. He instead enlisted in an artillery unit. Amedeo served with distinction in the ensuing conflict and ended the war as a major. In 1932 he became a pilot in the Italian Air Force. As squadron commander, he led a group of Italian airmen who helped defeat Libyan opponents in the conflict there.

In 1937 Amedeo was appointed viceroy of Ethiopia. His rule there is considered to be one of the most benevolent and beneficial that Ethiopia has experienced. He directed an overhaul of the country's infrastructure to rebuild the country and improve the standard of living. He enacted sweeping social changes that included outlawing slavery.[7]

The British deception plan apparently conveyed the image of a large force positioned to invade from Aden. The duke concluded that the British force would be too strong to resist. He instead ordered his troops to fall back from the coastal cities to the more defensible mountainous areas. He believed that his best chance for victory would be to wear down his attackers on defense, and then to deliver a counterattack once the British had impaled themselves on his lines.[8]

Could the British have reasonably foreseen the duke's decision? The profile that the British should have had was that of a competent and experienced military officer with an excellent understanding of the British military. Furthermore, the duke comes across as a noble and compassionate leader who was intimately familiar with the Ethiopian terrain and who placed a high priority on protecting his troops—in sum, a rational man. His experiences in World War I appear to have convinced him of the advantages that come with defending. Perhaps the British should have put more time into studying their deception target and at least have considered the alternative outcome scenarios in planning the deception.

A rational decision estimate, based on expected utility theory, is the place to start any decision simulation, but it is not the end point. Some other models should be considered, and they may be more accurate individually or in combination in assessing an opponent's likely decision. Sometimes, administrative or emotional models are more appropriate. Let's look at them each in turn.

Administrative Models

The utility theory (rational) approach is useful in decision estimates, but it must be used with caution. Why? Because people won't always make the effort to find the optimum action to solve a problem. The complexity of any realistic decision problem dissuades them. Instead, people tend to select a number of possible outcomes that would be "good enough." They then choose a strategy or an action that is likely to achieve one of the good-enough outcomes.[9]

This tendency of leaders to make suboptimal choices leads to a variant of the rational decision-making model called the *administrative model*. It discards the three assumptions in the rational model and treats decision makers as people having incomplete information, under time pressures, and perhaps beset with conflicting preferences—a situation often encountered in conducting deception. In this situation, decision makers typically look for shortcuts to find acceptable solutions. They do not try to optimize; they instead identify and accept a good-enough alternative. The optimal solution is the alternative with the highest value; but what is called "satisficing" requires no more than finding the first alternative with an acceptable value.[10]

There are limits, though, on how well we can simulate (and therefore predict) decisions based solely on either the rational or the administrative model. To improve decision estimates, we have to include emotional and cultural factors. These are the factors that often cause a target's decision, or the action of a group or population, to be labeled "irrational."

Emotional Models

A third aspect of the decision process to consider when analyzing behavior is the emotional. While we discuss it last as a factor in individual decision making, it often dominates as a factor. Pride, envy, and revenge are all emotional motivators. All types of targets, from national leaders and military generals to business professionals, make some decisions simply because they want to pay back an opponent for past wrongs. (Consider again the reason that Gondorff places his massive bet in *The Sting*.) The emotional aspect of behavioral prediction cannot be ignored, and personality profiling is one way to grasp it.

Intelligence analysts have developed many methodologies for personality profiling of opponents based on their experience that personal idiosyncrasies and predispositions have a greater bearing on an opponent's decisions than will a calculated assessment of resources and capabilities.[11] The resulting profile is a model that can be used to assess likely decisions.[12]

One methodology, the Myers-Briggs model, has been a standard since 1962. Sixteen personality types were identified, with emotion (in terms of sensing, feeling, and perceiving) being an integral component for each. A decision by one Myers-Briggs personality type will be predictably different from a decision made by another Myers-Briggs type. Obviously, an executive who was a linebacker on a college football team will have a completely different decision-making style than an executive who was president of the chess club.[13] Former national leaders such as Saddam Hussein and Chile's dictator Augusto Pinochet have been assessed as ESTJ on the Myers-Briggs scale—a type defined as "The Executive," possessed with confidence about their superior decision-making ability, relative lack of empathy for others, and reluctance to admit mistakes.

Many countries create emotional models or psychological profiles of the leaders with whom they must deal. In 2017 it was noted that the Russian government had developed a dossier on newly elected US president Donald Trump. The dossier reportedly concluded that Trump is a risk-taker and naïve in regard to international affairs.[14]

Emotional models also can be the dominant ones to consider in planning deceptions against target groups or even entire populations rather than individuals; that is, in social deception. Chapter 3 describes how, during 2015, a widespread belief developed among Iraqis (probably with Iranian help) that the United States was secretly supporting Daesh. That belief endured because many Iraqis had a strongly negative view of the United States and of US motives in Iraq. They had a propensity to believe. Groups, discussed next, can be swayed by emotion—including emotion induced by religious beliefs.

COLLECTIVE DECISION MODELING

The preceding section focused on decisions made by one person. But decisions are often made by a collective entity or reached by organizational consensus. In deceptions that support counterintelligence operations, for example, the target is a foreign intelligence service, and the objective usually is to convince that service rather than a single individual.

Such cases require a collective decision-prediction approach. It is somewhat easier to estimate what a group will decide than to estimate what an individual will decide—which is not to say that it is easy. In such decision modeling, one must identify the decision makers—often the most difficult step of the process—and then determine the likely decisions.

The collective decision-making model has been referred to as a *political model*. Its dominant features are that

- power is decentralized; therefore,

- in place of a single goal, value set, or set of interests of a single decision maker, there exist multiple and often competing goals, values, and interests among the decision makers; therefore,

- decisions result from a bargaining among individuals and coalitions.

So the collective decision-making model is a complex process of conflict resolution and consensus building; decisions are the products of compromises.[15]

In spite of this complexity, some analytic tools and techniques are available to estimate the likely outcome of group decision-making. These tools and techniques are based on the theories of social choice expounded by the Marquis de Condorcet, an eighteenth-century mathematician. He suggested that the prevailing alternative should be the one preferred by a majority over each of the other choices in an exhaustive series of pairwise comparisons. Another technique is to start by drawing an influence diagram that shows the persons involved in the collective decision. Collective decisions tend to have more of the rational elements and less of the emotional. But unless the decision participants come from different cultures, the end decision will be no less cultural in nature. In assessing collective decision-making, the Hofstede individualism index, discussed later in this chapter, is an important consideration.

Game Theory

One branch of the operations research discipline, known as *game theory*, is a powerful tool for decision modeling of both individual and group decisions. Game theory, in brief, is about analyzing the decision processes of two or more parties (referred to as the "players") in conflict or cooperation. It can be applied as a thought exercise or, because it makes use of mathematical models, by using simulations. It is, in a sense, a mathematical model of a sequence of OODA loops.

The game assumes the existence of two or more interdependent player strategies. Each player must determine how the other players will respond to his or her current or previous move. Each player next determines how he or she will respond to the estimated move of the other players, and the game cycle of action and response continues. The idea is for players to anticipate how their initial decisions will determine the end result of the game. Using this information, a player identifies an initial preferred decision.

The success of game theory depends on understanding the decision processes of the other players. So solid cultural models, as discussed later in this chapter, are essential. Game theory usually assumes that the other players will follow a rational decision process. When that is not the case, it becomes even more important to place oneself in the shoes of the other player(s).

The most prominent figure in applying game theory to intelligence issues may be Bruce Bueno de Mesquita. Over a thirty-year period, he has developed and refined a simulation model that applies game theory to produce political estimates. The estimates have an impressive success record:

- Five years before the death of Iran's Ayatollah Khomeini in 1989, Bueno de Mesquita identified Khomeini's successor, Ali Khamenei.

- In February 2008 he predicted correctly that Pakistan's president, Pervez Musharraf, would be forced out of office by the end of summer.

- In May 2010 he predicted that Egypt's president, Hosni Mubarak, would be forced from power within a year. Mubarak left the country nine months later, amid massive street protests.[16]

Bueno de Mesquita's estimates are not always on target—no predictive simulations are. But he reportedly has produced a large number of accurate political estimates as a consultant for the US Department of State, the Pentagon, the US intelligence community, and several foreign governments.[17]

A worthy opponent will apply game theory as well, and intelligence has a role in identifying the opponent's deceptive moves. Edieal J. Pinker, a Yale University professor of operations research, has applied game theory to the 2015 P5+1-Iranian negotiations and developed a hypothesis that the Iranians are carrying out a long-term deception. According to Pinker,

> Using game theory, we treat the situation as a leader/follower game, like chess, where opponents take turns moving. The first move goes to the West: to choose a threshold for action. The second move goes to Iran: to choose how to manage its weapons development program, taking into account the West's threshold for action.
>
> What is Iran's best strategy, assuming that it wants to develop nuclear weapons? If you're Ayatollah Khamenei and you want to obtain a destructive nuclear military capability, the fastest way to achieve that goal is to do two things in parallel: enrich uranium and develop military delivery systems. But knowing your opponents, the United States and Israel, you know that the fastest way is not the best way. You're aware that if you clearly demonstrate your military intentions, they will be forced to attack you. Another piece of intelligence: you know that there isn't very much political support for war in the United States, especially in the wake of the recent conflicts in Afghanistan and Iraq. Your strategy, therefore, is to not cross the threshold that will compel the United States to act forcefully until the last moment possible.
>
> Therefore your best choice is the slower choice: First, you declare that you are enriching uranium solely for peaceful purposes, like generating energy and providing nuclear materials for treating cancer patients. Second, you refrain from weaponizing the uranium until the very last moment possible. Since your enemies have already shown that they are reluctant to attack, if you don't step across their threshold, you can continue your nuclear program. Once you are ready, you will need to make a mad rush to complete the final steps toward a weapon before the United States and Israel react.[18]

The Pinker hypothesis illustrates the value of game theory in assessing the motivation behind an opponent's actions. Interestingly, Bueno de Mesquita in 2008 ran a game theory simulation that came to a different conclusion; it predicted Iran would reach the brink of developing a nuclear weapon and then stop as moderate elements came to power.[19] The part about moderates coming to power did occur when Hassan Rouhani assumed the presidency in 2013. But whether Pinker's hypothesis or Bueno de Mesquita's simulation more accurately describes the Iranian situation remained an open question in 2018.

Modeling Alternative Decisions

Whether dealing with individual or group decisions, we need to carefully think through possible alternative decisions that the target(s) will make when presented with a story. We've covered several different factors that affect decision-making in this chapter. In practice, though, how does one make use of these factors to identify the most likely decisions of an opponent? The opponent doesn't always make the decision that you expect. The example of the duke of Aosta, cited earlier, illustrates that point. A more recent historical example from Operation Desert Storm illustrates the importance of modeling the target's alternative decisions in case the target doesn't choose what appears to be most likely.

OPERATION DESERT STORM

In late 1990 a US-led coalition was planning for Operation Desert Storm—the campaign to retake the country of Kuwait, which Iraq had invaded and occupied earlier that year. The coalition forces numbered nearly one million troops in Saudi Arabia, over 70 percent of which were US combat units. They faced a comparable number of Iraqi troops deployed in Kuwait.

A frontal assault from Saudi Arabia into Kuwait would meet strong resistance from Iraqis in prepared defensive positions, and the coalition could expect heavy casualties. The more attractive option was a flanking maneuver into Iraq from the west to encircle and cut off the Iraqi forces in Kuwait—a tactic that later became known as the "left hook" or "Hail Mary" maneuver. From the coalition point of view, this was an obvious tactic. It would work; but if the Iraqis saw it coming, they would undoubtedly deploy forces to counter it.

The coalition objective was for the Iraqis to believe a scenario in which the ground attack would come from the South, along with an attack from the Persian Gulf into Kuwait. If successful, this would divert Iraqi attention away from a flanking maneuver through the desert.

Media channels were used to stage a diversion that had two major components:

- One component aimed to portray a Marine amphibious assault. A Marine Expeditionary Force conducted several amphibious training exercises, the most significant being Operation Imminent Thunder. The press was given access to cover these training operations that included an amphibious rehearsal in nearby Oman. The coalition also dropped propaganda leaflets on the occupying Iraqis that depicted a tidal wave shaped like a Marine washing over Iraqi soldiers. General Schwarzkopf, the US commander, was careful not to lie to the press. He simply conveyed the idea that the Marines were in the Gulf, ready to conduct an amphibious landing.

- Military units in Saudi Arabia, meanwhile, constructed replicas of Iraqi defensive positions across the border and conducted extensive training

(Continued)

(Continued)

against them. The press pool was allowed to observe and report on this training.

As the invasion date approached, coalition units conducted operational deceptions to reinforce the deception scenario. These demonstrations had the intended effect of causing seven Iraqi divisions to shift to the Kuwaiti Coast.

- In the week preceding the invasion, coalition aircraft conducted strikes against coastal targets and attacked Iraqi warships in Kuwait's waters, conveying the impression of an impending landing.

- A week before the main attack began on February 23, 1991, Marines crossed over the Saudi Arabia border to attack Iraqi forces in the south of Kuwait.

- On the morning of February 24, SEAL Task Force Mike conducted an amphibious feint, supported by naval gunfire, again to convey the impression of preparing the beach for an amphibious assault.[20]

The deception was helped by Iraqi perceptions about the danger of desert operations. They believed that any coalition force moving through the desert would become lost and pose no threat. The Iraqis had little operational experience in the desert, and their limited experiences there had convinced them that desert travel was hazardous. They somehow failed to appreciate how much the global positioning system (GPS) would affect desert operations.[21]

As with any major deception, there were a few flaws—aircraft and vehicle operations on the left flank that could have caught Iraqi attention—but these either weren't observed or weren't acted upon.[22] The deception was a success in that the Iraqis were caught by surprise when the coalition forces in the "Left Hook" maneuver swept into Iraq, cutting off supply lines and retreat for many Republican Guard troops.

While the deception was an unquestioned success, it had one unintended consequence. As was the case with the Ethiopian campaign, the deception operations led opposition leaders to make an unexpected decision.

The First Marine Expeditionary Force met little resistance as it advanced along the coast. The Iraqi commanders, it turned out, were concerned that they would be flanked by an amphibious landing. They accordingly had pulled their forces back some forty kilometers. The resulting quick advance of coalition units forced General Schwarzkopf to launch the "Hail Mary" attack some eighteen hours earlier than he had planned.

Like the Ethiopian campaign example, the Iraqi reaction could have been at least foreseen as a possibility by looking at the situation through the viewpoint of the Iraqi commanders. Iraq's recent experience in the Iraq-Iran war had taught them to emphasize defensive operations. And Iraqi concerns about a flanking maneuver should not have been difficult to foresee, given their assessment of the opposing deployments.

The preceding sections discussed the target when a decision or specific outcome was intended. But some scenarios don't aim for a specific decision or outcome. In some instances, the desired scenario is designed to shape the perceptions or beliefs of the target group or population to the advantage of the deceiver. It may or may not result in the target group taking any action. Planning this outcome scenario typically requires modeling the target culture—which is an important factor in both decision-making and the development of perceptions and beliefs.

CULTURAL MODELING

We treat cultural modeling last, because it can apply to deceptions targeting individual and group decision-making and to deceptions, usually PSYOPS, targeting populations when no decision is expected—perhaps only a perception or belief that benefits the deceiver. It is an essential first step when one plans to engage in memetic conflict (discussed in Chapter 8).

A critical component of decision modeling is the prediction of a human's behavior, within some bounds of uncertainty. But behavior cannot be predicted with any confidence without putting it in the target's social and cultural context. A deception planner needs to understand elements of a culture such as how it trains its youth for adult roles and how it defines what is important in life. In behavioral analysis, culture defines the ethical norms of the collective to which a group or decision maker belongs. It dictates values and constrains decisions.[23] In general, culture is a constraining social or environmental force. Different cultures have different habits of thought, different values, and different motivations. Straight modeling of a decision-making process without understanding these differences can lead the deception planner into the "irrational behavior" trap, which is what happened to US and Japanese planners in 1941.

Before Japan attacked Pearl Harbor, both the United States and Japan made exceptionally poor predictions about the other's decisions. Both sides indulged in mirror imaging—that is, they acted as though the opponent would use a rational decision-making process as *they* defined *rational*.

US planners reasoned that the superior military, economic, and industrial strength of the United States would deter attack. Japan could not win a war against the United States, so a Japanese decision to attack would be irrational.[24]

The Japanese also knew that a long-term war with the United States was not winnable because of the countries' disparities in industrial capacity. But Japan thought that a knockout blow at Pearl Harbor would encourage the United States to seek a negotiated settlement in the Pacific and East Asia.[25] To validate this assumption, the Japanese drew on their past experience—a similar surprise attack on the Russian fleet at Port Arthur in 1904 had eventually resulted in the Japanese obtaining a favorable negotiated settlement. The Japanese did not mirror image the United States with themselves, but with the Russians of 1904 and 1905. Japan believed that the US government would behave much as the tsarist government had.

Such errors in predicting an opponent's decision-making process are common when cultural factors are not taken into account. Cultural differences cause competitors not to make the "obvious" decision. During the Cold War, US analysts of the Soviet leadership within and without the intelligence community—known as "Kremlinologists"—often encountered a cultural divide in assessing likely Soviet moves. Soviet leader Nikita Khrushchev reportedly disparaged US Kremlinologists, remarking, "They are from a highly educated nation and they look upon us as being highly educated. They don't know that we are dominated by an unimaginative and unattractive bunch of scoundrels."[26]

Given that cultural differences are a significant factor in decision-making, we'd like to have some sort of cultural "template" to assist in constructing a decision model for any given target for a deception operation. Such templates do exist, and a commonly applied set of templates is known as the Hofstede cultural dimensions.

National cultures can be described according to the analysis of Geert Hofstede. These ideas were first based on a large research project into national culture differences across subsidiaries of a multinational corporation (IBM) in 64 countries.[27] Subsequent studies detailed four independent dimensions of national culture differences. Later on, Hofstede and others identified two more dimensions. Hofstede characterized the dimensions with numerical ratings, or indices, for different cultures.[28] The Hofstede dimensions have been used in planning deceptions, but they should be used with caution; leaders and groups within a country do not always fit the cultural dimension for that country—if there is one; it is difficult, for example, to characterize the "national culture" of Lebanon or South Africa.

Power Distance Index

The power distance index describes how people belonging to a specific culture view power relationships, specifically superior-subordinate relationships. It is defined as the extent to which the less powerful members of organizations and institutions, which include families, accept and expect that power is distributed unequally. A high index number indicates that hierarchy is clearly established and unquestioned in that society. A low index number characterizes a society in which people question authority and expect to participate in decisions that affect them. Table 4-1 illustrates the contrast between the two types of societies.

Latin America, Africa, the Arab world, and Asia have high power distance index scores. Countries with long-established democratic traditions, not surprisingly, have low scores on this index.[29]

Operation Fortitude—the deception aimed at leading the Wehrmacht into concentrating its forces around Pas-de-Calais (described in Chapter 2), succeeded, in part because under Hitler, Germany had a large power distance index score. Convinced that Calais was the real target, Hitler bullied his generals to defend the area and ignored their recommendations to release forces to counter the Normandy invasion.

TABLE 4-1 ■ Differences between Small- and Large-Power Distance Societies

Small Power Distance	Large Power Distance
Use of power should be legitimate and is subject to criteria of good and evil.	Power is a basic fact of society antedating good or evil: Its legitimacy is irrelevant.
Parents treat children as equals.	Parents teach children obedience.
Older people are neither respected nor feared.	Older people are both respected and feared.
Education is student centered.	Education is teacher centered.
Hierarchy means inequality of roles, established for convenience.	Hierarchy means existential inequality.
Subordinates expect to be consulted.	Subordinates expect to be told what to do.
Pluralist governments based on majority vote and changed peacefully.	Autocratic governments based on co-optation and changed by revolution.
Corruption rare; scandals end political careers.	Corruption frequent; scandals are covered up.
Income distribution in society is rather even.	Income distribution in society is very uneven.
Religions stress equality of believers.	Religions have a hierarchy of priests.

Creative Commons Attribution ShareAlike License

Individualism versus Collectivism

The individualism index measures the degree to which people in a society view themselves as part of a group. Individualistic societies have loose ties, and the ties that exist are mostly familial. People emphasize the "I" instead of the "we." Community is not valued as highly in individualistic societies.

Collectivist societies value group over individual interests. They are characterized by closely integrated relationships that tie extended families and others into clans. These clans emphasize loyalty to the group. They stress joint decision-making and group goals. They support each other in conflicts with other clans. Table 4-2 distinguishes the two societies.

TABLE 4-2 ■ Differences between Individualist and Collectivist Societies	
Individualism	Collectivism
Everyone is supposed to take care of himself or herself and his or her immediate family only.	People are born into extended families or clans that protect them in exchange for loyalty.
"I" consciousness.	"We" consciousness.
Right of privacy.	Stress on belonging.
Speaking one's mind is healthy.	Harmony should always be maintained.
Others are classified as individuals.	Others are classified as in-group or out-group.
Personal opinion is expected: One person, one vote.	Opinions and votes are predetermined by in-group.
Transgression of norms leads to guilt feelings.	Transgression of norms leads to shame feelings.
Languages in which the word "I" is indispensable.	Languages in which the word "I" is avoided.
Purpose of education is to learn how to learn.	Purpose of education is to learn how to do.
Task prevails over relationship.	Relationship prevails over task.

Creative Commons Attribution ShareAlike License

The individualism index has a strong East-West and North-South divide. North America and Europe have high scores on individualism. Asia, Africa, and Latin America are strongly collectivist. The Arab world and Japan score in the middle of the index.[30]

Arguably, the many pseudo operations described in Chapter 1 were more effective, and more devastating to the morale of the targeted insurgents, because they violated the norms of the collectivist societies where they were used.

Uncertainty Avoidance

The uncertainty avoidance index defines a society's tolerance for ambiguity and situations in which outcomes and conditions are unknown or unpredictable. The index measures the extent to which people either accept or avoid the unexpected or unknown. Societies that score high on uncertainty avoidance usually have guidelines and laws that define the boundaries of acceptable behavior. They tend to believe in absolute truth, or that a single truth dictates behavior and that people understand what it is. A low score on this index indicates general acceptance of differing thoughts and ideas. Societies with low scores tend to impose fewer restrictions on behavior, and ambiguity is more generally accepted in daily life. The differences between the two types of societies are summarized in Table 4-3.

TABLE 4-3 ■ Differences between Weak- and Strong-Uncertainty Avoidance Societies	
Weak Uncertainty Avoidance	**Strong Uncertainty Avoidance**
The uncertainty inherent in life is accepted and each day is taken as it comes.	The uncertainty inherent in life is felt as a continuous threat that must be fought.
Ease, lower stress, self-control, low anxiety.	Higher stress, emotionality, anxiety, neuroticism.
Higher scores on subjective health and well-being.	Lower scores on subjective health and well-being.
Tolerance of deviant persons and ideas: What is different is curious.	Intolerance of deviant persons and ideas: What is different is dangerous.
Comfortable with ambiguity and chaos.	Need for clarity and structure.
Teachers may say "I don't know."	Teachers are supposed to have all the answers.
Changing jobs is no problem.	People stay in jobs, even those they dislike.
Dislike of rules—written or unwritten.	Emotional need for rules—even if not obeyed.
Citizens are interested in politics, and protests are tolerated.	Citizens have low interest in politics, and protests are repressed.
In religion, philosophy, and science: relativism and empiricism.	In religion, philosophy, and science: belief in ultimate truths and grand theories.

Creative Commons Attribution ShareAlike License

Latin America, much of Europe, Russia, the Arab world, and Japan all score high in uncertainty avoidance. English-speaking, Scandinavian, and Chinese cultures tend to be more accepting of uncertainty. Few countries, though, score low on the uncertainty avoidance index.[31] How this cultural index might apply in planning deception is illustrated by the British experience with failed deceptions in World War II.

DECEPTION CAMPAIGNS AGAINST THE JAPANESE IN WORLD WAR II

Thaddeus Holt, in his book about Allied deception operations during World War II, has documented the difficulties that the British had in conducting deception against Japan. The British, from their experience in running deceptions against the Germans, had learned to use subtlety in providing information. A set of clues that was too obvious would be suspect. In dealing with the Japanese, the British repeatedly presented a subtle set of indicators to support deceptions only to see it apparently disappear into Japan's intelligence services without any response. Only when information was provided that pointed to an obvious conclusion did the Japanese respond. German intelligence would have rejected as a deception a level of information that pointed to an obvious conclusion. This result is all the more puzzling because the Japanese military routinely integrated deceptive operations into their own campaigns. Holt concluded that the Japanese intelligence service was incompetent.[32]

In fact, the apparent willingness of Japanese intelligence to ignore the subtle deceptive information may have had a more fundamental cause in the Japanese culture. Applying the Hofstede models produces an instructive result. Japanese have a very high uncertainty avoidance index (92 out of 120) according to a study that estimated the Hofstede indices of many countries.[33] So the natural tendency of Japanese intelligence services was not to act on ambiguous intelligence.

Masculinity versus Femininity

Masculinity here is defined as a preference in society for achievement, heroism, assertiveness, and material rewards for success. Femininity is characterized by a preference for cooperation, modesty, caring for the weak, and quality of life. Women in feminine societies share modest and caring views equally with men. In masculine societies, both are more assertive and competitive, but women notably less so than men. Table 4-4 contrasts the two societies.

TABLE 4-4 ■ Differences between Feminine and Masculine Societies	
Femininity	**Masculinity**
Minimum emotional and social role differentiation between the genders.	Maximum emotional and social role differentiation between the genders.
Men and women should be modest and caring.	Men should be and women may be assertive and ambitious.
Balance between family and work.	Work prevails over family.

Sympathy for the weak.	Admiration for the strong.
Both fathers and mothers deal with facts and feelings.	Fathers deal with facts, mothers with feelings.
Both boys and girls may cry, but neither should fight.	Girls cry, boys don't; boys should fight back, girls shouldn't fight.
Mothers decide on number of children.	Fathers decide on family size.
Many women in elected political positions.	Few women in elected political positions.
Religion focuses on fellow human beings.	Religion focuses on God or gods.
Matter-of-fact attitudes about sexuality; sex is a way of relating.	Moralistic attitudes about sexuality; sex is a way of performing.

Masculinity index scores are extremely low in Scandinavia. They are high in China, Japan, and central Europe and relatively high in English-speaking countries. Despite popular perceptions of masculine dominance, the Arab countries score in the mid-range of the masculinity index.[34]

Long-Term Orientation versus Short-Term Orientation

Long-term versus short-term orientation was added as a dimension after the original four in order to distinguish the difference in thinking between the East and West. Long-term orientation means that individuals are focused on the future. They are willing to delay short-term material or social success or even short-term emotional gratification in order to prepare for the future. Cultures having this perspective value persistence, perseverance, saving, and being able to adapt.

Short-term-oriented cultures are focused on the present or past and consider them more important than the future. People with a short-term orientation value tradition, the current social hierarchy, and fulfillment of their social obligations. They care more about immediate gratification than long-term fulfillment. Table 4-5 illustrates the contrasts between these two orientations.

High long-term orientation scores are typically found in East Asia, with China having the highest in the world and Japan not far behind. Moderate scores characterize Eastern and Western Europe. A short-term orientation characterizes the Anglo countries, the Muslim world, Africa, and Latin America.[35]

TABLE 4-5 ■ Differences between Short- and Long-Term-Oriented Societies	
Short-Term Orientation	**Long-Term Orientation**
Most important events in life occurred in the past or take place now.	Most important events in life will occur in the future.
Personal steadiness and stability: A good person is always the same.	A good person adapts to the circumstances.
There are universal guidelines about what is good and evil.	What is good and evil depends on the circumstances.
Traditions are sacrosanct.	Traditions are adaptable to changed circumstances.
Family life is guided by imperatives.	Family life is guided by shared tasks.
Pride in one's country.	Trying to learn from other countries.
Service to others is an important goal.	Thrift and perseverance are important goals.
Social spending and consumption.	Saving and thrift; funds available for investment.
Students attribute success and failure to luck.	Students attribute success to effort and failure to lack of effort.
Slow or no economic growth of poor countries.	Fast economic growth of countries up to a level of prosperity.

Creative Commons Attribution ShareAlike License

Indulgence versus Restraint

This dimension is essentially a measure of whether or not people enjoy the simple pleasures of life. Indulgent societies tend to allow relatively free gratification of natural human desires related to enjoying life and having fun. People in these societies believe themselves to be in control of their own lives and emotions. Indulgent cultures will tend to focus more on individual happiness and well-being; leisure time is more important; and there is greater freedom and personal control.

Restrained societies are more likely to believe that gratification of needs should be curbed and regulated by strict norms. Positive emotions are less freely expressed, and happiness, freedom, and leisure are not given the same importance. Table 4-6 summarizes the differences between these societies.

TABLE 4-6 ■ Differences between Indulgent and Restrained Societies	
Indulgent	**Restrained**
Higher percentage of people declare themselves very happy.	Fewer very happy people.
A perception of personal life control.	A perception of helplessness: What happens to me is not my own doing.
Freedom of speech is seen as important.	Freedom of speech is not a primary concern.
Higher importance of leisure.	Lower importance of leisure.
More likely to remember positive emotions.	Less likely to remember positive emotions.
In countries with educated populations, higher birthrates.	In countries with educated populations, lower birthrates.
More people are actively involved in sports.	Fewer people are actively involved in sports.
In countries with enough food, higher percentages of obese people.	In countries with enough food, fewer obese people.
In wealthy countries, lenient sexual norms.	In wealthy countries, stricter sexual norms.
Maintaining order in the nation is not given high priority.	Higher number of police officers per 100,000 population.

Creative Commons Attribution ShareAlike License

Indulgence scores are highest in Latin America, parts of Africa, the Anglo world, and Nordic Europe; restraint is mostly found in East Asia, Eastern Europe, and the Muslim world.

A final note about the Hofstede indices: The averages of a country do not automatically define the behavior or decisions of individuals of that country. Most countries have existed as such for less than a century, and many comprise multiple ethnicities and religious groups. Even though these models have proven to be quite often correct when applied to the dominant ethnic or religious group, not all individuals or even regions with subcultures fit into the national mold. The indices should be used as a guide to understanding the difference in culture between different groups when planning deception, not as law set in stone. As always, there are exceptions to the general rule.

NOTES

1. The material in this section was taken from Robert M. Clark, *Intelligence Analysis: A Target-Centric Approach*, 5th edition (2016) and modified.

2. Barry G. Silverman, Richard L. Rees, Jozsef A. Toth, Jason Cornwell, Kevin O'Brien, Michael Johns, and Marty Caplan, "Athena's Prism—A Diplomatic Strategy Role Playing Simulation for Generating Ideas and Exploring Alternatives," University of Pennsylvania, 2005, http://repository. upenn.edu/cgi/viewcontent.cgi?article=1321&context=ese_papers.

3. Jamshid Gharajedaghi, *Systems Thinking: Managing Chaos and Complexity* (Boston, MA: Butterworth-Heinemann, 1999), 34.

4. Oskar Morgenstern and John von Neumann, *Theory of Games and Economic Behavior* (Princeton, NJ: Princeton University Press, 1980).

5. Nanyang Technological University, Singapore, "Models of Organizational Decision-Making," http://tx.liberal.ntu.edu.tw/~purplewoo/Literature/!Theory/MODELS%20OF% 20ORGANIZATIONAL%20DECISION%20MAKING.htm.

6. Thaddeus Holt, *The Deceivers: Allied Military Deception in the Second World War* (New York: Skyhorse Publishing, 2007), 21–22.

7. "Prince Amedeo Savoia-Aosta: The Warrior Prince of Italy," biography posted by PELELIU81, June 3, 2010, http://www.comandosupremo.com/prince-amedeo-savoia-aosta.html.

8. Ibid.

9. David W. Miller and Martin K. Starr, *Executive Decisions and Operations Research* (Englewood Cliffs, NJ: Prentice-Hall, 1961), 45–47.

10. Nanyang Technological University, "Models of Organizational Decision-Making."

11. Walter D. Barndt Jr., *User-Directed Competitive Intelligence* (Westport, CT: Quorum Books, 1984), 78.

12. Ibid., 93.

13. Comment by Michael Pitcher, vice president of i2Go.com, in *Competitive Intelligence Magazine* 3 (July-September 2000): 9.

14. Bill Neeley, "Russia Compiles Psychological Dossier on Trump for Putin," *NBC News*, February 21, 2017, http://www.msn.com/en-us/news/world/russia-compiles-psychological-dossier-on-trump-for-putin/ar-AAn9TBD? li=BBnb7Kz.

15. Nanyang Technological University, "Models of Organizational Decision-Making."

16. Clive Thompson, "Can Game Theory Predict When Iran Will Get the Bomb?" *New York Times*, August 12, 2009, http://www.nytimes.com/2009/08/16/magazine/16Bruce-t.html?_r=0.

17. "Game Theory in Practice," *Economist*, Technology Quarterly, September 3, 2011, http://www .economist.com/node/21527025.

18. Edieal J. Pinker, "What Can Game Theory Tell Us about Iran's Nuclear Intentions?" in *Yale Insight* (Yale School of Management), March 2015, http://insights.som.yale.edu/insights/ what-can-game-theory-tell-us-about-iran-s-nuclear-intentions.

19. Thompson, "Can Game Theory Predict When Iran Will Get the Bomb?"

20. James F. Dunnigan and Albert A. Nofi, *Victory and Deceit: Dirty Tricks at War.* (New York: William Morrow, 1995), 322.

21. Ibid., 319–21.

22. Major Henry S. Larsen, "Operational Deception: U.S. Joint Doctrine and the Persian Gulf War," US Army Command and General Staff College, Ft. Leavenworth, Kansas, May 26, 1995, 18.

23. Gharajedaghi, *Systems Thinking*, 35.

24. Harold P. Ford, *Estimative Intelligence* (Lanham, MD: University Press of America, 1993), 17.

25. Ibid., 29.

26. Dino Brugioni, *Eyeball to Eyeball: The Inside Story of the Cuban Missile Crisis* (New York: Random House, 1990), 250.

27. Geert Hofstede, *Culture's Consequences: International Differences in Work-Related Values* (London: Sage, 1984).

28. Geert Hofstede, "Dimensionalizing Cultures: The Hofstede Model in Context," *Online Readings in Psychology and Culture* 2, no. 1 (2011). doi:10.9707/2307-0919.1014.

29. "Power Distance Index," Clearly Cultural, http://www.clearlycultural.com/geert-hofstede-cultural-dimensions/power-distance-index/.

30. "Individualism," Clearly Cultural, http://www.clearlycultural.com/geert-hofstede-cultural-dimensions/individualism/.

31. "Uncertainty Avoidance," Clearly Cultural, http://www.clearlycultural.com/geert-hofstede-cultural-dimensions/uncertainty-avoidance-index/.

32. Holt, *The Deceivers: Allied Military Deception in the Second World War*, 289.

33. "Uncertainty Avoidance."

34. "Masculinity," Clearly Cultural, http://www.clearlycultural.com/geert-hofstede-cultural-dimensions/masculinity/.

35. "Long-Term Orientation," Clearly Cultural, http://www.clearlycultural.com/geert-hofstede-cultural-dimensions/long-term-orientation/.

THE STORY

After thinking through the desired outcome scenario and determining the opponent's decisions and actions that would help create that outcome, the next step is to craft a separate scenario, often called the "story" in deception textbooks. The deception story is the picture that the target must believe in order to make the desired decisions that lead to the desired actions and, thus, the desired outcome.

Successful script writers, novelists, and news reporters all know how to tell a story. Some think that it's a lost (or perhaps undiscovered) art in intelligence writing. Several years ago, American movie director Steven Spielberg reportedly told a group of senior US intelligence community officials that they needed to learn to tell a story.

But what constitutes a story, or more specifically, a *good* story?

WHAT MAKES A GOOD STORY?

The story and the art of storytelling are as old as the human capacity to communicate. Storytelling is an essential and often defining element of human society. In fact, the idea of a good story is instilled almost immediately in children soon after they have begun to decode spoken words. From an early age, children are told (or they read) stories and remain captivated by the genre throughout their lifetimes. Recently, a class of eight-year-olds in Denmark was asked to describe the characteristics of a good adventure story. The resulting consensus was that a good adventure story had to have these characteristics:

1. It must begin with "once upon a time."

2. There must be talking animals.

3. The number "3" must appear (3 wishes, 3 riddles, 3 kingdoms, etc.).

4. There must be a princess.

5. There must be a conflict between good and evil.

6. There must be a resolution of the conflict where good defeats evil.

A story having these characteristics engages young children and makes them want to hear more. The first five characteristics include the elements that children *expect* to see in an adventure story. The last one is the one that almost everyone *wants* to see. It reinforces the belief that good should triumph in the end.

The point is, whether or not a story is judged as good is decided entirely by the audience. Like a good adventure story for an eight-year-old, a good deception narrative should have characteristics that fit with the deception target's expectations and desires.

CHARACTERISTICS OF A GOOD DECEPTION STORY

A well-known literary theory called "reader response" focuses attention not on what the author meant when she wrote the story, but instead on what the reader thinks and feels as he reads it. The theory asserts that the same narrative is responded to differently, based on the unique experiences of each reader. Put another way, it doesn't matter what the author was trying to convey. The person reading the story interprets the elements of it based on his personal world view. This is exactly how a deception planner must think when creating the story. The target has to be the focus. Godson and Wirtz confirm this in their description of what makes for a good deception narrative:

> To be successful, the deceiver must recognize the target's perceptual context to know what (false) pictures of the world will appear plausible. History, culture, bureaucratic preferences, and the general economic and political milieu all influence the target's perceptions. False information should conform to the idiosyncrasies of strategic and even popular culture. Mistakes are easily detected and often appear comical to the target audience. Thus, deception requires creative planning: experience shows that successful deception planners manage to escape the routine and culture of large bureaucracies. . . . In sum, deception planners "need to know a great deal about the worldview of those they are trying to manipulate, and recognize the human proclivity for self-deception."[1]

In short, neither a generic story nor one that reflects the deception planner's culture or characteristics will succeed. Instead, the deception planner must contemplate what circumstances and set of "facts" would lead the target to take the desired action. Those circumstances and "facts" will combine to create the story. Returning to the basic principles outlined in Chapter 1, the deception planner must ask: What combination of truth, denial, deceit, and misrepresentation is needed to produce a successful story for this particular opponent?

But to answer those questions, the deception planner first needs to understand the factors that are important in the opponent's decision-making process and what his or her state of mind is likely to be at the point of decision-making. For example, when dealing with a specific type of target—such as a decision maker who is prone to paranoia—a good start would be to develop a story that includes a conspiracy against that target. This knowledge usually requires some decision-modeling, as discussed in Chapter 4. It is also profitable to know the target's preferences in receiving information and intelligence. A story that finds its way to the opponent from a trusted source can lead to a false sense of security, a topic returned to in the next chapter.

Taking all of these elements into account, the earlier Godson and Wirtz description identifies two characteristics that make for a good story in deception. To have any chance for success, the story should have one, preferably both, of these characteristics:

- *Plausibility.* What story would fit with the target's beliefs and expectancies? What would convince the target that the deception story is the real one?

- *Reinforcement.* What story would reinforce the target's desires? What would reinforce the target's fears?

Let's look at each of these characteristics, with examples.

Plausibility

A story must be plausible to the opponent—which is not the same thing as what the deception planner would find plausible. A story that the deceiver sees as flawed might be highly acceptable to the target. Such was the case in the Operation Desert Storm deception, described in Chapter 4. A flanking attack was, in the eyes of the coalition leaders, obvious. To the Iraqis, it was foolhardy because of the dangers they perceived in moving through uncharted desert.

The *Argo* story, described next, in retrospect might seem downright fantastical to an American audience, but the Iranian government found it plausible.

ARGO

Chapter 1 introduced the similarity between deception operations and a con game, via *The Sting*. It also showed that the movie industry well understands both how to tell a good story and how to pull off a deception. In a few cases,

(Continued)

(Continued)

the US government has called on the movie industry for assistance because of these talents. The story of Argo is one such instance.

When the Iranians took over the US embassy in 1979 and seized the Americans there, six embassy employees with no intelligence background managed to find shelter in the Canadian embassy. Their presence there was not acknowledged to the Iranian government, and could not be acknowledged; the Iranian Revolutionary Guard had already shown its willingness to disregard the sanctity of embassies. The United States, in cooperation with the Canadians, had to find a way to exfiltrate the six, and the plan *had* to succeed. A failure would put both US hostages and Canadian embassy personnel at risk and would be politically embarrassing for both the United States and Canada.

The CIA was called on for a covert operation to rescue the six. It developed a plan in coordination with senior policymakers in the US and Canadian administrations. The plan called for an elaborate narrative in which a "Hollywood film production crew" would travel to Tehran for the purpose of making a movie that would be appealing to Iran's revolutionary government. After investigating possible filming locations, a party of eight (now including the six) would depart for home.

A fictional production company, Studio Six Productions, was created in the space of four days. The rescue team found a script that had science fiction elements, a Middle Eastern setting, and mythological elements along with features about the glory of Islam. The script also had some other elements that made it attractive to the target of the deception, the Iranian government—for example, building a large production set that later could be turned into a theme park.

An exfiltration team of two CIA officers obtained entry visas in Europe and proceeded to Tehran. At about the same time the two arrived at Mehrabad Airport, six studio executives—American and Canadian—arrived on a flight from Hong Kong to join them; at least, airline tickets showed that they did. In Tehran, the two CIA officers who actually made the trip contacted the six Americans and briefed them on the movie executive roles they had to play. The notional film crew of eight was now complete, comprising the two CIA officers and six embassy employees, and all had a cover story showing that they had traveled to Tehran. The two CIA officers, who were skilled at creating authentic forgeries, spent the next two days creating false passports and other exit documents to fit with the cover story. With considerable assistance from Canadian embassy staff, the eight then departed Mehrabad Airport via Swissair for Zurich.

The deception was successful, but it did not remain a secret for long. The press caught wind of it within a few days. The Iranians were publicly embarrassed, and the Canadians got a rousing "thank you" all across the United States for their role. When Studio Six folded several weeks after the rescue, they had received twenty-six scripts, including some potential moneymakers. One was from Steven Spielberg.[2]

The story created for the Argo deception was plausible, being both credible and appealing to the Iranian government. Contrast it with the alternate story proposed but rejected in the 2012 movie titled *Argo*. In the movie, a proposal is made to send the exfiltration team in as agricultural experts. The story was to be that they would consult with Iranians about how to improve their agricultural practices. That story failed the plausibility test: The operation was scheduled to take place in January. It made no sense to send experts to assist with Iranian agriculture in the middle of winter.

Again, all deception works within the context of what is true. To be plausible, the story should be based as much as possible on truth. Even the Argo operation, farfetched as it was, had true elements—such as an actual script that could be shown to the Iranians.

Where deception must be maintained over a long period without being detected, the ideal is for the activity or objects being concealed to be portrayed as true or plausible but uninteresting to foreign intelligence. The deception surrounding the GRAB satellite, discussed in Chapter 7, had exactly that objective. It was based heavily on truth. It carried a real but uninteresting (to Soviet intelligence) experiment in addition to the satellite's primary payload. In Project Azorian, the subject of the next case, the story was not true, but it was both plausible and, for Soviet intelligence, uninteresting.

PROJECT AZORIAN

In March 1968 a Soviet Golf-class submarine on patrol northwest of Hawaii was racked with explosions and sank in 17,000 feet of water, carrying all ninety men aboard down with it. Soviet salvage vessels were unable to locate the sunken craft, but the US Navy subsequently pinpointed its location using more sophisticated search equipment.

The submarine contained a number of items of intelligence value to the United States, especially the books containing Soviet naval codes. Also, the missiles aboard would provide valuable intelligence about nuclear warhead design. So an operation to salvage the submarine appeared to be worthwhile. Of course, an openly acknowledged salvage operation was out of the question. The submarine arguably was still Soviet property, and salvage of a foreign naval vessel is a violation of international law. Furthermore, cipher books have less value if the opponent knows that they have been acquired. Any salvage would need to be concealed from the Soviets. The CIA proposed to conduct the salvage operation, codenamed Project Azorian, protecting it with an elaborate deception.[3]

To accomplish the task, Howard Hughes's Summa Corporation built a 620-foot-long deep sea recovery vessel named the *Glomar Explorer* at a cost of $200 million. The deception story gave the ship a publicly acknowledged purpose: to do deep sea research and mining on the ocean floor for manganese nodules.

The choice of this story, and of Hughes's company to build it, offered several advantages. Manganese nodules are golf ball–sized rocks rich in valuable manganese, nickel, copper, cobalt, and other elements. They are found in large numbers miles down on the ocean bottom. They are very difficult to mine because of the difficulties in operating equipment at such depths. This story was chosen because, according to a CIA memorandum sent to Secretary of State Henry Kissinger,

(Continued)

(Continued)

The determination reached was that deep ocean mining would be particularly suitable. The industry was in its infancy, potentially quite profitable, with no one apparently committed to a hardware development phase and thereby possessing a yardstick by which credibility could be measured. Hughes Tool Company's (later Summa Corporation's) participation as the sponsor and sole source of funding was a logical selection. Mr. Howard Hughes is the only stockholder; he is recognized as a pioneering entrepreneur with a wide variety of business interests; he has the necessary financial resources; he habitually operates in secrecy; and, his personal eccentricities are such that news media reporting and speculation about his activities frequently range from the truth to utter fiction.[4]

The story choice proved to be a good one. Parts of the media enthusiastically popularized the story, highlighting it as the beginning of a race to exploit mineral wealth of the ocean bottom and claiming that the *Glomar Explorer* had the capacity to "suck up 5,000 tons of ore per day."[5]

During July and August 1974 the *Glomar Explorer* located the submarine and began recovery operations. Cables were looped around the submarine, and winches began slowly pulling the submarine up toward the barge. About halfway up, the hull broke apart and two-thirds of the submarine fell back and was lost on the bottom. Though the sought-after prizes—code books and nuclear warheads—were reportedly lost, the remaining one-third of the submarine was recovered and yielded valuable intelligence.[6]

The deception target was the Soviet intelligence services (the KGB and GRU). There has been some controversy about how well the deception succeeded. Much of the time, the *Glomar Explorer*'s operations were monitored by Soviet ships in the immediate area. The truth about Project Azorian was disclosed in a *New York Times* article in March 1975. By June 1975 the Soviets certainly were aware of the ship's covert mission and had assigned one of their ships to monitor and guard the recovery site. With the mission exposed, President Ford canceled further recovery operations.[7]

There have been claims since then alleging that the Soviets had foreknowledge of the salvage operation. Soviet naval leaders reportedly believed such a recovery to be impossible and disregarded the intelligence warnings.[8] If true, that again illustrates the importance of plausibility: A deep sea research and mining story was plausible; a submarine recovery mission was, from a Soviet perspective, implausible.

Reinforcement

A good cover story should reinforce what the opponent already believes or wishes to believe. A story that plays to or reinforces an opponent's fears can be equally effective. Operation Quicksilver, described in Chapter 2, fit nicely with the German belief that Pas-de-Calais was the logical site for an Allied invasion of Europe. And if the opponent's wish to believe something is strong enough, it may be possible (though never recommended) to conduct a deception that does not even have plausibility. One component of the Ultra deception, described in

Chapter 3, projected a story that the British had a radar that could detect submerged submarines. A radar expert would find such a story implausible, but the Germans accepted the story because it played to their fears.

The example of German rearmament after World War I is another case of an implausible story that succeeded because it reinforced the opponents' desire to believe.

GERMAN REARMAMENT

In the period between World Wars I and II, from 1920 to 1935, Germany conducted what may have been the longest-running deception operation in history. The 1919 Treaty of Versailles mandated German disarmament and provided for an inspection regime to ensure compliance with its terms. German military and civilian leadership successfully evaded the treaty restrictions, concealing their production of tanks, artillery, military airplanes, and U-boats.

U-boats were developed by a Krupp arms manufacturer subsidiary in the Netherlands and Spain. Daimler-Benz, BMW, and Porsche, companies later to become famous in the automobile industry, designed the first tank and armored car models. Krupp subsidiaries in Sweden produced heavy artillery and tanks. Tanks and armored cars were tested at the Red Army's tank complex in Kazan, USSR, under a secret agreement with the Soviet Union. They were shipped under the disguise of "heavy tractors."

The deception extended to the formation and training of combat units. Throughout the 1920s and early 1930s, Germany consistently violated treaty restrictions on the size of its army and navy, and trained its aviators for the future Luftwaffe. Pilots received flight training with Lufthansa, ostensibly as commercial airline pilots. They later received military training in Mussolini's Italy, wearing Italian Air Force uniforms.[9]

German rearmament is an example of strategic deception. The German goal was to rearm without provoking a response from other European countries. The target of the deception was the political leadership of those countries. The primary channel was the Inter-Allied Military Commission of Control comprising British, French, and American inspectors.

It is almost impossible to run an elaborate deception over a long term, as the Germans did, without it being exposed. And in fact, the inspectors did suspect violations and occasionally observed them. British and French military advisors repeatedly warned their foreign ministers that the Germans were violating the treaty, but the leadership simply did not want to hear the message. The operation succeeded because the Germans had estimated well the reluctance of the decision makers in the British and French governments to act. Their leadership was tired of war and did not want to deal with the question of Germany's rearmament.

This fatigue factor is something that deceivers continue to rely on in violating arms limitation agreements. As Godson and Wirtz have noted, "most governments are reluctant to act against murky evidence of arms violations" and "targeted nations 'take the easy way out' by believing palatable lies and half-truths rather than confront disturbing information."[10]

(Continued)

(Continued)

The commission was withdrawn in 1927, and its final report concluded that Germany had not disarmed and had over a seven-year period deceived the Allied powers about its rearmament.

The tactics applied in this deception operation set a pattern that has been repeated in recent years in WMD proliferation efforts. They relied heavily on skillfully managing the plant inspection visits. When warned of a commission inspection, the Germans would remove aircraft and components from production hangars and conceal them in the countryside.

The operation also relied on the concept of dual-use products: demonstrations of ostensibly civilian materiel that was in fact intended for military use. Aircraft designated as commercial or sporting types were developed with the intent of converting them to military use. Prototype fighter aircraft were designed as civilian to compete in air races. The Junkers trimotor aircraft was openly designated as a transport but originally designed to be a bomber. Since then, dual-use chemicals (that can be used in commercial products or in chemical warfare agent production) have been the subject of similar deception operations by several countries.

In constructing a complete story, a deceiver should make use of the different perspectives discussed in Chapter 3. That is, all of the PMESII factors that could be a part of the story have to be considered. There are several possible ways to put together each of these elements into a story. The next section describes one such method.

INFLUENCE NETS

A good story should present a consistent picture to the opponent—meaning that it should fit well with all of the evidence available to the opponent. So after constructing the deception story, it is a good idea to check it, adopting the opponent's perspective.

One way to check to see if the story meets the characteristics described in this chapter is to create an influence net. Influence net modeling is an intuitive graphical technique. It is useful in deception planning because it requires its creator to consider the factors, forces, or influences that are part of the story and that drive an opponent's decision both toward and away from the desired outcome scenario. It forces the deception planner to look at both the influences projected by the story *and* at the outside evidence (provided by other channels) that might support or undermine the story.

To create an influence net, the deception planner defines *influence nodes,* which depict factors that, taken together, compose the story. The next step is to create "influence links" between the nodes and the desired decision. These links graphically illustrate the cause-and-effect relationship between the nodes (factors) and the decision. The influence can be either positive (supporting a given decision) or negative (decreasing the likelihood of the decision), as identified by the link "terminator." The terminator is either an arrowhead (positive influence) or a filled circle (negative influence). The resulting graphical illustration is called the "influence net topology."

Consider Operation Fortitude, the deception to keep German forces away from Normandy prior to D-Day; and Operation Quicksilver, the part of the deception that encouraged the Germans to reinforce the area around Pas-de-Calais (see Chapter 2). An example topology, showing some of the influences on Adolf Hitler's decision to concentrate German defenses against an invasion at Calais, is pictured in Figure 5-1. The decision is stated as "Defend against an Allied invasion at Calais." The influence net began with three of the factors shown, none of which the Allies could change:

1. Calais is the most direct route to take for an invasion, involving the shortest sea route into Europe from the United Kingdom, and posing the least difficulty in handling logistics.

2. The Germans already had put extensive defenses in the Calais area by 1944.

3. A deception portraying Calais as the target had to contend with past successful British deceptions, such as Operation Mincemeat, that should have made the Germans suspicious.

The latter two factors weighed against that decision (shown as solid circles terminating the connectors). The positive factors (with arrows terminating the connectors) show three key parts of the deception plan that were being considered:

1. Assemble a fictional first US army group (FUSAG) being near Dover.

2. Appoint General Patton, whom the German military regarded as the most capable Allied commander, to head the FUSAG.

3. Have British-controlled double agents that the Germans trust report that Pas-de-Calais is the target.

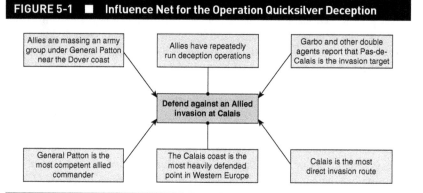

FIGURE 5-1   ■   Influence Net for the Operation Quicksilver Deception

Note: The arrows come from boxes that support a German decision to expect an invasion in the Pas-de-Calais region. The filled dots come from boxes that do not support that decision.

With an established desired outcome scenario, a target, and a story employed to induce the target toward decision and action, it's time to select the channels to be used to convey the story.

NOTES

1. Roy Godson and James J. Wirtz, "Strategic Denial and Deception," *International Journal of Intelligence and Counterlntelligence* 13 (2000): 426–37.

2. Antonio J. Mendez, "A Classic Case of Deception," CIA *Studies in Intelligence*, Winter 1999/2000, https://www.cia.gov/library/center-for-the-study-of-intelligence/csi-publications/csi-studies/studies/winter99-00/art1.html.

3. CIA, "Project AZORIAN," July 23, 2012, https://www.cia.gov/about-cia/cia-museum/experience-the-collection/text-version/stories/project-azorian.html.

4. *Foreign Relations of the United States, 1969–1976, Vol. XXXV, National Security Policy, 1973–1976,* p. 871, https://history.state.gov/historicaldocuments/frus1969-76v35/d186.

5. "Ripping Off the Ocean Bed," *New Scientist*, August 16, 1973, 388.

6. *Newsday*, April 11, 1989, 2.

7. CIA, "Project AZORIAN."

8. Michael White, documentary, "AZORIAN: The Raising of the K-129," Vienna: Michael White Films 2009, http://projectjennifer.white.at/.

9. Barton Whaley, "Covert Rearmament in Germany 1919–1939: Deception and Misperception," in *Military Deception and Strategic Surprise*, ed. John Gooch and Amos Perlmutter (New York: Frank Cass, 1982).

10. Godson and Wirtz, "Strategic Denial and Deception," 430.

THE CHANNELS

The channels (sensors and sources) used to project a deception are mostly traditional intelligence channels, which are covered in detail in Chapter 7. But a number of channels for projecting deception exist that don't fit in the traditional intelligence domain, and these have assumed more importance in recent years. Many of them fall into the cyberspace category, covered in Chapter 8.

Further, some channels exist that fall into neither the intelligence nor the cyberspace category. Open source is readily available outside of intelligence channels, though for convenience we treat it as an "INT" in Chapter 7. Telephones, postal mail, and emails are used to project deceptions.

An example of a completely different type of deception is one that targets the global positioning system (GPS) channel. On January 12, 2016, two US Navy patrol boats were seized by Iran's Islamic Revolutionary Guard Corps Navy after they entered Iranian territorial waters near Iran's Farsi Island in the Persian Gulf. It was later determined that the two US patrol boats entered Iranian waters because of navigational errors. Some observers speculated at the time that Iran had used deception of GPS signals to lure the boats off course. The hypothesis was based in part on a precedent that had been set five years earlier. In 2011 Iran had claimed that it had captured a US RQ-170 Sentinel drone by deceiving its GPS receiver to lure it from Afghanistan into Iranian airspace.

Both the hypothesis and the Iranian claims are open to doubt, but they indicate a new potential channel for projecting deception. The US military uses a different set of codes than do civilian GPS systems to receive broadcasts from GPS satellites. The military codes are encrypted. The civilian GPS systems are not encrypted, and it is possible to deceive these GPS receivers—not easily, but it has been done. In June 2013 a Cornell University researcher demonstrated the ability to deceive the GPS navigation system on a private yacht in the Mediterranean, luring the ship one kilometer off course.[1]

With that background on the channels, let's turn to how deceivers can understand and make use of them.

UNDERSTANDING THE CHANNELS

To execute any deception, deception planners must have an understanding of both their own and their adversary's capabilities for observing and orienting to the operational environment. Though related, the two steps differ in character. Managing the observation phase of one's own channels (sensors and sources), or of the target's, is usually relatively straightforward through the identification of intelligence, surveillance and reconnaissance platforms, and physical capabilities. However, understanding how an intelligence organization orients information can be challenging, as it is the product of that organization's culture and past experiences.

For example, during World War II, Allied deception operations in the European theater often succeeded because the Allies were culturally close to the Germans and Italians. The Allies also had a good understanding of how German and Italian intelligence services operated. In the Pacific theater, Allied deception operations were less successful. This lack of success has been blamed on the disinclination of Pacific US forces to use deception and on the inadequacy of Japan's intelligence services, as noted in Chapter 4.[2] More likely, the causes were the cultural differences between the Americans and the Japanese, and the inadequate US knowledge of how Japanese intelligence actually functioned.

To appreciate how channels are used to deceive an opponent, let's revisit the deception, introduced in Chapter 4, that preceded Operation Desert Storm. The discussion in Chapter 4 illustrated a skillful use of media channels to portray an invasion of Kuwait from the south across Wadi Al-Batin accompanied by an amphibious assault from the east.

The operation featured a situation one rarely encounters in deception: The coalition not only made good use of the media channels that the Iraqis could receive, but it also was able to control what other sources and sensors were available to Saddam Hussein and his generals and manipulate what could be seen through those. This part of the operation included two major components:

- The first step was the removal of Saddam's primary channels for intelligence: IMINT by the Iraqi Air Force, and most SIGINT by air and ground-based units in the theater. After more than a month of coalition air strikes, that mission was a success. The Iraqis were left with two channels for intelligence: OSINT, and what their forward deployed units could observe by sight and sound (aided a bit by surviving SIGINT units). Better yet, the coalition was positioned to manipulate what the enemy still could see.

- Once the threat of imagery collection was gone, two coalition corps moved from their positions south of Wadi Al-Batin to staging areas in the western desert. Units remaining behind continued to transmit what appeared to be the two corps' radio traffic, to give surviving Iraqi SIGINT units the impression that the corps had not moved and were preparing to attack from the south.

A first step in planning how to feed information to the target is to map the sensors in his or her OODA loop (observation) and then characterize those channels (orientation). Then the planner decides how to exploit the channels. Let's go through each step.

SENSOR MAPPING

Sensor mapping requires the deception planner to model the observation stage of the adversary's loop in order to eventually manipulate that adversary's OODA loop and decision-making process, as Figure 6-1 indicates. To succeed in deception, your side must commit both collection and analytic resources to model the target's collection capabilities. The purpose is not only to develop a fundamental knowledge as to what types of sensors the target has available in any given operational environment, but also to develop an understanding of any timelines or time restrictions related to the different channels. There is no point making a great effort to deceive a sensor if it is not in use. As an example, dummy tanks

---

FIGURE 6-1 ■ Adversarial Sensor Map

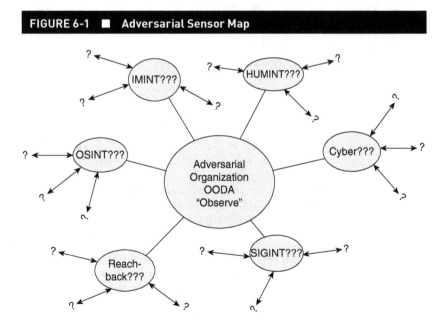

were not deployed in Operation Quicksilver because, as noted in Chapter 2, the Germans could not send reconnaissance aircraft over the UK to observe them.

Observation

The process of identifying adversarial sensors can include a variety of methods that stretch from in-depth research as to what the opponent had before the conflict, to targeted collection and general knowledge. It could be something simple, for example, a few lines written by a patrol leader in his or her report that refer to "enemy roving patrols" at a specific time and place (the enemy patrol is therefore an adversarial sensor for exploitation), to something more complicated like working out the access times of an imaging satellite over the area of interest or operations. It could also be the social network surrounding "legal" spies in your country, such as military attachés, or maybe more clandestine "illegal" HUMINT networks. It could include understanding in detail how the channel functions in accepting information to pass through it, as illustrated in the next case—an example of a counterintelligence deception.

THE DOCUMENT BINDER DECEPTION

In November 2010 Igor Sporyshev arrived in New York on assignment as a trade representative of the Russian Federation. The FBI took an immediate interest in Sporyshev—his father had served as a major general in the Russian Federal Security Service (FSB). Service in both the KGB and its successors—the FSB and Foreign Intelligence Service (SVR)—tends to run in families. The FBI subsequently set up an elaborate counterintelligence operation targeting Sporyshev.[3]

A critical part of assessing and using channels for deception is understanding how the opponent likes to use them. In the case of HUMINT, it is well known that the Russians prefer to initiate a contact, and are suspicious of contacts initiated by another, especially by Americans. So the FBI offered Sporyshev an attractive target: an agent posing as a Wall Street analyst in the energy sector who attended the energy conferences that Sporyshev seemed to frequent. Sporyshev sought out the agent and struck up an acquaintance based on their common interest in energy matters. As the relationship developed, the Russian inquired about the financial projections and strategy documents in the US energy sector that the agent claimed to possess.

The next stage of the deception relied on another quirk of Russian intelligence. The SVR, like the KGB before it, has a preference for clandestine HUMINT instead of open sources, and a strong preference for documentary material. The FBI agent accordingly, over time, provided Sporyshev with "confidential" corporate reporting on the energy sector. The reports were in numbered binders that, according to the agent, could not be kept for very long because his superiors would notice their absence.[4]

The reports must have looked like a treasure trove to Sporyshev and his SVR associates. After all, subsequent reporting seems to show that they led rather boring lives by espionage standards. That at least might explain what happened next.

The Russian made a basic tradecraft mistake: Foreign material (that has not been under friendly control from the outset) should never be taken into a secure facility. But as he received each binder, Sporyshev took it into the SVR's secure facility in Russia's UN office in New York, presumably to be photocopied before it was returned. The binders all had concealed voice-activated audio devices that recorded conversations among SVR officers in the facility. Over a period of several months, as binders went into and out of the SVR facility, their voice recordings were downloaded and handed over to FBI translators.[5] The several hundred hours of conversations that the binders produced had a great deal of uninteresting material but probably provided a number of profitable leads for US counterintelligence. The result of one such lead became public because it wound up in a US court.

The discussions among SVR agents in their secure facility contained references to an SVR source working on Wall Street. The FBI subsequently zeroed in on Evgeny Buryakov, who was an executive in the New York branch of Vnesheconombank (VEB) a Russian development bank. Buryakov actually was what clandestine services call a nonofficial cover (NOC) officer, assigned by the SVR to obtain US corporate and financial secrets.[6]

The FBI subsequently turned its attention to Buryakov and exploited that source over the next year and a half. They placed audio taps on his telephone calls and audio and video surveillance sensors in his home, using them to acquire additional counterintelligence information.[7]

On January 26, 2015, FBI agents arrested Buryakov as he left a Bronx grocery store. On May 24, 2016, he was sentenced to thirty months in a US prison for being an unregistered foreign agent.[8] Buryakov was released from prison and deported to Russia on April 5, 2017.

Understanding the different INTs used by an opponent, as well as some of the key platforms available to the various INTs, is also key to planning how to execute deception. This includes identifying the "reachback" resources that are available to the adversary. These could be assets outside of the immediate adversary's command and control at the national level, such as satellites, or specialist analytic capabilities, databases, and allies or supporters that could provide intelligence if requested. Every adversary and context will be different, so making a concerted effort to sensor map your specific adversary is important. Visualizing the adversary's sensor map, as in Figure 6-1, helps maintain a focused effort on sensor mapping.

Identifying adversarial sensors should be a targeted, intentional process built on method. The exercises in Chapters 12 and 14 are designed to illustrate how this process works. In those exercises, all of the intelligence reports contain relevant information. Note, however, that a deception planner typically must apply skill and focus to identify and extract relevant information from a mass of reports. Many of these reports have nothing to contribute to building a target model of the sensors and sources the opponent uses for observation in its operational environment.

Orientation

Knowing how adversaries observe their operational environment is a prerequisite for executing an effective deception plan. However, knowing how they collect should not translate into certainty on how they *understand* what they collect. An adversary's intelligence service may not conduct analysis as your side does. So understanding requires assessing how the adversary orients what is collected—also known as characterizing the channels, discussed next.

CHANNEL CHARACTERIZATION

The preceding section emphasized the importance of knowing an opponent's intelligence collection system (or information channels). But their analysis capabilities also must be understood—if they have any. Nonstate actors may depend on leadership to do its own analysis. In fact, successful deception requires a solid appreciation of the target opponent's operational and intelligence cultures. One of the most effective counterintelligence (specifically, counterespionage) operations in the previous century depended on an intelligence service's ability to model the analytic processes and cultural propensities of an opposing intelligence service, as illustrated in the next case.

PROTECTING AMES AND HANSSEN

In the waning years of the Cold War, the Soviets scored a major intelligence coup that continued to pay dividends long after the Soviet Union itself ceased to exist. They acquired the services of two agents who, because of their positions in the counterintelligence services of the CIA and FBI, represented the gold standard for "moles" in an opposing intelligence service:

- Aldrich Ames served as a counterintelligence officer in the CIA's Soviet/East European Division. He began working for the Soviets in 1985 and in a short period of time identified for them many of the CIA's agents in the USSR. The Soviets quickly arrested and executed most of them.

- Robert Hanssen was an FBI agent who primarily worked on counterintelligence against Soviet targets in Washington, DC, and New York City. He volunteered to work for the Soviets in 1979.

Because these two assets had immense value for Soviet counterintelligence, the KGB went to great lengths to protect them. Over an extended period, the KGB ran several deception operations to protect Ames until his arrest in 1993. According to a report by the Senate Select Committee on Intelligence,

Beginning in October 1985 and continuing sporadically over the next several years, the KGB undertook a concerted effort to make the CIA and FBI believe that the sources compromised by Ames were either still alive or had been lost because of problems unrelated to a human penetration of the CIA.[9]

As they eliminated the agents, in some cases the KGB replaced them with double agents who fed false information to their CIA handlers. They also skillfully applied misdirection to lead CIA and FBI investigators away from Ames. The misdirection efforts had several phases, including the following:

- In 1985 Vitaly Yurchenko walked into the US embassy in Rome and defected to the United States. Yurchenko identified two Soviet agents—Edward Lee Howard, a former CIA officer; and Ronald Pelton, a former National Security Agency (NSA) employee. Suspicion fell on Howard as the source of the Ames compromises. Howard defected to the USSR before he could be arrested, and Yurchenko subsequently re-defected to the USSR. Some suspect that Yurchenko's performance was a deliberate KGB effort to lead investigators away from Ames—a suspicion supported by the Soviet government awarding him the Order of the Red Star after his re-defection.[10]

- In 1987 a CIA officer was contacted by a KGB officer named Aleksandr Zhomov, who offered to pass on information about KGB surveillance operations. Over a three-year period, Zhomov provided false information about KGB operations and helped the CIA recruit double agents. Zhomov's objective appears to have been to divert investigations away from Ames.[11]

The KGB deceptions bear a striking resemblance to the coalition deception that preceded Operation Desert Storm. In both cases, the deceivers controlled the channels. The KGB had long studied the CIA's operations and had a good understanding of how their opponent—the CIA's Counterintelligence Center—analyzed the operational intelligence it obtained. That understanding apparently allowed them to construct stories that were plausible and that played to the fears of counterintelligence officers.

After Ames was arrested in 1993, the SVR (successor to the KGB) continued to apply misdirection but now to protect its remaining asset: Robert Hanssen. Hanssen compromised a number of US intelligence operations before his arrest in 2001, and investigators at first naturally tended to blame Ames.[12] But some of the compromises could not have come from Ames, so the hunt began for another mole.

The Hanssen deception was helped, as most deceptions are, by the target's mindset. In this case, the FBI found it difficult to believe that one of their own could be a traitor. They focused the investigation instead on an innocent CIA employee. Hanssen made a number of mistakes beginning in 1993 that should have resulted in his arrest prior to 2001, but the FBI apparently failed to follow up on them. Whether or not the SVR recognized and exploited the FBI mindset is an open question. In any event, that mindset helped to protect Hanssen for another eight years.

Modeling the "Black Box" of Orientation

Much like using modeling to sensor map the adversary, modeling can also be an effective tool to assess how an adversary makes use of the raw intelligence it collects. Following the OODA loop paradigm, this is the orientation stage. Among deception planners, this is sometimes referred to as the "black box" because it is so difficult to comprehend.

Today's adversaries may build their decision-making organization in very different ways based on culture or simply to ensure survival. This means that they can organize their observation and orientation functions in many different ways, and it would be rare to find two organized in precisely the same manner. However, holding true to our generic OODA model, the function "observe and orient" will be used. It is identifying who and what performs those functions that is the challenge. Therefore, spending time to understand the intelligence structure of the adversary must include how it orients collected information. Once their sensors collect information, the deception planner must determine what they do with it in order to comprehend to what degree it affects decision-making.

The Case of the Daesh 2013–2014 Intelligence Organization

Daesh made an extraordinarily quick and successful military advance across northern Syria and into Iraq during 2013–2014. It was later recognized as the direct result of an extensive intelligence preparation of the battlespace. That preparation reduced the chance of organized military resistance in targeted cities and towns by taking them from the inside out. It was more a case of cities and towns themselves raising the Daesh flag than it was of the success of an invading army.

Efforts to understand the command and control (C2) structure of Daesh began in earnest with the establishment of western military assistance to counter Daesh in the spring of 2015. Understanding how the self-declared leader of Daesh and the so-called caliphate as an organization made decisions became a primary concern for the purposes of disrupting their efforts in Syria and Iraq. Several media outlets as well as terrorism experts and consultants proposed organizational diagrams of this new group based on open sources and analytic methods. The following fictional example is inspired by a *Der Spiegel* article, "Secret Files Reveal the Structure of Islamic State," and reflects its attempt to model the "black box" of Daesh.[13] Intelligence "roll-ups" are overviews of intelligence reporting collected on a specific topic and placed on a timeline; they include a short description of the source as well as a brief summary of relevant intelligence. The roll-up in Table 6-1 provides fictional sources and information for creating a model of the Daesh "black box."

Table 6-1 introduces the source evaluation and rating schema for HUMINT reporting that is used throughout the exercises in later chapters. The number (345 in the table) identifies the source. The two characters that follow indicate the evaluation of the source and the source's information, as shown in Table 6-2.

TABLE 6-1 ■		Roll-Up of Related Daesh "Black Box" Presented in Figure 6-2
REP #	**DTG (Date Time Group)**	**TEXT**
R1	1 AUG 2014	**OSINT:** Several major news reporting streams suggest that Daesh has divided Syria and Iraq into governances that are further subdivided into Walis such as Homs, Damascus, Raqqa, and Deir al-Zour in Syria, and Baghdad, Anbar, Diyala, and Euphrates in Iraq.
R2	1 AUG 2014	**OSINT:** Based on analysis of Daesh-owned media, civil governance in the caliphate is largely managed by the Cabinet, including Oil, Aid & Welfare, Communications, and Justice and Policing sectors.
R3	1 AUG 2014	**HUMINT-345-B3:** Abu Ahmed al-Alwani and Abu Abdul Salem work at the Military Council, while Shakir Omar, Haji Bakr, and Abu al-Fahdawi work in the Intelligence Bureau.
R4	3 AUG 2014	**HUMINT-345-B3:** Internal spying within Daesh-controlled or contested areas is managed by the tribal relations offices. Shakir Omar is responsible for Iraq while Abu al-Fahdawi is responsible for Syria.
R5	5 AUG 2014	**SIGINT:** Abu Kifa works at the Daesh War Office and is responsible for managing IED production and distribution while Abu Shema manages other logistics.
R6	8 AUG 2014	**SIGINT:** Haji Bakr is head of the Daesh Intelligence Bureau.
R7	8 AUG 2014	**CYBER:** Review of social media related to Daesh indicates a C2 structure where Abu Bakr al-Baghdadi is the caliph; he is supported by a Military Council, War Office, Cabinet, and Intelligence Bureau.
R8	9 AUG 2014	**CYBER:** Cyber activities related to governance of Walis within the Daesh political structure indicate that money and other resources are distributed from the Cabinet to the governances, who in turn move them to the Walis. This does not include military resources.
R9	9 AUG 2014	**OSINT:** Abu Suja openly acts as the caliph's representative for affairs concerning women and martyrs.
R10	9 AUG 2014	**OSINT:** Reporting from Daesh's own media resources indicate that Abu Luqman is responsible for Wali Raqqa, Amir al-Rafdan for Wali Deir al-Zour, Abdul Khadir for Wali Baghdad, and Abu Salema for Wali Anbar.

TABLE 6-2 ■ 6 × 6 Source Evaluation and Rating Schema

Reliability of the source	Credibility of the information
A Completely reliable	1 Confirmed by other sources
B Usually reliable	2 Probably true
C Fairly reliable	3 Possibly true
D Not usually reliable	4 Doubtful
E Unreliable	5 Improbable
F Reliability cannot be judged	6 Truth cannot be judged

Figure 6-2 illustrates the "Black Box" model that results from analysis of the reporting in Table 6-1. The "R.#" boxes refer to the specific reporting in the table.

In this example, the relationship between the Intelligence Bureau of Daesh and its leadership is established within the context of Daesh as an organization. In practice, the intelligence organization would be targeted for more collection, to establish more detail on how intelligence support is integrated into the Daesh OODA loop, and a variety of submodels describing capabilities and geographic responsibilities would be populated. A simple question regarding an adversary's black box that should be answered with regard to eventual deception planning is, to what extent does an organization's intelligence unit actually affect decision-making?

FIGURE 6-2 ■ Daesh "Black Box" Model

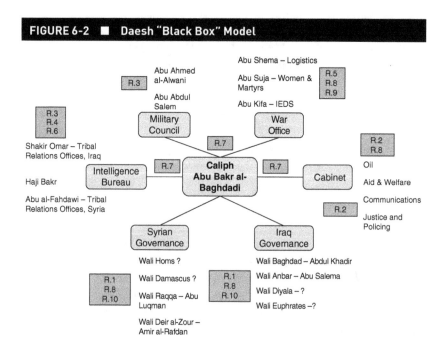

In this particular example of Daesh, the question to answer would be, to what extent does Abu Bakr al-Baghdadi base his decisions on intelligence provided by his Intelligence Bureau?

CHANNEL EXPLOITATION

Deception planning next requires answering the question, how can we best feed them? That is, which channels should be used to convey information to the target? Often this means using imagination both to exploit traditional channels used by the opponent and to develop new ones for the opponent to use.

A channel is more than just the sensor. It includes the tasking, processing, and exploitation phases of intelligence. Because of the flood of imagery, it's not uncommon for an image to be taken and processed but never exploited. More than once, a deception operation has been derailed when, unaccountably, the opponent either didn't receive the information that was provided or didn't understand or act on what it did receive. Chapter 4 discussed the Allied failures during World War II in attempts to deceive the Japanese. There, the problem was a failure to bridge a cultural divide. Often, however, the problem is the length of the opponent's communications chain. It's a basic rule of communications that, the more nodes between transmitter and receiver, the more likely a message is to be distorted or lost. The nodes (here, human) can misinterpret, lose, or falsify for their own purposes a message before transmitting it to the next node.

An example of what can go wrong in the intelligence channel was the Soviet decision to invade Afghanistan in 1979. The invasion was intended to support the existing Afghan government, which was dealing with an open rebellion. The intervention was based largely on flawed intelligence provided by KGB chairman Yuri Andropov. Andropov controlled the flow of information to General Secretary Brezhnev, who was partially incapacitated and ill for most of 1979. KGB reports from Afghanistan and passed on to Brezhnev created a picture of urgency and strongly emphasized the possibility that Prime Minister Hafizullah Amin had links to the CIA and to US subversive activities in the region.[14]

Most targets of deception have more than one channel available to them, though. They also have past experiences and predispositions to draw upon in making a decision. The ideal is for information provided in different channels to be *congruent* both with each other and with the target's experiences and predispositions. That is, they should all reinforce each other to lead the opponent to the desired decision. To the extent that the information provided is incongruent—that is, it conflicts with information in other channels or with the target's thinking—it will be rejected.

The Indian nuclear test deception, introduced in Chapter 1, was successful partially due to congruent information being fed through multiple channels. The United States had given India a model of its imagery intelligence channels—what its overhead IMINT systems could do and what its analysts looked for—in a demarche. Armed with that knowledge, the Indians could put together a congruent story in IMINT, OSINT, HUMINT, and diplomatic channels. Chapter 9 will address an example of incongruent use of channels. The Rabta Chemical plant deception described in that chapter failed because, though the Libyans knew about the IMINT sensors they had to deal with, they apparently understood neither the capability of the sensors nor the skill of the imagery analysts looking at Rabta. So the Libyans presented an incongruent picture to imagery analysts.

A key part of channel exploitation concerns the timing of the deception elements. Remember that an effective way to do this is to work backward from the desired outcome scenario. The deception planner develops what is called a *branch-point scenario*. This usually takes the form of a timeline. It identifies triggering events along the path—events that represent points at which a target's observations shape his or her decisions. The branch points later on can serve as indicators that the desired scenario is developing or failing to develop.

The main purpose of a branch-point scenario is to focus attention on the pivotal events rather than on the final outcome, because those are the moments where deception can lead the opponent to make the desired decisions and take the desired actions. The planner's skill at identifying and timing these branch points often determines the effectiveness of the deception. If the critical elements of intelligence arrive too early so that they can be vetted and dismissed as a deception, or too late, after a decision has been made, they are worse than useless.

To illustrate the use of branch-point scenarios, let's continue to revisit Operation Quicksilver (introduced in Chapter 2). Here, we focus on the specific timing of events in the second phase of the deception. Recall that for the pre-invasion, the scenario envisioned having the Germans concentrate their forces near Calais. Post-invasion, the objective was to keep the Germans from moving forces to Normandy for as long as possible. Figure 6-3 illustrates a timeline of the deception scenario. Although it contains several events, there are two critical points, each timed to convey a specific message to the Germans. The first, pre-invasion, is designed to convince the Germans that Calais is the target:

- Pre-invasion, dummy military equipment is displayed in what appears to be a marshalling area near Dover.

- Dummy landing craft are displayed at Dover port.

- On April 24 dummy radio traffic from notional FUSAG units commences, and continues until after the invasion.

- Two double German agents, nicknamed Garbo and Brutus, provide confirming reports of FUSAG dispositions near Dover.

As Figure 6-3 indicates, these observables were scheduled in late April, to allow time for the Wehrmacht to move additional units to the Calais area prior to June 6.

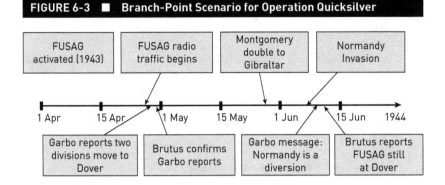

FIGURE 6-3 ■ Branch-Point Scenario for Operation Quicksilver

Near the end of May, the British added a temporal dimension to what was otherwise a deception about location. A double of Field Marshal Montgomery was publicly sent to Gibraltar, to deceive the Germans about the invasion date—it being unlikely that any invasion would occur while the key British commander was in Gibraltar.

Then, on the evening before the invasion, the second phase began, in an effort to convince Hitler that Normandy was a diversion:

- On June 5 Garbo sends an urgent message to his handler that an invasion of Normandy is imminent. The message intentionally arrives too late for a German response; its purpose is to make Garbo's next report credible.

- On June 8 Garbo reports that Normandy is a diversion. The message is timed to halt possible movement of forces toward Normandy and therefore goes directly to Hitler.

- Brutus then reports that the FUSAG is still in position at Dover, reinforcing Hitler's decision to hold his forces near Calais.

Because understanding the channels is a critical factor in the success of a deception, the next two chapters treat the subject more thoroughly. Chapter 7 examines the traditional intelligence channels: OSINT, COMINT, HUMINT, IMINT, and technical collection channels. Chapter 8 goes into detail on the channel that is becoming dominant in deception: cyberspace.

NOTES

1. Mark L. Psiaki and Todd E. Humphreys, "GPS Lies," *IEEE Spectrum*, August 2016, 26.

2. Thaddeus Holt, *The Deceivers: Allied Military Deception in the Second World War* (New York: Skyhorse Publishing, 2007), 289.

3. Garrett M. Graff, "The Spy Who Added Me on LinkedIn," *BloombergBusinessweek*, November 15, 2016, http://www.bloomberg.com/news/articles/2016-11-15/the-spy-who-added-me-on-linkedin.

4. Ibid.

5. US Department of Justice Press Release, "Evgeny Buryakov Pleads Guilty in Manhattan Federal Court in Connection with Conspiracy to Work for Russian Intelligence," March 11, 2016, https://www.justice.gov/usao-sdny/pr/evgeny-buryakov-pleads-guilty-manhattan-federal-court-connection-conspiracy-work.

6. Graff, "The Spy Who Added Me on LinkedIn."

7. Ibid.

8. Ibid.

9. "An Assessment of the Aldrich H. Ames Espionage Case and Its Implications for U.S. Intelligence," US Congress Senate Select Committee on Intelligence, 103d Congress (2nd Session), 1994, 29–30.

10. Alexander Kouzminov, *Biological Espionage: Special Operations of the Soviet and Russian Foreign Intelligence Services in the West* (London: Greenhill Books, 2006), 107.

11. B. Fischer, "Spy Dust and Ghost Surveillance: How the KGB Spooked the CIA and Hid Aldrich Ames in Plain Sight," *International Journal of Intelligence and CounterIntelligence* 24, no. 2 (2011): 284.

12. T. Weiner, D. Johnston, and N. A. Lewis, *Betrayal: The Story of Aldrich Ames, an American Spy* (New York: Random House, 1995), 249.

13. Christoph Reuter, "Secret Files Reveal the Structure of Islamic State," *Der Spiegel*, April 18, 2015, http://www.spiegel.de/international/world/islamic-state-files-show-structure-of-islamist-terror-group-a-1029274.html.

14. Svetlana Savranskaya, ed., "The Soviet Experience in Afghanistan: Russian Documents and Memoirs," *National Security Archive*, October 9, 2001, https://www2.gwu.edu/~nsarchiv/NSAEBB/NSAEBB57/soviet.html.

THE TRADITIONAL
INTELLIGENCE
CHANNELS

The deception planner's own intelligence channels have two distinct roles in deception. First, they are used to provide intelligence that supports the deception operation in several ways:

- *Identifying and assessing the target(s).* For example, providing information about the target's attitudes and decision-making process—the subject of Chapter 4.

- *Constructing the story,* the subject of Chapter 5.

- *Identifying the opponent's channels* to use for projecting the deception. For example, using OSINT might determine that the opponent has purchased SIGINT equipment; the nature of the equipment indicates a channel that the opponent will be using. Or a HUMINT source might report that an opponent has broken one of your communications encryption systems, and you can therefore use that communications channel to provide deceptive information.

- *Assessing the effectiveness of a deception operation.* Once the story has been provided to the target, it is important to determine whether the narrative has been accepted and acted upon—discussed in Chapter 9.

Second, your own channels have a critical role in detecting an opponent's deception. Looking for incongruences or suspicious congruences in the channels will help determine whether your side has been targeted for deception—the subject of Chapter 10. Extensive detail on intelligence channels for these purposes is contained in two separate publications: *Intelligence Collection*[1] and *The Five Disciplines of Intelligence Collection.*[2] An approach to analyzing the intelligence from these channels is detailed in *Intelligence Analysis: A Target-Centric Approach.*[3]

The focus of this chapter is instead on the *opponent*'s intelligence channels, that is, on projecting a deception by providing material to the target through his or her own channels, to support the deception. All channels used to collect intelligence can be targeted in a deception operation, with widely varying prospects for success.

This chapter goes into detail on five major channels that are used for projecting a deception. Chapter 8 focuses on cyberspace, a channel that has become prominent in deception and falls into a gray zone between operations and intelligence.

Deception must follow a careful path; it has to be subtle (too-obvious clues are likely to tip off the deception) but not so subtle that the opponent misses it. HUMINT is a commonly used channel for deception, but today it is seldom adequate on its own. An effective deception operation frequently has to be multi-INT or a "swarm" attack. Increasingly, carefully planned and elaborate multi-INT D&D is being used by various countries.

First, consider the channels that produce *literal* information—information in a form that humans use for communication. These are open source (OSINT), communications intelligence (COMINT), and human intelligence (HUMINT). All three have long been used to feed opponents deceptive information. The information they provide requires no special exploitation after the processing step (language translation) to be understood. It literally speaks for itself.

Nonliteral information includes imagery (IMINT) and a number of specialized technical collection disciplines; some are called measurements and signatures intelligence (MASINT), and some fall into the signals intelligence (SIGINT) domain. In contrast to literal information, this material usually requires sophisticated technical expertise applied in processing and exploitation in order for it to be understood and used. An opponent's nonliteral channels are increasingly used to project a deception, but they can be tricky to use, and there is less certainty (compared to literal channels) that the message gets to its intended recipient.

OSINT

Open source intelligence covers the traditional published and broadcast sources that are commonly available to anyone: media such as newspapers, magazines, radio, television; professional and academic material from conferences, symposia, professional associations, and academic papers; and government reports and official data. It also now includes user-generated web content such as social networking sites, video sharing sites, wikis, and blogs. Web content therefore overlaps with the CYBER channel and so is covered in the next chapter.

Open source has long been a means for planting deceptive information, and that role has increased now that OSINT is so prevalent on the web. News reporting via radio, TV, newspapers, and online naturally provides many opportunities to communicate deceptive information. These channels were used extensively to support the deception prior to Operation Desert Storm, as noted in Chapter 4. It's worth restating the challenge in using these channels, as was illustrated in that deception; one must avoid misleading one's own people and allies. The US government, for example, as a matter of policy does not lie to the press.

Open source is an excellent way to plant misleading material. It has the advantage of near-certain transmission and it's the only literal channel that an opposing service is almost certain to receive (other than diplomatic discussions). Following are two examples of the use of open source channels in deception.

GRAB SATELLITE

By the late 1950s the US Air Force Strategic Air Command (SAC) had developed an elaborate war plan for a retaliatory nuclear strike against the Soviet Union. The plan involved a coordinated air attack on key Soviet targets by SAC's B-47 and B-52 aircraft.

The success of the war plan depended critically on the ability of attacking aircraft to overcome Soviet air defenses. That meant avoiding or neutralizing Soviet air defense radars. And that, in turn, required that SAC's planners create a map of the locations and types of the radars for the entire Soviet Union.

For several years, SAC had been able to locate and identify the radars around the northern periphery of the USSR. Air Force and naval electronic reconnaissance aircraft, known as ferrets, flew from bases in the United Kingdom and Alaska on routes close to the Soviet border and used sensitive receivers to intercept and locate the radars. But radars in the interior could not be detected by aircraft without overflying the Soviet landmass.

For that mission, a satellite was needed, and in 1958 the Naval Research Laboratory (NRL) proposed to build one: an electronic intelligence (ELINT) satellite in low earth orbit that could intercept radar emissions and geolocate radars anywhere in the world. The problem was that, if the Soviets knew that a satellite was conducting ELINT missions, they could practice denial—shutting down critical parts of their air defense radars when the satellite was in view. This was already a common Soviet practice to defeat ferret aircraft flying near the USSR's borders. A simple unacknowledged mission launch was not an option; it would attract too much attention, and the Soviets might determine the satellite's real mission.

The solution was to create a cover story that would not attract undue interest. NRL proposed to put two payloads on the satellite: a highly classified ELINT receiver, and a publicly acknowledged research payload. The result was the GRAB

(Continued)

(Continued)

(Galactic Radiation and Background) experiment. The first GRAB satellite was launched on June 22, 1960; a second GRAB went into orbit on June 29, 1961, and operated until August 1962. GRAB transmitted its ELINT intercepts to a network of receivers at ground sites around the world. It also provided measurements of solar radiation (the SolRad experiment) that were publicly released in open source channels to support the deception.

The GRAB operation is an excellent example of a subtle deception. Interestingly, it didn't include all of the elements of deception that were defined in Chapter 1. The cover story was based on truth (the satellite was real; the SolRad experiment was real). It included denial (the ELINT package was concealed; the project had been placed under a tight security control system with access limited to fewer than 200 officials in the Washington, DC, area). And misdirection—the attention paid to the SolRad experiment—was part of it. But it did not include deceit; as noted earlier, the US government is not allowed to deceive the press. The press releases simply omitted an important feature.

BLACK BOOMERANG REDUX

Recall the Black Boomerang operation described in Chapter 3. There, the discussion was focused on the social component of the PMESII view that a deceiver takes when considering outcome scenarios for deception. The open source channel that the British relied on was radio, albeit a fake radio station. The radio was operated such that the British government could avoid being held to account. While the primary function of the station was to sow discord among German troops, it was also used for a second purpose in tandem with open source print publications. It made effective use of the truth against neutral targets, as the following illustrates.

During the war, the British government published a list of the neutral firms and businessmen who were breaking the Allied blockade by trading with Hitler. The list was used to impose sanctions. But the British also had a second list of firms that were only suspects. Their names were not published. British officials, however, had orders to counter their activities where possible.

The Black Boomerang team acquired this list of suspects along with files that revealed both the reasons for suspicion and the personal background of the suspect firms' directors. Subsequently, these suspects heard the secrets of their private and commercial lives being publicly exposed on the Atlantiksender radio. Usually their reaction was to protest to the nearest British authorities, who, of course, denied any connection with a German radio broadcast. Delmer, in his book *Black Boomerang*, describes the typical approach:

> We then waited to see whether they would mend their ways. If they did not, we followed up with further broadcasts about them. As a rule,

however, one broadcast was enough. One typical case was that of a firm of Swedish exporters who were buying ball-bearings in Sweden, and smuggling them to Germany, thereby undoing the effects of our bombing. Our story about the firm was so accurate and so ribald that the Swedish authorities felt deeply hurt in their national pride. They made unofficial representations about it to the British ambassador Sir Victor Mallet.

"We had our eye on this firm," said the Swedes with injured dignity, "we were waiting to prosecute them, when we had enough evidence. Now your broadcast has warned them." Sir Victor replied that he had no knowledge of the Atlantiksender, and nothing to do with it. . . . [T]he Swedish newspapers had taken up the story we had put out, and the directors of the Swedish firm, fearing more Atlantiksender publicity, had cancelled all further deliveries to Germany.[4]

COMINT

Communications intelligence, or COMINT, is the interception, processing, and reporting of an opponent's communications. Communications in this definition includes voice and data communications, facsimile, video, and any other deliberate transmission of information that is not meant to be accessed except by specifically intended recipients. This definition includes Internet transmissions, though their collection overlaps into the realm of CYBER collection, described in Chapter 8.

Communications are seen as more attractive than OSINT and HUMINT channels for projecting a deception. That's because COMINT is generally considered to be valid and, therefore, more trusted by intelligence organizations. The problem often is selecting the right communications channel for the deceiving information. There are many potential sources of COMINT: cell phones, satellite communications, microwave point-to-point, and optical fiber cables carry a large volume. In fact, there are simply too many sources that an opposing service might target. So the problem becomes determining which channels the opposing service is monitoring. A few of the channel types pose no problem: A tap into a fiber optic cable signals that a hostile COMINT service is monitoring the cable's traffic—though it may be difficult to identify exactly which hostile service emplaced it. A COMINT antenna aimed at a geostationary communications satellite indicates that the host country of the antenna is monitoring that satellite's communication downlinks. In contrast, it is very difficult to determine what cell phone traffic that a hostile COMINT service is monitoring.

But once the COMINT means that an opponent relies on are known, then deception become straightforward. For example, during the Cold War, the Soviets made extensive use of audio taps (bugs). US counterintelligence operatives occasionally used these bugs to feed the Soviets false information. In some cases, they used the bugs to take out troublesome Russian agents, either by hinting that the agent was on the US payroll or by reporting that he was having an affair with some Soviet minister's wife.

COMINT deception can be used for strategic or tactical deception. The deceptions that supported Operation Quicksilver and Operation Desert Storm fit more into the strategic deception class. But COMINT deception is most widely used at the tactical level, as it was in Operation Bolo.

OPERATION BOLO

During the Vietnam War, the pilots of the US Seventh Air Force were becoming frustrated with the tactics of their North Vietnamese opponents. The North Vietnamese Air Force carefully avoided confrontations that would pit their MiG-21 Fishbed fighters against the US Air Force's superior F-4C Phantoms. Instead, they selectively targeted US F-105 fighter/bombers that were conducting airstrikes in the theater—and in the process, racking up kills; the MiG-21 was superior to the F-105 in a dogfight.

In December 1966 the US Air Force developed a deception operation to change the odds. The plan was nicknamed Operation Bolo. Its objective was to create an aerial ambush.

F-4Cs flying from bases in Thailand and South Vietnam took the flight paths normally used by F-105s. Knowing that the North Vietnamese monitored aircraft communications, the F-4C pilots used the communications frequencies and call signs normally used by F-105s on bombing runs.

At the same time, other F-4Cs flew to positions off the coast of North Vietnam, positioning themselves to guard selected North Vietnamese airfields to prevent the MiG-21s from returning to them.

The mission was a success. When the MiG-21s took off and flew to intercept what appeared to be easy prey, the F-4s pounced, shooting down seven MiG-21s in twelve minutes—in effect destroying one-third of the enemy's MiG-21 inventory.[5]

Bolo is an example of COMINT deception, but it also illustrates the swarm or multi-INT type of operation noted in the opening of this chapter. Multiple channels were targeted, including North Vietnamese radar and COMINT channels. It also relied on a truth that was well established—the F-105 operational patterns and signatures had produced a conditioned response by the North Vietnamese. And of course it made use of deceit.

The end result indicates another basic characteristic of deception: Once a deception is exposed, its effectiveness usually is lost and future similar deceptions are unlikely to succeed. A number of other Bolo-type missions were flown over the ensuing months, the first on January 23, 1967, but either there was a pattern that alerted the North Vietnamese or other factors went wrong. Whatever the reason, none of the later missions were as successful as the initial operation.

Helping COMINT Deception Succeed

Intelligence is perceived to have more credibility by the other party if they must work hard or go to great expense to obtain it. So, the idea is to make the intelligence difficult to get, but not so difficult that it never gets through to the opponent. The credibility of the deception in Operation Mincemeat (see Chapter 2) was greatly enhanced because the information about the target of an Allied invasion was so difficult to obtain, and required substantial analysis to figure out.

In similar fashion the techniques for defeating COMINT can be applied to *enhance* the credibility of a deceptive communication. Following are a few examples of such techniques in the COMINT discipline.

Steganography

Steganography is defined as the art and science of hiding information by embedding messages within other, seemingly innocent messages. Secret writing traditionally made use of invisible ink to place a message between the visible lines of an apparently innocuous letter. Counterespionage routinely relies on opening suspect correspondence (known in the trade from pre-Internet days as "flaps and seals" operations) and testing for secret writing. So secret writing is not commonly used by sophisticated intelligence services. However, it still finds use in countries or organizations where technical methods of communication are not available. During World War II, agents used a sophisticated type of steganography called the microdot: a technique of photographing and reducing a page of text to the size of a pinhead, then making it look like the period at the end of a sentence.

A new version of steganography is today used by terrorists and narcotics traffickers to avoid the detection of compromising information—hiding messages inside computer files. It works by replacing bits of useless or unused data in graphics, audio, text, or HTML files. The message often is embedded in a map or a photograph. A digital image of a landscape, for example, might hold a communiqué or a map. A digital song file might contain blueprints of a targeted building.[6] Unless the COMINT processor has some idea that digital steganography is embedded in a specific file, it can be very difficult to find. When used for offensive deception, or planting material that you want the adversary to retrieve and find credible, again, the message or image has to be found—but not be too easy to find.

Code Words and "Talking Around"

It is widely known that cell phones are targeted for COMINT. So when using cell phones or the Internet, targets may talk around a topic, often by using prearranged code. As an example, the 9/11 attackers communicated openly and disseminated information using prearranged code words. For instance, the "faculty of urban planning" meant the World Trade Center, and the Pentagon was referred to as the "faculty of fine arts." Mohammed Atta's final message to the eighteen other terrorists who conducted the 9/11 attacks read, in code: "The semester begins in three more weeks. We've obtained 19 confirmations for studies in the faculty of law, the faculty of urban planning, the faculty of fine arts, and the faculty of engineering."[7] The number *19,* of course, referred to the number of cell members who were to board the four aircraft.

Because the use of code words and "talking around" a topic is a widely known tactic, it is a natural way to communicate deceptive information. Again, this deception method requires some subtlety when planting deceptive information; the communication has to look like a credible attempt to conceal information, but not be so difficult to analyze that the opponent's COMINT analyst misses it completely.

Encryption

Encryption is now widely practiced in many types of communication to deny COMINT exploitation. The result is that encrypted traffic is more likely to be the focus of intelligence interest, especially when encryption is used where it should not be found in a system. Al Qaeda long relied on unencrypted emails for communication because they knew that encrypted ones would attract attention.[8]

Like the "talking around" method with telephones, since unexpected encryption does attract attention, it is a natural way to communicate a deceptive message that your side wants the other side to believe and act on—either using a cipher that the opponent has broken, or using a cipher that the opponent can readily break. Recall that the case of protecting Ultra, described in Chapter 3, illustrates the tactic: The British sent a radio message to a notional spy in Naples, thanking him for warning them of a convoy departure. The message was sent using a cipher system that the Germans could decode. During World War II in the Pacific, the British on more than one occasion sent deceptive information to notional spies using a cipher that they knew the Japanese could decode.

Deceiving Traffic Analysis

Traffic analysis is a method of obtaining intelligence from what are called "externals," that is, from the characteristics of the communications signal, without looking at the information content. It is especially useful when message content is not available, for example, when encryption is used. The externals can be used, for example, to determine the location and movement of a communications emitter.

The usual objective of traffic analysis is to build a model of a communications network (or a network of associates) by observing communications patterns.

Traffic analysts look at these calling patterns to identify networks of personal or official associations. Traffic analysis is commonly used in assessing military communications and traffic within criminal cartels and within terrorist cells. Examples of judgments that can be made based on communications traffic patterns include the following:

- Frequent communications from one node can tell the traffic analyst who's in charge or the control station of a network.

- Correlating who talks and when can indicate which stations are active in connection with events.

- Frequent communications often indicate that an operation is in the planning stage.

- No communication can indicate either no activity, or that the planning stage is complete.

- Rapid, short communications are often connected with negotiations.

Traffic analysis can be deceived, to some extent, by techniques such as inserting dummy traffic in the network. The result can be that COMINT analysts looking for patterns will be led to the wrong conclusion. Traffic analysis can be targeted as part of a larger deception, for example, by making an outlying (and expendable) node appear to be the controlling node in a clandestine network.

HUMINT

HUMINT sources include familiar clandestine assets—spies—but also include émigrés, defectors, elicitation, and interrogation sources (described in the sections that follow). The common theme of this channel is that the intelligence is collected by one person interacting with another person to obtain information.

The products of governmental HUMINT activities include embassy officers' assessments, information elicited from contacts, information from paid agents, or documents or equipment clandestinely acquired by purchase or theft. The human sources can be diplomats and defense attachés, international conference attendees, defectors, émigrés, refugees, or prisoners. Volunteers—cooperating private individuals and organizations—also can supply privileged information that they encounter in the course of their work. Nongovernmental organizations have proliferated in recent years and are increasingly useful sources about foreign developments.

These different types of HUMINT divide into two broad classes—overt and clandestine HUMINT. They are treated differently in both conducting and detecting deception.

Overt HUMINT

Overt HUMINT is attractive for conveying deceptive information because the channel is direct: The deceiver has some degree of confidence that the information will reach its intended recipient. It has the attendant disadvantage that it is often used to pass deceptive information, so it is a suspect channel. There are a number of channels for collecting overt HUMINT, but three are prominently used: elicitation and its formal counterpart, liaison; facilities visits and public demonstrations; and interrogations.

Elicitation and Liaison

Elicitation is the practice of obtaining information about a topic from conversations, preferably without the source knowing what is happening. Elicitation is widely practiced in gatherings of diplomats and military attachés and in the commercial sector during business executives' social hours and sales conventions. In fact, elicitation may be the most valuable tool of a successful diplomat. But as a channel for deception, it must be used with skill because it is so often used in that capacity.

Liaison relationships also are conducted among intelligence organizations, though these are usually not overt. The relationships are mostly bilateral, and involve sharing intelligence, sometimes in exchange for intelligence collection equipment or diplomatic or commercial favors.

Both diplomatic and intelligence liaison provide many benefits, but they carry risks that the liaison partner will use the relationship to deceive. Even if the liaison partner doesn't intend to deceive, he or she may be the conduit for deception aimed at the other partner. Such was the case in Operation Mincemeat, described in Chapter 2; the British relied on the existence of a liaison relationship between Spanish and German intelligence to ensure that the deceptive information would be shared.

Liaison channels have the advantage of being less complex to execute transmission of intelligence, compared to using clandestine HUMINT for deception. But intelligence collectors and analysts charged with detecting deception know this. So the deceptive information acquired through liaison is less likely to be accepted without independent confirmation.

Facilities Visits and Demonstrations

During the Cold War, industrial plant visits often were used for obtaining advanced technology for military use. The Soviets, and later the Chinese, made numerous visits to US industrial facilities in attempts, often successful, to acquire advanced military and civilian technologies. And, because the host is able to control what the visitor sees, such facilities visits provide multiple opportunities to conduct deception.

International arms control treaties often require onsite visits. These visits have been used to promote the image that a chemical warfare plant, for example, is actually a pesticide production plant. Countering such deception frequently makes use of methods such as clandestine materials sampling.

Demonstrations to convey a deception have been used repeatedly in military conflicts, going back to Sun Tzu's time, at least. During the US Civil War, Confederate cavalry general Nathan Bedford Forrest had pursued and closed with a Union cavalry unit commanded by Colonel Abel Streight. Forrest, outnumbered three to one, persuaded Streight to surrender by a ruse. He paraded his forces back and forth in front of Streight in such a way as to make it appear that he actually had superior numbers.

Public demonstrations such as military parades are often used to project deceptive images. The deception carried off by the Soviets at the 1955 Moscow Air Show, detailed in Chapter 9, illustrates a use of the tactic of making a smaller force appear to be larger using a demonstration.

The story of German rearmament after World War I, described in Chapter 5, illustrates one of the most elaborate uses of both facilities visits and public demonstrations such as air shows to support deception.

Interrogation

Interrogation is a standard overt HUMINT technique, widely used by military forces and governments to obtain intelligence. Interrogation might best be described as elicitation in a controlled setting. The difference is that the interrogator has physical custody or some form of control over the fate of the source—who usually is a prisoner charged with a crime, a prisoner of war, an émigré, or a defector. The specific tactics used depend on the interrogator's degree of control and the willingness of the detainee to cooperate. Émigrés and defectors usually evince the greatest willingness to cooperate.

For the military, prisoner interrogations provide a wealth of material of immediate use about the morale, location, and combat readiness of opposing forces. It's an old technique, but it continues to be successful. During the US Civil War, Union interrogators at Gettysburg were able to determine that they had prisoners from every Confederate division except General George Pickett's—leading them to conclude correctly that Pickett, having fresh troops, would lead the attack on the following day.

Prisoner interrogations can be used as a primary channel for deception. Few such deceptions have proved as devastating to the deceived as the operation that the British conducted against the Irish Republican Army (IRA), in what was called the IRA Prison Sting.

THE IRA PRISON STING

Chapter 1 described the IRA Embezzlement Sting, a deception the British used to destabilize the IRA in Northern Ireland. Probably the most effective destabilization operation during that conflict, however, was conducted in 1974, and is often referred to as the IRA Prison Sting.

Vincent Heatherington and Miles McGrogan were two young Catholic men from Belfast. The two were trained by British intelligence for an interrogation deception and were then sent to Crumlin Road prison, purportedly to await trial for the

(Continued)

(Continued)

murder of two police officers. In the prison, they were placed in the IRA wing. Since neither had extensive ties with the IRA, both were viewed with suspicion. The prison's IRA leaders separated the two men and conducted intensive interrogations.

After several days of interrogation, Heatherington appeared to break down. He admitted to being a British informer. He said that he had been forced to work for the British since the age of sixteen. During the next week, he provided details of British operations against the IRA that were already known to IRA leadership, along with false information that fit with IRA suspicions. He also identified a number of IRA members that he claimed were British informers. Those identified were primarily from the younger emerging leadership of the IRA. Finally, Heatherington claimed that he was really sent there to assassinate the prison leadership. To check his allegations, the IRA apparently provided details of the assassination plot to the prison governor. A subsequent search of Heatherington's cell uncovered vials of poison. The IRA leadership in Crumlin Road then accepted Heatherington's story in its entirety. In the words of a key IRA lieutenant,

> We suddenly believed Heatherington. The names of all those he mentioned were passed on to relevant people in the IRA in Long Kesh (the Maze) and on the outside. Interrogations began, and in the Maze many men were badly treated by their interrogators. The IRA was carried away in hysteria. Men admitted, under interrogation, crimes they could not have committed. No one was safe from scrutiny.[9]

IRA leaders subsequently described these as the darkest days of their movement. The IRA almost disintegrated in the aftermath. Their leadership began a two-year witch hunt for informers. Within prisons and outside, IRA intelligence brought in and harshly interrogated suspects. The interrogations within prisons included torture with piano wire and electric current. Innocent IRA members were forced to confess, under harsh torture, to being British agents and then were executed.

The IRA did in fact survive, with unforeseen and unwelcome consequences from a British standpoint. The emergent IRA was a smarter organization. For example, in a move designed to slow its penetration by British intelligence and to limit the damage caused by informers, the IRA adopted a cellular structure replacing the traditional battalion formations.[10]

Clandestine HUMINT

A nation's clandestine service performs highly diverse but interdependent activities that span many intelligence channels, including, for example, COMINT and CYBER. The unifying aspect of these activities is the fact that they are conducted clandestinely or secretly. However, it is clandestine HUMINT that is most well-known because of its popular portrayals in print and movies. Obviously, clandestine HUMINT depends on deception to function. And it can be a vehicle for conducting deception against both intelligence and operational targets. Specifically, it depends on deception in the form of *cover*: a false picture of personal or organizational identity, function, or both.

Personal Cover

Clandestine services officers must conceal their actual role. So some form of personal cover (for example, an assumed identity) is needed. There are two types of cover—official and nonofficial. Persons under official cover work in official government positions. The deepest level of cover is nonofficial cover. Such operatives are called NOCs. NOCs are much more difficult for a counterintelligence service to identify but are much more vulnerable if identified.

All forms of overseas cover are increasingly a problem for all clandestine services. The increased availability of life history data to foreign governments and increasing worldwide availability of technologies such as facial recognition software and biometrics exacerbates the cover problem. (As an example, US law enforcement has amassed a facial recognition database of 117 million citizens or at least half of the adult population.)[11]

Crossing borders has become a particularly hazardous event for the clandestine officer. With the advent of biometric information, false documents are easier to discover. Furthermore, the ability to investigate the background of a suspicious person has grown rapidly with the Internet. Perhaps ironically, a person *without* a cyber footprint is also treated with suspicion.

As a result, nonofficial cover is becoming both more necessary and more difficult to maintain, and new types of NOCs have to be created. Nontraditional platforms for agent recruitment also are increasingly necessary, and these cost more to maintain than official cover platforms.[12]

Organizational Cover

Many intelligence agencies use organizational cover in the form of front companies and co-opted businesses for technology and materiel acquisition and to run agents. Countries such as Russia and China have a long history of using organizational cover to target Western Europe, the United States, and Japan because of the advanced technology that is available in those countries.

Front companies have several options for running deceptions to obtain technology and materiel. They often are used to solicit bids for technology or products from legitimate companies. The victim companies often will provide detailed technical knowledge in the hope of being competitive and making sales.[13] The front companies also are useful as transshipment points for purchasing materiel and then making prohibited exports. Dave Szady, the FBI's chief counterintelligence official, reported in 2005 that the Chinese operated over 3,000 front companies in the United States. The primary purpose of those companies, he said, is to purchase or steal controlled technologies.[14]

IMINT

Defeating visible imagery usually starts with denial: putting shielding over sensitive targets, camouflaging them, and placing facilities underground. When denying information to imaging satellites, awareness of the orbits allows security personnel to stop an activity, or perhaps cover the sensitive parts, when the satellite is overhead.

IMINT deception goes a step further by presenting the false. Typically, this relies on decoys. Their use during World War II and in Kosovo has already been described in earlier chapters, and decoys continue to be used in military conflicts. During 2016, Iraqi forces fighting to retake the city of Mosul from Daesh found a cache of wooden tanks, vehicles, and even dummy soldiers near the city. The decoys were intended to divert airstrikes away from actual targets.[15]

There are a wide range of techniques besides decoys to deceive imagery. Once again, the Indian nuclear test case, described in Chapter 1, is a classic because it illustrates an effective combination of denial (camouflage, concealing test equipment during daylight hours) with deceit (dressing test range personnel in military uniforms, reshaping excavated sand to look like natural sand dunes).

The Al Kibar case illustrates the level of sophistication that IMINT deception can achieve, and the effective use of other channels to defeat it. Al Kibar was an elaborate Syrian attempt to conceal efforts to develop nuclear weaponry.

THE SYRIAN DECEPTION AT AL KIBAR

In 2003 the Syrians began to construct a nuclear reactor near the town of Al Kibar. The reactor was a near-duplicate of one at Yongbyon, North Korea, and was built with North Korean assistance. The Syrians realized that US imagery analysts probably had a profile of the Yongbyon reactor and would quickly spot any similarity in imagery. They consequently developed an elaborate deception to conceal the reactor from imagery collection and, more important, from imagery analysis:

- They partially buried the reactor and erected a false roof and walls around it to conceal its characteristic shape from overhead imagery.

- They disguised the outer shell to look like a Byzantine fortress of the sort to be found in Syria.

- Several tactics for denial supported the deception. The Syrians did not construct new roads or put in place airfields, rail tracks, air defenses, or site security—any of which would have drawn the attention of imagery analysts.[16]

The Syrian strategy could be summed up as "minimize the visible signature of the facility and make it appear to be uninteresting." It appears to have been successful. Reportedly, in 2005, US imagery analysts found the building but could not figure out what it was for; it was "odd and in the middle of nowhere."[17]

The deception was exposed, as imagery deceptions often are, by a HUMINT operation or, more accurately, by a HUMINT-enabled cyber operation. On March 7, 2007, covert operations specialists from Israel's Mossad broke into the Vienna home of Ibrahim Othman, head of the Syrian Atomic Energy Agency. Once inside, they hacked into Othman's computer and copied about three dozen photographs. These proved to be photographs taken from inside the Al Kibar complex. The photos confirmed that Al Kibar indeed housed a copy of the Yongbyon reactor; they even included photographs of North Korean technicians at the facility.[18]

The Israelis decided on a direct approach to deal with the facility. During the night of September 5–6, 2007, four Israeli F-16s and four F-15s departed Israel Air Force bases, flew north along the Mediterranean coast, and then eastward along the border between Syria and Turkey. The attackers used electronic warfare en route to deceive and disrupt the Syrian air defense network. The seventeen tons of bombs that they dropped on Al Kibar totally destroyed the reactor building.

On April 28, 2008, CIA director Michael Hayden confirmed that Al Kibar would have produced enough nuclear material for one to two weapons a year, and that it was of a similar size and technology to North Korea's Yongbyon Nuclear Scientific Research Center.

Countering infrared, spectral, and synthetic aperture radar (SAR) has relied mostly on denial (camouflage and radar-reflective coverings) rather than deception. Deception using decoys against all of these imagers can be done, though, and is most effective when combined with denial to protect the real targets. The Serbian deception efforts in Kosovo, described in Chapter 3, involved creating heat sources to deceive infrared imagers, though that was a crude effort by current deception standards.

Introducing deception into SAR imagery is difficult, though possible. Usually, deception relies on radar decoys that simulate equipment—such as ships, missile sites, aircraft, and tanks—and that deceive visual as well as radar imagery. It helps to have extensive knowledge of the capabilities and limitations of the SAR. It is also important to understand the capabilities of the imagery analysts, because well-trained analysts can spot minor inconsistencies in the image that indicate deception.

TECHNICAL COLLECTION

Technical collection in a most general sense refers to all nonliteral collection, that is, IMINT, SIGINT other than COMINT, MASINT, and materiel acquisition. IMINT was treated separately because of its prominence both in conducting deception and in countering it.

Deception against technical collection has a history that dates back to World War II, when technical collection began to play an important role in warfare. It began with efforts to deceive enemy radar.

Radar

During World War II, Allied aircraft attacking European targets began to deceive German radars by dropping chaff—strips of tinfoil that, released from an aircraft, appeared on radar to be another aircraft. After the war, this type of misdirection was applied in more sophisticated versions. Because chaff moved slowly with the wind, a radar operator could distinguish it from the fast-moving target that was the aircraft. So deception moved into the purely electronic domain: Using a technique called spoofing, the attacking aircraft received and retransmitted the radar signals in such a way as to make the aircraft appear to be in several other locations, while hiding the reflected signal from the aircraft itself. As radars became more sophisticated, this type of deception moved back into the physical domain, with the use of air-launched decoys—small pilotless vehicles designed to present much the same radar return as the aircraft that launched them.

This type of deception is a part of what is called electronic warfare (EW) or electronic attack (EA). It is supported by operational electronic intelligence (OPELINT) or electronic support measures (ESM). Although it is narrowly focused on deceiving opposing radars in combat situations, it requires all of the elements of more elaborate deceptions. The operation must be planned well in advance, with a good understanding of how the radar works. And some means must be established to determine if the deception is succeeding.

Operation Bolo, discussed earlier, illustrates a clever tactical application of radar deception. The aircraft flight paths appeared on North Vietnamese radars as coming from Thailand, the normal F-105 attack route. The F-4s deliberately reduced their airspeed to that used by the F-105s and carried radar reflectors that, on radars, simulated the larger signature of the F-105.

Electronic Intelligence (ELINT)

Electronic intelligence refers to the information extracted through the collection, processing, exploitation, and analysis of signals transmitted by radars, beacons, jammers, missile guidance systems, and altimeters. Most ELINT is conducted against radar targets.

Deception against electronic intelligence also dates back to World War II. During that time, the radar communities developed deception techniques to counter both ELINT and EA. In the post–World War II period, reconnaissance aircraft began flying regular ELINT missions to locate an opponent's radars and to assess each radar's purpose, performance, and weaknesses. Many such flights targeted radar test ranges to assess new radars in development.

To counter such ELINT collection, radar developers conducted deceptive tests, concealing what were called "wartime modes" so that, during conflicts, attackers would be surprised by encountering radars operating on unexpected frequencies or in unexpected modes.

A number of more sophisticated deceptive techniques also are used against ELINT. For example, ELINT uses the signature (frequency, transmission patterns, and operating modes) of a radar to identify it, and often to identify the ship, aircraft, or vehicle carrying the radar. By simulating the signature of an uninteresting radar, one can (for example) make a naval ship appear to be a commercial vessel.

Foreign Instrumentation Signals Intelligence (FISINT)

A number of platforms used for military purposes—missiles, aircraft, and satellites—carry instrumentation to monitor conditions on the vehicle. The instrumentation measures such things as velocity, pressures, temperatures, and subsystems performance. There are two situations where it is necessary to transmit the instrumentation readings to a ground station for analysis: missile and aircraft testing, and satellite status monitoring. Such radiofrequency transmissions are called *telemetry*. The collection of telemetry signals is sometimes called telemetry intelligence but more often is called foreign instrumentation signals intelligence (FISINT).

FISINT deception involves transmitting a bogus signal while in some fashion hiding the actual telemetry. It can be used to mislead about the mission of a satellite or the performance of a missile or aircraft, or to demonstrate a level of performance (range, payload, accuracy) that is much better or worse than actual. There are no publicly disclosed instances of telemetry deception being practiced, perhaps because it is a difficult operation to execute successfully. One has to know a great deal about the FISINT collector—especially its location and performance—and to manipulate the false telemetry signal's characteristics accordingly.

Acoustic and Infrasound

Signatures of intelligence value are collected in the acoustic spectrum in the audible (above 20 Hz) and infrasound (below 20 Hz) parts of the spectrum. Typically, this collection depends on the unintentional emission of sound waves created by some kind of disturbance. Deception is targeted against two broad types of acoustic signature collection: ACOUSTINT and ACINT.

ACOUSTINT Deception

Some acoustic sensors detect sound traveling through the atmosphere or in the ground near the surface and therefore function only at comparatively short ranges (a few meters to a few kilometers). The intelligence product of such collection is usually called *ACOUSTINT.* These sensors are used both in military operations and in intelligence to identify and track land vehicles and airborne platforms. They can locate these targets and determine their speed and direction of motion based on sound transmitted through the air or earth. Such sensors can be readily deployed and disguised in all types of terrain.[19] Most of the sensing of sound in air or underground finds tactical military or law enforcement use because detection can be made only at short ranges.

Acoustic sensing has been used to detect enemy ground movements for millennia. Armies routinely send out patrols or establish listening posts to listen for the sounds of tanks, trucks, and marching troops. Deception—creating deceptive sounds to simulate such movements—also has a long history. During World War II an Allied military unit in Europe made use of massive loudspeakers mounted on trucks to simulate the movements of tanks and infantry.

ACINT Deception

Acoustic intelligence derived from underwater sound is usually called *ACINT*. ACINT relies on a class of acoustic sensors that detect sound in water. Sound travels much better in water than in air. Underwater sound created by ships and submarines can be detected at distances of several hundred kilometers. Tactical deception to counter ACINT has been practiced for decades, in the form of decoys deployed to simulate the sound produced by a ship or submarine.

NOTES

1. Robert M. Clark, *Intelligence Collection* (Washington, DC: CQ Press, 2014).

2. Mark M. Lowenthal and Robert M. Clark, *The Five Disciplines of Intelligence Collection* (Washington, DC: CQ Press, 2015).

3. Robert M. Clark, *Intelligence Analysis: A Target-Centric Approach,* 5th ed. (Washington, DC: CQ Press, 2017).

4. Sefton Delmer, *Black Boomerang* (New York: Viking Press, January 1962), 47–48.

5. NSA Cryptologic History Series, "Working against the Tide," Part 1, June 1970, 149–53.

6. United States Institute of Peace, "Terror on the Internet: Questions and Answers," http://www.usip.org/publications-tools/terror-internet/terror-internet-questions-and-answers.

7. Ibid.

8. Devin D. Jessee, "Tactical Means, Strategic Ends: Al Qaeda's Use of Denial and Deception," *Terrorism and Political Violence* 18 (2006): 367–88.

9. Mark L. Bowlin, "British Intelligence and the IRA: The Secret War in Northern Ireland, 1969–1988," September 1999, 83–89, https://archive.org/stream/britishintellige00bowlpdf/british intellige00bowl_djvu.txt.

10. Ibid.

11. Steven Nelson, "Half of U.S. Adults Are in Police Facial Recognition Networks," *US News and World Report*, October 18, 2016, https://www.law.georgetown.edu/news/press-releases/half-of-all-american-adults-are-in-a-police-face-recognition-database-new-report-finds.cfm.

12. "A Tide Turns," *The Economist*, July 21, 2010, http://www.economist.com/node/16590867/.

13. E. M. Roche, *Corporate Spy: Industrial Espionage and Counterintelligence in the Multinational Enterprise* (New York: Barraclough, 2008), 131–35.

14. P. Devenny, "China's Secret War," FrontPageMagazine.com, March 31, 2005, http://archive.frontpagemag.com/Printable.aspx?ArtId=9146.

15. John Bacon, "Islamic State Used Fake Tanks to Confuse Airstrikes," *USA Today*, November 14, 2016, http://www.msn.com/en-us/news/world/islamic-state-used-fake-tanks-to-confuse-airstrikes/ar-AAkhs2f.

16. Frank V. Pabian, "Strengthened IAEA Safeguards-Imagery Analysis: Geospatial Tools for Nonproliferation Analysis," June 22, 2012, Los Alamos National Laboratory, LA-UR-12-24104.

17. Andreas Persbo, "Verification, Implementation, and Compliance," May 13, 2008, http://www.armscontrolverification.org/2008/05/syrian-deception.html.

18. David Makovsky, "The Silent Strike," *New Yorker*, September 17, 2012, http://www.newyorker.com/magazine/2012/09/17/the-silent-strike.

19. B. Kaushik and Don Nance, "A Review of the Role of Acoustic Sensors in the Modern Battlefield," paper presented at the 11th AIAA/CEAS Aeroacoustics Conference, May 23–25, 2005, https://ccse.lbl.gov/people/kaushik/papers/AIAA_Monterey.pdf.

THE CYBERSPACE CHANNEL

Within the complex domain that we call CYBER, there are three basic types of deception. One supports cyber offense; one is a part of cyber defense; and one supports deception operations that transcend the cyber domain. Many of the examples in this chapter are of the first two types: They describe deception where the objective was a cyber target, and the deception remained entirely in cyberspace. But deception can be conducted in cyberspace to support operations across all of the PMESII domains. It is used to support covert actions and influence operations. It is used to manage perceptions, beliefs, and understanding, and to create a flawed situational awareness among individuals or groups, thus increasing the chance that deception will succeed. It can be a powerful tool for conducting deception against a defined group as discussed in Chapter 1.

Cyberspace is especially important for today's military. Some military leaders consider it a complementary domain to support real-time operations by land, sea, air, and special operations components. Others argue that, from a military doctrinal perspective, cyberspace is an independent domain for operations. As conflict is moving more into cyberspace, it appears to be etching out a fifth battlespace domain—cyber—to join air, land, sea, and space. The last five years have seen many countries in the West establishing cyber commands for the express purpose of managing cyber warfare as a fully integrated battlespace domain. Consequently, deception—one of the important tools for winning conflicts—must move there also. And it has.

Chapter 7 addressed the deceiver's own intelligence channels as having two distinct roles in deception. One role is to provide intelligence that supports the deception: assessing the targets, constructing the story, identifying the opponent's channels, and assessing deception effectiveness. The second role is to identify an opponent's deception attempts. Chapter 7 also noted the importance of knowing the opponent's intelligence channels for projecting a deception.

The cyberspace channel serves all of these functions in deception operations. But the cyberspace channel has become a key one for projecting a deception, and for that reason it is treated in this separate chapter. Before discussing the various subchannels, let's review some of cyberspace's unique features.

DECEPTION IN CYBERSPACE

Up front, an important definition must be understood. Although this chapter is about deception in cyberspace, the term *cyber deception* is applied in only one section. The term has a specific meaning in the cyber community and, from its perspective, a narrow one. Cyber deception refers to a set of deceptive tactics and strategies in cyberspace that is used to defeat cyber attack and exploitation—that is, to defeat hacking. This type of deception is discussed extensively in many books and articles.[1] But cyber deception also potentially has a useful role in projecting deception; that role is discussed in the last section of this chapter.

Deception in the cyber domain shares features with counterintelligence, specifically counterespionage. Counterespionage has often been referred to as a "wilderness of mirrors"—a term credited to the CIA's former head of counterintelligence, James Jesus Angleton, when he described the confusion and strange loops of espionage and counterespionage. Deception in cyberspace shares similar characteristics.

For the purposes of this book, and to remain within the focus of intelligence support to a deception plan, CYBER here is treated as a two-way channel from which information can be extracted to support planning, as well as a communication platform from which to project information in executing the deception. The cyber realm therefore divides into two broad types: computer network exploitation (CNE), which is basically passive, and computer network attack (CNA), which is unquestionably active. Both have roles to play in deception: CNE, for collecting intelligence, and CNA, for projecting a deception by providing material to the target to support the deception.

So the World Wide Web via the Internet is a primary channel for conducting CNE/CNA. But the web can be an effective channel for projecting a deception without using CNA, as discussed next.

WEB-BASED DECEPTION

In 2012 a popular US television commercial featured a young woman proclaiming, "They can't put anything on the Internet that isn't true." In response to the question "Where'd you hear that?" she responds, "The Internet."

The Internet and its associated social media provide what is probably the most commonly used channel for deception by governments, organizations, and individuals today. The extensive development of cyber-based social media and information sources over the past fifteen years has opened a richly dynamic environment in which to conduct deception and counterdeception. It literally provides the communication backbone for a wide variety of possible channels to and from adversaries that can be used to monitor, analyze, and exploit.

In the world of cyber operations, much attention is paid to malware—computer viruses and those who develop and deploy them. The succeeding sections delve into these more aggressive techniques of cyber operations. But first, let's investigate the web as a channel for projecting deception much as it is done in traditional open-source publications.

News and Reference Media

Over several centuries, first newspapers, then radio (think of the Atlantik-sender case described in Chapters 3 and 7), then television, became the primary sources of news reporting. Today the Internet seems on its way to dominating such reporting. Yet it is the most vulnerable of all media for conducting deception by planting false news reporting. More recently, the dominant deception has taken the form of *fake news*. Fake news websites promulgate false information and hoaxes, often by appearing to be legitimate journalistic reporting. The sites then rely on social media (discussed later) to spread the message. They offer a major new tool for applying deception in psychological warfare. As such, they can be used to affect elections and consequently to shape government policy. Fake news, during 2016, reportedly had an effect on the outcome of the UK referendum on exiting the European Union (Brexit) and on the US presidential election—a phenomenon that led the Oxford dictionary to choose *post-truth* as its word of the year. *Post-truth* is defined as circumstances in which "objective facts are less influential in shaping public opinion than appeals to emotion and personal belief."[2] German chancellor Angela Merkel, alarmed at this trend and the prospect of fake news affecting the 2017 German elections, observed, "Something has changed—as globalization has marched on, [political] debate is taking place in a completely new media environment. Opinions aren't formed the way they were 25 years ago. Today we have fake sites, bots, trolls—things that regenerate themselves, reinforcing opinions with certain algorithms and we have to learn to deal with them."[3]

The web also has become the primary source for research about almost any topic. The web pages that search engines lead to, and online reference sites, are excellent places to plant misleading information. Sites that have editors or a validation process, such as Wikipedia, are somewhat better suited to defend against deceptive inputs, but they are not immune. Ironically, on its own site, Wikipedia displays an article noting that it has been banned by many academic institutions as a primary source due to reliability and credibility issues.[4] The increased access to CYBER has increased the depth and scope of "common knowledge" available, leaving artists of deception projection an easily accessible canvas for "designing common knowledge" through sites such as Wikipedia and blogs.

E-mails

E-mails that appear to come from a trusted source have a well-known role in emplacing malware. But such e-mails also can be used to project a deception. Sometimes, it isn't even necessary to impersonate a trusted source. Prior to operation Desert Storm, PSYOPS specialists from the coalition called senior Iraqi officers directly on their personal cell phones and sent e-mails to their personal accounts, attempting to induce them to surrender and providing deceptive information about the upcoming conflict. These measures developed a level of discord and mistrust among the senior Iraqi leadership that had a definite adverse impact later on in the conflict.[5] To return to the terms introduced in Chapter 1, this was an "A" type deception.

Cyber operations to acquire e-mails can be a powerful tool in PSYOPS, as demonstrated in Russian cyber activities prior to the 2016 US elections. US intelligence agencies concluded that Russia conducted a cyber operation to obtain—and subsequently release—information from e-mails that damaged the campaign of Democratic nominee Hillary Clinton, while withholding damaging information they had collected from e-mails of Republican nominee Donald Trump.[6]

Social Media

Social media may be the most widely used channel for deception today. Individuals, organizations, and governments convey deceptive information via social media for both worthy and nefarious purposes. Because it is difficult to determine that a profile presented on the Internet is that of an identifiable person, deception is easy to pull off. Such deception is, in effect, an online version of pseudo operations.

Law enforcement uses social media, for example, to ensnare online sexual predators via posts that appear to come from young girls. Websites pretending to recruit for Daesh are used to identify and arrest would-be Daesh volunteers.

Social media is readily used in deception to further government objectives. A Harvard University study found that the Chinese government produces about 488 million false social media posts a year in an effort to divert attention away from sensitive issues. Most of the bogus posts are designed to indicate popular support for the government. They appear to be written by workers at government agencies assigned to make the posts in addition to their regular duties.[7]

Deceptive posts such as the Chinese example often are the work of Internet trolls—persons either anonymous or using assumed names. These posts typically are intended to advance causes and influence thinking through emotional appeals. The Russian government has developed a sizeable team of Internet trolls who regularly post deceptive information in an ongoing psychological operations campaign to undermine NATO and US interests and promote Russian interests.[8]

Social media such as Twitter, YouTube, Facebook, Instagram, and blogs are just the tip of the iceberg of available cyber social networks that contribute significantly to the formation of public opinions and perspectives across national borders. It has been demonstrated repeatedly that "going viral" in social media can quickly inspire violent events in the physical domain. A single picture illustrating political hypocrisy can in a matter of seconds weaken international alliances abroad, and undermine support for policy at home. Perhaps the most dramatic outcome of this online mobilization, Internet activism, and grassroots organization occurred in 2011. The events of that year that became known as the Arab Spring started in Tunisia and spread rapidly to Egypt and Libya, toppling governments in all three countries, and to Syria, sparking what seems to be an endless conflict that has drawn in major powers.

Memetic Conflict

Deception plays a major role in a new area of interstate and intercultural conflict known as memetic warfare or *memetic conflict*. A meme (derived from the word *gene*) is an idea or type of behavior that spreads from person to person within a population. It is a carrier of cultural ideas, symbols, or practices from one person to another through writing, speech, gestures, symbols, or rituals.

The term *meme* was introduced by Oxford professor Richard Dawkins in his 1975 book *The Selfish Gene*. Though the name is of recent origin, the meme obviously has been around for a long time in human affairs. But it has become a powerful tool for shaping opinions and actions in the era of social media.

Memetic conflict has been defined as "competition over narrative, ideas, and social control in a social-media battlefield. One might think of it as a subset of 'information operations' tailored to social media."[9] In contrast to cyber conflict,

> Cyber warfare is about taking control of data. Memetic warfare is about taking control of the dialogue, narrative, and psychological space. It's about denigrating, disrupting, and subverting the enemy's effort to do the same. Like cyber warfare, memetic warfare is asymmetrical in impact.[10]

So memetic conflict is a new type of psychological warfare. In this conflict, Internet trolls play a critical role. They are the warfighters of the Internet, and memes are their weapons.[11] For nonstate actors such as Daesh, memetic warfare has been a powerful tool for spreading their message, motivating their supporters, and attracting recruits to the cause.

Of course, the tools of these conflicts can be used by both sides. In a memetic conflict campaign against Daesh, for example, it has been suggested that one could

- Systematically lure and entrap Daesh recruiters

- Create fake "sockpuppet" Daesh recruiting sites to confuse sympathizers and recruits

- Expose and harass those in the Daesh funding network, along with their families

- Weaken the Daesh appeal to supporters and possible recruits by enlisting gay activist trolls to start and spread a #ISISisgay hashtag[12]

Techniques such as these are easily applied by, for example, the Russian government. They would pose both political and legal problems for many Western governments that tried to apply them. The United States, for example, is not allowed to spread propaganda domestically, and social media knows no borders.[13]

WEB-BASED CNE/CNA

The preceding section discussed a straightforward use of the cyber realm to project a deception; such use requires no specialized technical expertise. This section is about applying the tools of cyber operations for obtaining intelligence or to project a deception. Cyber offense falls into two broad objectives when conducted against networks:

- *Computer network exploitation (CNE).* The objective here is to target the Internet or an intranet (a privately maintained computer network that requires access authorization and may or may not be connected to the web via an administrative computer), but not for attack. Instead, the focus is on *collection* operations where the network continues to function normally.

- *Computer network attack (CNA).* CNA operations are conducted with the intent to degrade, disrupt, deny, or deceive. The effects of CNA typically are readily observed. In this chapter, the term *CNA* is used as a convenience, for any projection of deception that uses CYBER means— via the Internet or placing deceptive information directly on an intranet or standalone computer.

Although these terms refer to offensive deception against a network, the same principles and tools apply in attacking or exploiting a single computer that is not connected to a network; only the techniques for obtaining access are different. Let's look at some of the channels for CNE/CNA and then examine some of the tools for using them to obtain access and implant malware.

Web-Based Channels

A basic rule of deception is that the more trustworthy a channel is believed to be, the more effective it is as a channel for deception. Several components in cyberspace are designed to provide a trusted environment for sharing information or conducting daily activities. Making use of these generally requires CNE/CNA tools, but the channels can then be effective in projecting a deception.

Intranets

An intranet is an internal network that people can access only from within their organization or trusted group. It is intended as a place to securely share files or sensitive documents. Some intranets are not connected to the Internet; others have Internet access, but only through a gateway administrator from within the organization. In this section, we're looking at the type of intranet that connects to the Internet but has some form of protection. They're usually called virtual private networks (VPNs), and they allow people to operate with an expectation of privacy on the Internet. An intranet that does not connect directly to the web requires a different approach and is discussed in a later section.

A VPN is an attractive channel for projecting deception because people using intranets for communications and sharing sensitive documents tend to blithely accept the material in their system as valid—far more so than they would if it came directly from the Internet rather than through the organization or group's intranet. But because these VPNs connect to the web, they are relatively easy for an attacker to get into via a web-based attack.

The Deep Web and the Dark Web

The terms "deep web" and "dark web" are often used interchangeably. Some argue that the two should be differentiated, while others disagree. Both are based on the concept of privacy; the dark web emphasizes anonymity.

The deep web refers to the vast part of the Internet that is not indexed and therefore not normally visible or accessible from search engines. Access-restricted commercial databases, websites, and services comprise much of the deep web. Special browser software such as Tor (originally created by the US Navy to transfer files securely) is required for access. The Tor software makes use of a set of VPNs, allowing users to securely travel the deep web and remain anonymous. It protects users by bouncing their communications around a distributed network of relays run by volunteers around the world, which prevents others from watching users' Internet connections to learn what sites they visit, prevents the sites that users visit from learning their physical location, and lets users access sites that are blocked to anyone unless granted permission. Government databases, such as those maintained by NASA and the US Patent and Trademark office, also use the deep web space for obvious reasons.

Within the deep web lies what is often referred to as the dark web. Much of the dark web content fits well with the name: It includes all types of black markets, illicit drug traffic, fraud-related material, and child pornography. It is used for a number of scams and hoaxes, but it also is used for political discussion groups, whistleblowing sites, and social media sites often to avoid government censorship. These legitimate uses of the dark web offer attractive channels for projecting a deception, because many governments pay close attention to the material posted on these sites. Tracing the source of a post in the dark web is very difficult—an added advantage in executing deception.

Blockchains

Blockchains are another example of a seemingly secure channel for projecting a deception. The challenge is to find a way to make use of it.

A blockchain is software that allows the creation of a digital ledger of transactions that is then shared among participants in a distributed network. It relies on cryptography to allow each participant on the network to manipulate the ledger securely without the control of a central authority. Once software is deployed on a blockchain, programs run automatically and are accessible to any Internet user. This design makes them basically autonomous and uncontrollable by governments.

Blockchains are best known as the technology underpinning the bitcoin cryptocurrency. Commercial enterprises are now using blockchains to make and verify transactions on a network instantaneously without a central authority. Once an item is entered into the blockchain ledger, it is extremely difficult to change or remove. If a participant wants to change it, others in the network run algorithms to evaluate and verify the proposed transaction. If a majority of participants agree that the transaction looks valid, then it will be approved and a new block added to the chain. The key feature is that the entire network, rather than a central authority, is responsible for ensuring the validity of each transaction.[14]

Like Intranets, blockchains tend to be trusted. So if they can be compromised, the resulting deception is more likely to succeed. Of course, compromise of a blockchain is much more difficult than some of the softer targets on the Internet.

The Internet of Things

The Internet of Things (IoT) is the network of physical objects—devices, vehicles, buildings, and other items—embedded with electronics, software, sensors, and network connectivity that enables these objects to collect and exchange data. The objects can be sensed and controlled remotely via the web.

Experts estimate that 6.4 billion connected things were in use worldwide in 2016, up 30 percent from 2015. The Internet of Things is expected to consist of almost 50 billion objects by 2020. It includes a wide class of cyber-physical systems, which also encompasses technologies such as smart grids, smart homes, intelligent transportation, and smart cities. Each thing is uniquely identifiable through its embedded computing system but is able to interoperate within the existing Internet infrastructure.

These network-connected devices automatically collect and exchange data, allowing enterprises to be more efficient and productive. However, IoT networks also incorporate an extensive set of connected devices that can introduce multiple points of vulnerabilities in the networks.

The Internet of Things can be used in a cyber attack on infrastructure, as the Mirai attack suggests. But it can be used to convey a deception, often as part of an attack, by presenting a false picture of security systems or the status of equipment that has been altered. The Stuxnet malware, described later in this chapter, was not web-based but did exactly that: The sensors that Stuxnet infected provided the monitoring personnel at Iran's Natanz nuclear facility with a false picture of their enrichment centrifuges while the centrifuges were being destroyed.

MIRAI

On October 21, 2016, the US East Coast encountered Internet outages from a massive distributed denial of service (DDoS) attack that overwhelmed web service with traffic. The attack was targeted on servers maintained by Dyn, a company that controls many of the Internet's domain names. The attack took down many popular websites in Europe and the United States, including Twitter, Netflix, Reddit, CNN, and *The Guardian*.

The attack relied on a malware package called Mirai, which organized what is called a *botnet* to conduct the attack. The controller of a botnet is usually referred to as a command-and-control (C&C) server. This server issues instructions to the botnet, directing the activities of infected computers (referred to as zombies) through communication means such as Internet Relay Chat or HTTP.

The Mirai botnet used vulnerable IoT technology to launch an attack. One of the major IoT resources used was the security cameras sold by a Chinese firm, Hangzhou Xiongmai. Millions of these cameras are sold in the United States. The DDoS attack exploited the default passwords in the equipment and organized them into a botnet. Hangzhou Xiongmai issued a recall for the cameras on October 24, 2016, while complaining that users should have changed the default passwords.

Botnets such as Mirai exploit weak security measures in IoT devices. Most such devices, if they have any protection at all, are delivered with a standard password and username combination—"admin" and "1111" are typical ones. The botnet scans the Internet for IoT systems using these standard passwords and infects them with malware that directs them to the C&C server; the server then uses them as hosts to launch cyber attacks.

The Tools of Cyber Operations

CNE and CNA use the same tools. There are many of them—thousands, in fact, with new ones and improvements being added daily. This introduction touches on some traditional ones, and some of the latest developments in tools at the time of publication. But it scratches just the surface of the field.

An attacker must gain access to the target network, have tools to exploit it, and remove any evidence of the operation. Attackers can exploit a vulnerability that occurs in the network or is presented by the supply chain. They can masquerade as an authorized user or use human assets to gain physical access to the network. Once they gain access, they usually leave behind a software implant called a *backdoor*. The implants communicate back to the controlling organization, allowing the attackers to acquire data from the network and introduce malware.

In poorly defended systems, a backdoor can give unlimited access to data in the system. Valuable corporate proprietary information has been acquired time and again from competitors through backdoors.[15]

This can happen, for example, when the target receives an e-mail that appears to come from a trusted source—an acquaintance or someone within the same organization. The e-mail might ask the target to open an attachment. Adobe PDFs, images, and Microsoft Office files are commonly used. When the file is opened by the vulnerable program on the victim's computer (such as Adobe Acrobat or Microsoft Excel, PowerPoint, or Word), a backdoor program executes and the computer has been compromised. At the same time, a seemingly normal file or image appears on the target's computer screen, so that the recipient has no reason to suspect that something is amiss. E-mails are widely used for deception because it is possible to identify an employee's trusted relationships and professional networks by looking at his or her e-mail patterns.[16]

Alternatively, the e-mail may direct the target to a website that contains the backdoor, with much the same outcome. Such a website is called a *drive-by download* site. It typically relies on vulnerabilities in web browsers and browser add-ons. Users with vulnerable computers can be infected with malware simply by visiting such a website, even without attempting to download anything.[17] The attacker can then acquire files from the computer or e-mail or send data from the computer, or force the compromised computer to download additional malware. From there, the attacker can use the infected computer to exploit the victim's contacts or other computers on the target network.[18]

The basic tools of malware are known as *exploits*, discussed next.

Exploits

An exploit takes advantage of software vulnerabilities to infect, disrupt, or take control of a computer without the user's consent and preferably without the user's knowledge. Exploits take advantage of vulnerabilities in operating systems, web browsers, applications, or other software components.[19]

The preferred target of exploits changes constantly as vulnerabilities are found and corrected in all of these targets. For example, exploitation of the Adobe Flash Player had been quite low until 2011, when it suddenly became a major target. Adobe provided patches and updates to eliminate the vulnerabilities, only to encounter new versions of malware year after year as hackers went after the patched versions and even moved to place Trojans (discussed below) on mobile versions of Flash Player.[20] In 2016, new malware targeting Flash Player continued to be discovered.

Four of the most widely known exploits are Trojan horses (usually abbreviated "Trojans"), worms, rootkits, and keystroke loggers.

- A *Trojan horse* is a seemingly innocent program that conceals its primary purpose. The purpose is to exfiltrate data from the target computer system.

- A *worm* can do many of the things that a Trojan does, and can also do such things as install a backdoor. But in contrast to the Trojan, the worm is designed to be completely concealed instead of masquerading as an innocent program.

- A *rootkit* is software code designed to take control of a computer while avoiding detection. The rootkit is often concealed within a Trojan.

- *Keystroke loggers,* or keyloggers, can be hardware or software based. Their general purpose is to capture and record keystrokes. For CYBER collection, they specifically are intended to capture passwords and encryption keys.

Although all of these exploits can be used for cyber deception, they are most effective when they are used against a *zero day* vulnerability. Also called a *zero hour* or *day zero* vulnerability, this is an application vulnerability that is unknown to defenders or the software developer. It derives its name from that time (called the zero hour or zero day) when the software developer first becomes aware of the vulnerability. Until that moment of awareness, the developer obviously cannot develop a security fix or distribute it to users of the software. Zero day exploits (software that uses a security gap to carry out an intrusion) are highly valued by hackers and cyber espionage units because they cannot be defended against effectively—at least not until sometime after zero day arrives.[21]

Exploits are usually emplaced via the web, but they can be emplaced directly on machines, as discussed later. Deception via the web requires more than the deployment of exploits. The cyber espionage organization must control the exploits and use them to insert the desired information while maintaining the secrecy, or at least the deniability, of the operation. Often this is done by botnets such as Mirai, used in the DDoS attack described earlier. The botnet's command-and-control server can't be easily shut down because it's hard to determine its real location.

Advanced Persistent Threats

An advanced persistent threat (APT) might be thought of as an integrated system of exploits. It is a set of stealthy and continuous computer hacking processes. The term *advanced* refers to the use of multiple malware components to exploit system vulnerabilities that are tailored to defeat detection by software security firms.

Persistent refers to the existence of a continuing external command system that controls the malware package and extracts data from the infected machine or network.[22]

APTs originally appear to have been government-sponsored efforts used for intelligence gathering or CNA, but increasingly they are being used by organized criminal groups. Some of the first to be observed have been named Duqu, Flame, and Gauss.

DUQU, FLAME, AND GAUSS

Duqu. Duqu was a sophisticated piece of malware discovered in 2011, having been used in a number of intelligence-gathering attacks against a range of industrial targets. Duqu has a number of similarities to the Stuxnet APT discussed later, though it appears to have the purpose of CNE, not CNA. It attacks Microsoft Windows systems using a zero day vulnerability. It uses a stolen digital certificate to create the façade of being secure software.

Duqu was detected on servers in Austria, Hungary, Indonesia, the United Kingdom, Sudan, and Iran. It may have had a number of CNE roles, but one clear role was to compromise certificate authorities and hijack digital certificates. These certificates could then be used on attacked computers to cause malware to appear as secure software.[23]

Flame. In 2012, malware was discovered that appears to have targeted Microsoft Windows computers in the Middle East for intelligence purposes. Called Flame, it reportedly had been operating for five years in these countries.[24] Flame is more powerful and flexible than Stuxnet and has a number of features that illustrate the level of sophistication and precise targeting that is possible today in cyber espionage:

- Flame incorporates five distinct encryption algorithms and exotic data storage formats both to avoid detection and to conceal its purpose.

- It does not spread itself automatically, doing so only when directed by a controlling entity (the command-and-control server).

- It allows the controlling entity to add new malware at any time for targeted collection.

- It enables the controlling entity to remotely change settings on a computer, gather data and document files, turn on the computer microphone to record conversations, log keystrokes, take screen shots, and copy instant messaging chats.[25]

Flame is a very sophisticated piece of malware, far more complex than Duqu—so sophisticated, in fact, that it almost certainly is the product of a government that has an advanced software industry. It functions as a backdoor and a Trojan. It also has wormlike features, so that it can replicate itself in a local network and on removable media if it is instructed to do so by its controller. Flame's sophistication earned it the "Epic Ownage" award from the 2012 Black Hat convention—the equivalent, among cyber security experts, of an Oscar. (So far, no one has come forward to accept the award.)[26]

Gauss. In 2012 a new CYBER collection toolkit appeared—apparently created by the same government that developed and deployed Flame. Called Gauss, it has many similarities to Flame: architecture, module structures, and method of communicating with command-and-control servers are strikingly similar. The owners of the Gauss command-and-control server shut it down shortly after its discovery.

Gauss is an example of a highly targeted intelligence collector. It infected personal computers primarily located in Lebanon, and stole browser history, passwords, and access credentials for online banking systems and payment websites from its targets. More than 2,500 infections were identified; total infections probably numbered in the tens of thousands.

It appears that the targeting was intended to collect intelligence about financial transactions. The targets included a number of Lebanese banks such as the Bank of Beirut, EBLF, Blom Bank, Byblos Bank, FransaBank, and Credit Libanais. Flame also targeted specific Citibank and PayPal accounts.[27]

The current state of the art in APTs has been named Duqu2. It had an unusual target, though a logical one for a government that is in the cyber espionage business.

DUQU 2

Kaspersky Lab is one of the world's major software security companies, operating in almost 200 countries from its Moscow headquarters. Its founder, Eugene Kaspersky, reportedly has ties to Russia's intelligence services (he is a graduate of the FSB academy; the FSB is the successor to the KGB). Kaspersky Lab has been the most prominent of software security firms in identifying, analyzing, and countering the malware described in this chapter.

In 2016, Kaspersky Lab was itself the target of a malware attack. The attack successfully accessed the company's intellectual property and proprietary technologies and its product innovations. It was targeted specifically on the Kaspersky tools used for discovering and analyzing advanced persistent threats, and the data on current Kaspersky investigations into sophisticated malware attacks. The attack was discovered only after it had been inside the company's intranet for several months.[28] It was, in counterespionage terms, a wilderness of mirrors event—using computer espionage to target the web's equivalent of a counterespionage organization—presumably so that the attacker could better evade discovery by Kaspersky in future cyber attacks.

The malware, which Kaspersky named Duqu 2, has very little persistence, making it difficult both to detect and to eliminate. It exists almost entirely in the memory of the targeted system. As a result, according to the Kaspersky Lab report, "the attackers are sure there is always a way for them to maintain an infection—even if the victim's machine is rebooted and the malware disappears from the memory."[29] Duqu 2 was so named because it shares much of the code of the original Duqu and of Stuxnet, leading observers to believe that it was developed by the same unidentified organization.

STANDALONE COMPUTERS AND INTRANETS

Attacking a network that is physically isolated from the Internet (a private intranet) or a single computer that never connects to the Internet requires a different type of effort from that used in CNE. The collector has to gain access to the computer or the intranet in some way. Once access has been gained through a USB drive, a network jack or cable, a utility closet, or some similar device—almost anything can be done. From the defense point of view, the game is over and the defense has lost.

One of the simplest targets is a personal notebook computer that is carried on trips or to conferences. With a few minutes of uninterrupted access, a collector can download the contents of a notebook's hard drive or upload malware. Computers or any devices containing electronic storage—separate hard drives or USB flash drives, for example—can be legally searched when they are taken across international borders, and they often are. Encrypting the material does not provide protection. Customs officials can demand the encryption key, deny the traveler entry to their country, or confiscate the computer. In many cases, customs officials are looking for terrorist material, pornography, or hate literature, but countries that have a reputation for commercial espionage also are likely to make intelligence use of the material acquired.

Gaining direct access to an isolated intranet or a standalone computer on a continuing basis requires some effort. But IT systems rarely exist for long periods in isolation. Upgrades, patches, software fixes, and new software have to be added to these systems. All of those provide opportunities for a determined attacker to use methods such as social engineering to implant malware or obtain information from the system.

Social Engineering

Isolated intranets are not connected to the Internet most often as a security measure. They therefore are viewed generally as safe from attack and placement of deceptive information. But this perceived trust makes them more vulnerable to deception. The challenge, of course, is to get into the intranet to place the misleading information. Social engineering is one means of doing that. It's used to facilitate both CNA and CNE.

In cases where computers never leave a secure facility, and where remote access is not possible, it is necessary to use field operations to access networks. This category encompasses deployment of any CNA or CNE tool through physical access or proximity. In intelligence, these are called HUMINT-enabled operations; in the world of hackers, they are usually referred to as social engineering.[30] They encompass such classic HUMINT techniques as gaining access under false pretenses, bribery or recruitment of trusted personnel in a facility, and surreptitious entry.[31] HUMINT-enabled operations are often facilitated by human error or carelessness, and complex intranets are particularly susceptible to both.

The case of Stuxnet, which has attracted much international attention and even been the source of a 2016 TV documentary titled *Zero Days*, illustrates the importance of direct access to an intranet as well as the value of social engineering. Although Stuxnet is an example of CNA, it relied heavily on deception for its success.

STUXNET

Stuxnet illustrates the type of precision attack that is most effective in both CNA and CNE. Stuxnet was a worm designed to infect and disable a specific type of computer performing a specific task. The target, investigators believe, was the computer controlling the isotope separation centrifuges in Iran's Natanz uranium enrichment facility.

Stuxnet was used in a sustained and directed attack, conducted over a ten-month period beginning in 2009. Reportedly, at least three versions of the program were written and introduced during that time period. Investigators found that the first version had been completed just twelve hours before the first successful infection in June 2009. One attack, in April 2010, exploited a zero day vulnerability in Windows-based computers.

Once introduced, the Stuxnet worm infected all Windows-based industrial control computers it found while searching for specific equipment made by the Siemens Corporation. Upon finding its target, the worm was programmed to damage a centrifuge array by repeatedly speeding it up and slowing it down, while at the same time hiding its attack from the control computers by sending false information to displays that monitored the system.[32]

The attack appears to have been at least partially successful. International inspectors visiting Natanz in late 2009 found that almost 1,000 gas centrifuges had been taken offline. Investigators therefore speculated that the attack disabled some part of the Natanz complex.

How the complex became infected has been a matter of speculation, because there are several possible ways the worm could have been introduced. A classified site like Natanz is unlikely to be connected directly to the Internet. The attacker could have infected an organization associated with Natanz that would be likely to share files, and therefore the malware, with Natanz. An infected e-mail sent to one of the Natanz operators could have carried the worm. Or a USB flash drive carrying the worm could have been provided to one of the Natanz staff as part of routine maintenance.[33]

A sophisticated and targeted worm such as Stuxnet would need to be tested to ensure that it would succeed against its target, preferably without causing damage to unintended targets. Stuxnet recorded information on the location and type of each computer it infected, indicating a concern about protecting unintended

(Continued)

(Continued)

targets.[34] Israel reportedly built an elaborate test facility at its Dimona nuclear weapons development center. The facility contained a replica array of the Natanz Iranian uranium enrichment plant.[35] Such a test site would have been necessary for the design of the attack software.

Although Stuxnet was an attack malware, it illustrates what can be done in CNE. Stuxnet operated by fingerprinting any computer system it infiltrated to determine whether it was the precise machine the malware was looking for. If not, it left the computer alone.[36] The Duqu program that was associated with Stuxnet could gain access to a specific computer on a network, acquire classified or proprietary information from it, manipulate the defense system so that everything appeared to be operating normally, and exfiltrate the data via the operator's apparently secure mechanisms (probably USB drives) for placing data on the infected computer or network.[37]

Stuxnet represents the pre-2009 state of the art in attacks on standalone computers and intranets. Malware has improved substantially since then. In 2016 the current state of the art was represented by another malware package known as Project Sauron.

PROJECT SAURON

In October 2016 the research teams at Kaspersky Lab and Symantec published separate reports about a new malware package called Project Sauron. According to their reporting, it was responsible for large-scale attacks on government agencies; telecommunications firms; financial organizations; and military and research centers in Russia, Iran, Rwanda, China, Sweden, Belgium, and Italy. It appears to have specifically targeted communication encryption software used in those countries.

Project Sauron relies on a zero day exploit, presumably delivered by a USB drive that is inserted into a computer on the secure intranet. When a user logs in or changes a password, the malware logs keystrokes and acquires the password. It also acquires documents and encryption keys. It then waits for another USB drive to be attached to the infected machine and downloads its payload to the USB drive.

The malware appears to have been carefully designed to defeat efforts by software security experts at companies such as Kaspersky Lab and Symantec. These experts rely on finding patterns or signatures that can identify malware. Project Sauron creates no distinguishable patterns and relies on an almost random selection of disguises. It uses file names similar to those used by software companies such as Microsoft. It regularly changes its method of sending data back to the attacker. And, of course, it relies on very powerful encryption to conceal its presence on a USB drive or victim machine.[38]

Deception in Hardware

Even better than getting access to a target's computer is to manufacture the computer. Technology has allowed us to hide malware in many places, and the supply chain (all the way from component manufacturer to end user) is a very attractive place. Anyone in the supply chain before sale has the access necessary for inserting malware in a computer or other electronic device. Such embedded malware is difficult to detect, and most purchasers do not have the resources to check for such modifications.

The hardware can be modified in ways that are not readily detectable, but that allow an intelligence service to gain continuing entry into the computer or communications system. Targeted components can be add-ons that are preinstalled by the computer manufacturer before the computer is sold. A user may not even use the vulnerable add-on or be aware that it is installed. [39] Malware inserted in a computer before sale can call home after being activated, exfiltrate sensitive data via USB drives, allow remote control of the computer, and insert Trojan horses and worms. Such backdoors are not limited to software installed on the computer. Hardware components such as embedded radio-frequency identification (RFID) chips and flash memory can be the sources of such malware.

CYBER DECEPTION

This chapter is about the use of cyberspace means to project a deception. But, as previously stated, the term *cyber deception* has a specific meaning within the cyber community. The target of this type of deception is the cyber attacker. The objective is to deceive the attacker and cause him or her to behave in a way that gives the defender an advantage.

Much effort is spent worldwide on cyber defense—to protect organizational networks from hacking. Cyber deception is a technique to complement the defense with an aggressive offense. It offers a way to penetrate the opponent's cyber espionage system, identify the source of cyber attacks, and raise the cost of intrusion into protected networks. These three go together; without knowing the source, it is difficult to retaliate. It is important, for example, to distinguish casual hackers from foreign intelligence services.

The idea of using deception in cyber defense developed after it became apparent that traditional cyber security measures taken alone were losers. The cyber defender could defend against known types of attack. But the attacker could repeatedly develop new ways to counter network defenses. The pattern reinforced the basic maxim of strategic conflict: *The offense always wins.* The best that traditional cyber security defenses could do was slow the attacks or make them more expensive. Winning on defense was not an option.

The deception-based defense changes that equation. Instead of monitoring for known attack patterns, the defender instead uses sophisticated techniques and engagement servers to entice attackers away from its sensitive servers. Attackers tend to work on the fundamental assumption that the infrastructure data they see are real. Deception technology uses carefully designed lures to attract attackers during infiltration and instantly identify them.

In brief, cyber deception conceals your real network, while deceiving attackers into believing that they have hacked into your network; or at the least, it leaves attackers uncertain and confused about what they are seeing. It levels the cyber battlefield. It leads opponents into an alternate reality, and when they apply their attack methods and insert malware, all of it is captured for later examination by a cyber forensics team. An advantage of the cyber deception approach is that a hacking attack typically takes weeks to identify and deal with using purely defensive measures. Deception, in contrast, detects hackers immediately and allows the defender to obtain intelligence about the hacker's strategies, methods, and identity.

How Cyber Deception Works

Cyber deception is like all other deceptions: It works by hiding the real and showing the false. It might manipulate network activities to mask the actual network while creating a notional one. The notional network takes the form of a *honeypot* or *honeynet*—a server or network that attracts and traps would-be attackers. This type of defense generally includes the following steps:

- *Install an engagement server.* This is a separate server that appears to be an integral part of an organization's network or network of networks but is intended to lure hackers, trap them, and analyze their attacks.

- *Place a special operating system on the server.* Engagement servers can use either an emulated operating system or a real one. Emulation is simpler to deploy, but it is easier for the hacker to identify deception. In the simplest versions, when the hacker breaks in, he finds nothing there. If he attempts to run malware, it has no impact. Real operating systems make deception harder for an attacker to identify. They can be designed with applications and data to closely match the actual network environment, both adding credibility to the deception and allowing better assessment of the threat as the attacker moves around in the engagement server.

- *Misdirect the attacker.* This step relies on lures that work with deception engagement servers to draw attackers away from the organization's servers and instead pull them into the engagement server. Publishing misleading details about the organization's network can sometimes help in this step.

- *Assess the threat.* This step makes use of forensics to capture the methods and intent of the hacker. It then identifies the indicators of compromise so that defensive systems across the real network can identify and block subsequent attacks.

- *Counterattack.* This optional step depends on the forensics being able to identify the attack source; retaliation can then take the form of placing malware on the attacker's machine or network.

- *Recover.* The operating system should have a self-healing environment that, after containing and analyzing an infection, destroys the infected virtual machine and rebuilds itself to prepare for the next attack.[40]

Cyber deception offers a substantial advantage over conventional cyber defense. The conventional approach generates a high volume of alerts that are not attacks (false positives). Cyber deception doesn't have this problem: It only delivers an alert based on actual engagement with the deception server.

During 2016, cyber deception began to be deployed to defeat attacks on the Internet of Things. The defense used special servers and decoys designed to appear as production IoT sensors and servers. When attackers engage with a decoy, believing that it is a standard production device, they are quarantined and subjected to detailed forensics to support countermeasures development.

Projecting a Deception

Cyber deception obviously is a form of deception in and of itself. But it also can be used as a channel to project a deception. You simply place the deceptive material in the engagement server so that it appears to be valid protected files. When opponents hack into your site, they obtain files that lead them into the story that you want to project.

This has been a brief introduction to the topic. Cyber deception to protect against cyber attack is a complex subject that is treated in detailed texts elsewhere. Readers who wish more detail may want to peruse Gartzke and Lindsay's article on the subject[41] or the 2016 book *Cyber Deception.*[42]

Let's next turn to the planning and execution part of the process.

NOTES

1. See, for example, Sushil Jajodia, V. S. Subrahmanian, Vipin Swarup, and Cliff Wang, eds., *Cyber Deception: Building the Scientific Foundation* (Switzerland: Springer, 2016).

2. Oxford Dictionary, "Word of the year is . . . ," https://en.oxforddictionaries.com/word-of-the-year/word-of-the-year-2016.

3. Amar Toor, "Germany Is Worried about Fake News and Bots ahead of Election," *The Verge,* November 25, 2016, http://www.theverge.com/2016/11/25/13745910/germany-fake-news-facebook-angela-merkel.

4. See https://en.wikipedia.org/wiki/Reliability_of_Wikipedia.

5. Wang Yongming, Liu Xiaoli, et al., *Research on the Iraq War* (Beijing, PRC: Academy of Military Science Press, 2003).

6. Intelligence Community Assessment, "Assessing Russian Activities and Intentions in Recent US Elections," ICA 2017-01D, January 6, 2017, https://www.dni.gov/files/documents/ICA_2017_01.pdf.

7. Gary King, Jennifer Pan, and Margaret E. Roberts, *How the Chinese Government Fabricates Social Media Posts for Strategic Distraction, Not Engaged Argument*, working paper, August 26, 2016, http://gking.harvard.edu/50c.

8. Timothy Thomas, "Russia's 21st Century Information War: Working to Undermine and Destabilize Populations," *Defence Strategic Communications* 1, no. 1 (winter 2015): 13.

9. Jeff Giesea, "It's Time to Embrace Memetic Warfare," *Defence Strategic Communications* 1, no. 1 (winter 2015): 70.

10. Ibid, 71.

11. Ibid, 69.

12. Ibid, 68.

13. Ibid, 75.

14. Steve Norton, "The CIO Explainer: What Is Blockchain," *Wall Street Journal*, February 2, 2016, http://blogs.wsj.com/cio/2016/02/02/cio-explainer-what-is-blockchain/.

15. John McAfee and Colin Haynes, *Computer Viruses, Worms, Data Diddlers, Killer Programs, and Other Threats to Your System* (New York: St. Martin's Press, 1989), 79.

16. Bryan Krekel, "Capability of the People's Republic of China to Conduct Cyber Warfare and Computer Network Exploitation," Northrop Grumman Corporation, October 9, 2009, https://nsarchive2.gwu.edu/NSAEBB/NSAEBB424/docs/Cyber-030.pdf.

17. *Microsoft Security Intelligence Report*, Vol. 12, http://www.microsoft.com/security/sir/default.aspx.

18. *Shadows in the Cloud: Investigating Cyber Espionage 2.0*, Joint Report JR03-2010, of the Information Warfare Monitor and Shadowserver Foundation, April 6, 2010, http://www.scribd.com/doc/29435784/SHADOWS-IN-THE-CLOUD-Investigating-Cyber-Espionage-2-0.

19. *Microsoft Security Intelligence Report*, Vol. 12.

20. Ben Weitzenkorn, "Adobe Flash Player Hit by Hackers on Both Ends," *Security News Daily*, http://www.securitynewsdaily.com/2191-adobe-flash-player-iphone-android.html.

21. *Microsoft Security Intelligence Report*, Vol. 12.

22. Sam Musa, "Advanced Persistent Threat–APT," March 2014, https://www.academia.edu/6309905/Advanced_Persistent_Threat_-_APT.

23. Kim Zetter, "Son of Stuxnet," *The Intercept*, November 12, 2014, https://theintercept.com/2014/11/12/stuxnet/.

24. Damien McElroy and Christopher Williams, "Flame: World's Most Complex Computer Virus Exposed," *Telegraph*, May 29, 2012, http://www.telegraph.co.uk/news/worldnews/middleeast/iran/9295938/Flame-worlds-most-complex-computer-virus-exposed.html.

25. Ibid.

26. Bernt Ostergaard, "Black Hat Roundup: Keeping Tabs on the Ones That Got Away," July 31, 2012, https://itcblogs.currentanalysis.com/2012/07/31/black-hat-roundup-keeping-tabs-on-the-ones-that-got-away/.

27. Kaspersky Lab, "Kaspersky Lab Discovers 'Gauss'–A New Complex Cyber-Threat Designed to Monitor Online Banking Accounts," August 9, 2012, http://www.kaspersky.com/about/news/virus/2012/Kaspersky_Lab_and_ITU_Discover_Gauss_A_New_Complex_Cyber_Threat_Designed_to_Monitor_Online_Banking_Accounts.

28. David Gilbert, "Duqu 2: The Most Advanced Cyber-Espionage Tool Ever Discovered," *International Business Times UK*, June 10, 2015, http://www.ibtimes.co.uk/duqu-2-most-advanced-cyber-espionage-tool-ever-discovered-1505439.

29. Gilbert, "Duqu 2."

30. Kevin D. Mitnick and William L. Simon, *The Art of Intrusion* (Indianapolis, IN: Wiley, 2005), ch. 10.

31. "War in the Fifth Domain," *The Economist*, July 1, 2010, http://www.economist.com/node/16478792? story_id=16478792.

32. John Markoff, "Malware Aimed at Iran Hit Five Sites, Report Says," *New York Times*, February 11, 2011, http://www.nytimes.com/2011/02/13/science/13stuxnet.html.

33. Ibid.

34. Ibid.

35. William J. Broad, John Markoff, and David E. Sanger, "Israeli Test on Worm Called Crucial in Iran Nuclear Delay," *New York Times*, January 15, 2011, http://www.nytimes.com/2011/01/16/world/middleeast/16stuxnet.html.

36. Mark Clayton, "Stuxnet Malware Is 'Weapon' Out to Destroy . . . Iran's Bushehr Nuclear Plant?" *Christian Science Monitor,* September 22, 2010.

37. Ibid.

38. Michael Mimoso, "ProjectSauron APT on Par with Equation, Flame, Duqu," *Threatpost.com*, August 8, 2016, https://threatpost.com/projectsauron-apt-on-par-with-equation-flame-duqu/119725/.

39. *Microsoft Security Intelligence Report,* Vol. 12.

40. Carolyn Crandall, "The Ins and Outs of Deception for Cyber security," *Network World,* January 6, 2016, http://www.networkworld.com/article/3019760/network-security/the-ins-and-outs-of-deception-for-cyber-security.html.

41. Erik Gartzke and Jon R. Lindsay, "Weaving Tangled Webs: Offense, Defense, and Deception in Cyberspace," *Security Studies* 24, no. 2 (2015): 316–48, doi:10.1080/09636412.2015.1038188.

42. Jajodia et al., eds., *Cyber Deception: Building the Scientific Foundation.*

9

PLANNING AND EXECUTING DECEPTION

The preceding chapters have addressed planning backwards through the inverse OODA loop. The final step in planning a deception is to go through the loop forward and answer three questions:

1. Will the deception plan result in the desired decision and action?

2. Will it produce the desired outcome scenario, or an unexpected and undesired one?

3. Will it affect only the desired target?

CHECKING THE DECISION/ACTION MODEL: RED TEAM ANALYSIS

Red team analysis requires that an analyst or analytic team (ideally, not the one who developed the deception plan) take a fresh look at it. The analyst or team examines the story, as conveyed in the deception plan, from the point of view of the deception target. At its core, red teaming is intended to avoid the trap of ethnocentric bias or the mirror imaging problem.[1]

The methodology requires that a person or team with detailed knowledge of the situation and an understanding of the target's decision-making style put themselves in the target's circumstances and react to foreign stimuli as the target would. That is, the red team goes through the opponent's OODA loop to see if the proposed deception produces the desired outcome scenario. For that reason, it is especially useful for checking the results of a game theory decision model. The CIA's tradecraft manual recommends these steps for performing red team analysis:

- Develop a set of "first-person" questions that the target (leader or group) would ask, such as "How would I perceive incoming information?" "What would be my personal concerns?" or "To whom would I look for an opinion?"

- Draft a set of policy papers in which the target makes specific decisions, proposes recommendations, or lays out courses of action. The more these papers reflect the cultural and personal norms of the target, the more they can offer a different perspective on the analytic problem.[2]

It's most important to ask the question: "What different decisions could an opponent make, besides the intended one?" In answering that question, the red team analysis must consider all relevant PMESII factors. This is a check on the analytic logic that supports the assessment of an opponent's likely decision. What might the likely decisions be, both with and without deception?

CHECKING FOR UNFAVORABLE OUTCOMES: ALTERNATIVE ANALYSIS

Alternative analysis is closely related to the idea of red teaming. Its purpose is to identify possible outcome scenarios other than the expected one. Cultural or organizational assumptions, biases, and preferences often shape analytic conclusions, so applying structured techniques to challenge them and force consideration of other possible outcomes is essential.[3] Chapter 4 addressed the importance of modeling alternative decisions an opponent could make. Alternative analysis takes that one step farther and considers not only an opponent's possible alternative decisions, but possible alternative outcomes that result.

Stated another way, this step requires that we identify unintended consequences in the form of unfavorable scenarios that might develop as a result of deception. Several of the cases cited in earlier chapters illustrate such outcomes. Chapter 1 described Saddam Hussein's WMD deception operations prior to Operation Desert Storm. Recall that Saddam officially denied possession of WMD while simultaneously portraying the possibility that Iraq indeed had them. He managed to create what had to be his worst possible scenario—the United States employing a "shock-and-awe" bombing campaign followed by an invasion that swiftly overtook Iraqi forces and, three years later, Saddam's execution at the hands of his own military court. An Iraqi alternative analysis team could have told him that telegraphing two opposite messages with one deception effort is a recipe for an unfavorable result. Of course, as was also noted in Chapter 4, Saddam's personality type indicated a dictator possessed with a superiority complex—not a candidate for listening to criticism.

Both the United States and the USSR failed to identify possible unfavorable outcomes in some deception operations that they conducted during the Cold War, and they proved to be costly mistakes. Two examples stand out, and they have common features. Both deceptions—one by each country—succeeded. And both were strategic disasters for the deceiving country.

MOSCOW AIR SHOW, 1955

During the 1950s and 1960s, the USSR leadership saw a compelling need to display the image of a militarily powerful Soviet Union, in order to protect and promote its interests worldwide. The Soviets accordingly conducted a number of deceptions designed to depict this projection of strength. One such deception occurred in July 1955, during the Soviet Aviation Day demonstrations at Tushino Airfield, near Moscow.

The Aviation Day demonstrations annually provided Western military attachés with an opportunity to see the newest hardware in the Soviet Air Force—a fact well known to Soviet intelligence agencies. It was the custom for the attachés to take pictures and movies (the video clips of the 1950s) of the hardware displayed.

During the 1955 event, a highlight of the show occurred when a flight of ten M-4 Bison bombers flew past the reviewing stand, followed shortly thereafter by another flight of eighteen Bisons.

It later became apparent that the flyover was a deception. After the first ten bombers had passed the reviewing stands and were out of sight, they quickly turned around in a racetrack pattern and flew past the stands again with eight more Bisons joining the formation, presenting the illusion that there were twenty-eight aircraft in the flyby.

The deception was a tactical success but turned out to be a strategic mistake. The total of twenty-eight Bisons came as a surprise to Western military analysts, who were expecting a much smaller inventory. Starting from that count, the analysts extrapolated that by 1960 the Soviets would have 800 long-range bombers, presenting a substantial threat to the United States in the event of a major war. This threat became a political issue during the presidential campaign, when John F. Kennedy accused the Eisenhower administration of allowing a "bomber gap" to develop. In fact, only ninety-three Bisons were produced before the assembly lines shut down in 1963.

The deception was a strategic failure, because it led to a US response that the Soviets neither anticipated nor desired. Alarmed at the prospect of a "bomber gap" along with a "missile gap" (another Soviet strategic deception), the US government embarked on a military buildup of both its bomber fleet and ballistic missile attack capabilities that gave it a substantial strategic edge.

During the Cold War, the United States conducted a series of deceptive operations to convince the Soviets that it was making advances in chemical warfare and subsequently in biological warfare capabilities. The deceptions proved to be at least as counterproductive for the United States as the Moscow Air Show deception had been for the USSR.

THE CW AND BW DECEPTIONS

In 1959 the GRU (Soviet military intelligence) recruited US Army sergeant Joseph Cassidy and used him as an agent for more than twenty years. During all that time, Cassidy was actually serving as a double agent, run by the FBI and US Army intelligence. Cassidy passed to the GRU secret information about the Army's chemical warfare (CW) program being conducted at Edgewood Arsenal in Maryland, in order to build up his credentials for a subsequent deception.[4]

The objective of the deception was to convince the Soviets to expend resources on a CW agent that wouldn't work. The United States had for some time researched the potential of a super nerve agent called GJ. The researchers had finally concluded that it would never become useful as a weapon. The deception was intended to send the Soviets down the same path, and it succeeded. Information provided by Cassidy and by others convinced the Soviet leadership that the United States was developing a super-agent, and they ramped up their own CW programs. That conviction was reinforced by reporting from a second double agent stationed in the United States, GRU colonel Dmitri Polyakov.[5]

The problem was that the expanded Soviet program actually succeeded in developing a highly toxic and effective nerve agent called Novichok. It is not clear whether Novichok was a result of their work to duplicate GJ or something completely different. What appears to be the case, though, is that the agent resulted from an expanded program in response to a US deception.[6]

At the end of the 1960s, though, the deception appeared to be a success, convincing US intelligence to begin a second round of deception, this time focused on biological warfare (BW).

The story to be conveyed in this deception was that the United States was pursuing a clandestine BW program at the same time that it was negotiating the Biological Weapons Convention outlawing such weaponry. The objective of this plan remains unclear. Under the circumstances, it is hard to see how such a deception could have a good outcome.

The deception was carried out through a number of channels, but Colonel Polyakov was the key one. Alarmed by this new threat, the Soviet leadership ordered the creation of a new program for research and development of biological weaponry. That program, nicknamed Biopreparat, involved a number of military and civilian research and production institutes and at least one test site.[7]

The Biopreparat program took on a life of its own and continued throughout the 1970s and 1980s, at least. Scientists working on the program were encouraged to keep up with the United States or to pull ahead. Their managers and program directors used the reports of US progress to obtain continued funding for their own programs.[8]

These two cases illustrate the difficulties in identifying the long-term, unintended consequences of deceptions, especially at the strategic level. The Moscow Air Show deception was driven by the need to project an image of Soviet power, without thinking through the possible US responses to such an image. The US biological warfare deception was especially egregious; it apparently didn't consider the implications of convincing the Soviets—always suspicious of US intentions—that the United States could not be trusted in arms control negotiations.

DECONFLICTION

The final step in deception planning usually is *deconfliction*. The idea is to plan deception so that it affects only the intended target.[9] In military terms, the goal always is to avoid collateral damage. That's the tactical view of deconfliction.

In a strategic sense, deconfliction is a much broader concept. Strategically, it is the process of anticipating and avoiding undesirable consequences of a deception operation. Its objective is to ensure, as much as possible, that the deception affects only the intended target in the intended fashion. So deception planners must put considerable thought into the possible unintended consequences of the operation on others than the intended target. Deconfliction thus is closely related to the idea of avoiding unfavorable outcomes that resulted from the Moscow Air Show and CW and BW deceptions.

Any deception operation therefore must be carefully coordinated during the planning stage to avoid having different parts of the deceiver's organization or partner organizations working at cross purposes. Then during execution of tactical operations, the deception operation must be monitored to avoid fratricide. For example, units involved in pseudo operations (and, therefore, dressed as insurgents) very much want *not* to be targeted by their own forces. The operation also must avoid adverse consequences to civilian populations. Some of the cyberspace channels discussed in Chapter 8 can be observed by not only intended targets but also by friendly and neutral parties, with attendant risks of bad outcomes.[10]

At the strategic level, the effect of deception on innocent parties, neutral or allied, has to be considered. In the globalized economy of today, that can be a problem. A result of the Farewell operation, described in Chapter 3, was a gas pipeline explosion that disrupted the Soviet plans to supply natural gas to European countries. That outcome certainly was not a welcome one for several US allies. As a hypothetical example, a deception indicating that a major economic power planned to devalue its currency could trigger a global recession. Small changes can produce major consequences, thanks to globalization.

Deconfliction can be especially tricky in deception to support counterintelligence, because there are so many intelligence compartments having limited access—as the following example illustrates.

A few years ago, one US agency had developed a new technology for tracking vehicles of high intelligence interest. They needed to provide the resulting intelligence to military units in the field. But the potential for a compromise to the intelligence was high because of such wide access, so a cover story was needed.

The program leaders developed a deception plan to attribute the raw intelligence about vehicle locations to a novel collection program run by a completely different "INT." So far as they knew, no such program existed. The problem was that the novel collection program *did* exist, protected by very tight compartmentation. Only one person below the top levels of the US intelligence community was aware of both programs. Fortunately, the proposed deception was briefed to a senior intelligence community officer who was able to halt the deception effort. If the cover story had been used, it would have compromised a highly successful billion-dollar intelligence effort.

CYBER poses some unique problems in managing deconfliction. One of the major challenges for a nation in terms of managing a cyber capability is the deconfliction between national authorities with different objectives in the cyber domain. CYBER has the inherent ability to traverse organizational and national boundaries with a single click or keystroke, making it a flexible conduit for deception projection. But that also makes it a challenge for deconfliction: while a military cyber operations unit is emplacing deceptive information in an opponent's intranet, a national intelligence organization might be collecting intelligence from that same intranet—and consequently fall victim to a deception executed by its own military. Shutting down a website that is a good source of intelligence is a typical deconfliction problem. Furthermore, CYBER as a channel for projecting a deception can easily affect both cognitive and physical domains. For example, promoting a deception narrative through social media is cognitive; planting a virus in a system that disrupts radar images on a screen is physical. Lack of coordination across these domains could lead to great information operations sites being destroyed by viruses planted by a deceiver's own side.

OVERVIEW OF THE EXECUTION PROCESS

Field Marshal Helmuth Karl Bernhard Graf von Moltke (known as Moltke the Elder) once observed that "no plan survives contact with the enemy." In any deception, not just military deceptions, there is a desired outcome and a plan to use deception to help accomplish it. But it seldom if ever happens that events transpire to bring about that perfect outcome. So executing deception becomes a dynamic process. Two OODA loops—the deceiver's and the opponent's—are in operation, and the deceiver's loop has to operate inside the opponent's loop—a subject returned to later.

Executing deception requires carefully managing the channels. From a generic operational perspective, this phase occurs only after adversarial sensors and sources have been mapped and/or modeled, the adversarial processing and decision-making structures are understood, and the channels for communicating deception

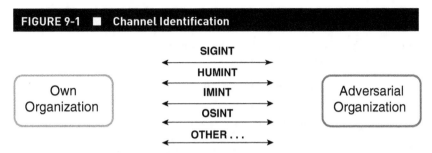

FIGURE 9-1 ■ Channel Identification

Any communication channel can transmit...
- Relevant and true information
- Irrelevant information (noise)
- Relevant but false information

are defined and, most important, determined to be manageable. Like the planners, those who are responsible for execution must understand how the adversary receives, analyzes, and understands information being provided through the channels. Therefore, execution requires resources to be specifically set aside in order to monitor the opponent's channels as information is collected or disseminated across them. It is here that the concept of channels plays a key role. Deception execution is in fact the exploitation of how the adversary observes, orients, and decides.

Figure 9-1 depicts a generic framework for understanding the dynamics behind channel management. Essentially the channels for projecting and detecting deceptions are the observation/collection platforms available to both your side and the adversary. Where it concerns projecting deception, understanding which adversarial collection platform to target in order to affect their situational understanding is the key. For detecting deception, knowing how the adversary understands your side's collection platforms is central.

ACHIEVING SURPRISE

Chapter 1 validated the importance of achieving surprise in military operations. To secure the advantage of surprise, the execution of a deception plan has to be included in the overall concept of operations (CONOPs). That requires delegating enough resources to the deception to ensure that it has the chance to succeed. Consider the example described here.

Your side wants to launch an amphibious landing at a certain location against an adversary but would like to deceive him into thinking it is at another location in order to reduce resistance at the real location. There are several ways to generate the surprise needed to accomplish this. The obvious goal is to deceive with regard to place; but at the same time the use of cross-cutting deceptions will provide effective support to the overall task. For example, you can deceive as to timing—when the assault will actually take place—in order to support the place

TABLE 9-1 ■ Barton Whaley's Five Modes of Surprise	
Place	Point, location, or area threatened—the axis or direction of operations (where?)
Time	Unexpectedness of timing measured in minutes, hours, days, and weeks (when?)
Strength	The amount of forces or assets committed to the operation (who?)
Intention	The scope of fundamental preferences—meaning the desired situational effects of the surprise (what?)
Style	The form or fashion in which the operation is carried out (how?)

Source: Barton Whaley, *Stratagem, Deception and Surprise in War* (Norwood, MA: Artech House, 2007/reprint of 1969 edition), 111–14.

deception. Or, it can be effective to disguise your side's strength and capability to support the place deception. The modes of surprise presented by Barton Whaley from his comparative analysis of historical cases provide a simple but useful taxonomy of surprise that illustrates how to manage the components of deception execution (see Table 9-1). Note that these five modes of surprise address the who-what-when-where-how question set that intelligence analysts ask and answer in assessing any situation.

Let's return to the deception that was part of Operation Desert Storm, described in Chapter 4, with some additional facts to illustrate how this works in practice:

- *Place.* The Iraqis were led to expect an attack on their positions from the south, not one across the desert to the west.

- *Time.* The Iraqis were led to believe that some days would pass after the 0600 hour deadline on February 24, 1991, before any large-scale ground assault by coalition forces into Iraq would occur. (The Iraqis were slowly complying with coalition demands for withdrawal from Kuwait.) However, a full ground campaign was set in motion before 0600 hours on February 24.

- *Strength.* The Iraqis were led to believe the US VII Corps was not yet at full strength just to the west of Kuwait; the corps was in fact at full strength.

- *Intention.* Iraq was led to believe the coalition's primary intended effects were the liberation of Kuwait and the withdrawal of Iraqi forces from Kuwait. The Iraqis assumed those actions would quickly halt further coalition action. However, just as important to the coalition was the destruction of Iraqi forces. (The Iraqi decision to withdraw made them easier targets as they raced to the perceived safety of the Iraqi border in open terrain.)

- *Style.* An amphibious landing instead of an armored attack through the western desert was a major part of the deception.

As another example, let's reconsider Operation Fortitude, described in Chapter 2, the deception that preceded the Normandy invasion in 1944:

- *Place.* The Germans were led to expect an invasion of Norway (Fortitude North) and at Pas-de-Calais (Fortitude South).

- *Time.* The deception included a visit by Field Marshal Montgomery's double to Gibraltar on the eve of the invasion to mislead German intelligence about the date.

- *Strength.* The Allies portrayed a fictitious force (FUSAG) near Dover and another in Scotland. They concealed the strength of the units assembling in south England.

- *Intention.* The deception reinforced perceptions that, because of logistics concerns, Pas de Calais was a preferable landing site over a Normandy site that required extended seaborne supply lines.

- *Style.* The Germans were led to believe the aggressive General Patton would be leading the invasion plan. Patton was known to often overextend supply lines when exploiting success. This reinforced the importance of not placing German mobile armor reserves too close to the coast in order to retain a strong pincer capability out of reach of Allied air power.

Once again, the projection of deception is about managing the adversary's available channels. Management across channels primarily consists of synchronizing individual channel deceptions in order to provide synergy, and to ensure a minimum of abnormal congruences or incongruences that might tip off the adversary to deception. Synergy in deception is also created by using the channels to promote cross-cutting modes of surprise, as shown in the notional amphibious assault as well as the two real-world examples described earlier. A deception projected through all available channels to the opponent reinforces his or her perspective that the assault will occur at the wrong place.

Specifically, as Figure 9-2 indicates, synchronization management requires that there are no abnormal patterns in the projected deception that might trigger the adversary to look in the correct direction.

In executing a deception, the deceiver is managing how the deception appears to an opponent in all of the channels and across the channels. Figure 9-3 illustrates what might happen if this management is not done or is handled poorly.

As the figure indicates, both abnormal congruences and abnormal incongruences were present in the total picture presented to the opponent—likely leading to failure of the deception.

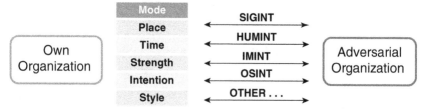

FIGURE 9-2 ■ Managing Deception Execution

Task: Support an amphibious assault on X by projecting a deception portraying amphibious assault on Y.

Are there abnormal congruences in the channel projection of an attack on Y?
Are there abnormal incongruences in the channel projection of an attack on Y?
Can there be more synergy?

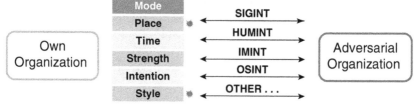

FIGURE 9-3 ■ Synchronizing Deception Execution

Task: Support an amphibious assault on X by projecting a deception portraying amphibious assault on Y.

Are there abnormal congruences in the channel projection of an attack on Y?
Yes, in terms of style, our information operations (for their cyber collection) are intensifying and seem aimed at an imminent attack on Y; we have almost never relied on information operations in the past.

Are there abnormal incongruences in the channel projection of an attack on Y?
Yes, in terms of place, our communications (for their SIGINT) point to an attack on Y, while our IMINT collection platforms are visibly focusing on X.

Now let's shift focus to another part of the execution management process: the opponent's OODA loop.

OPERATING INSIDE THE OPPONENT'S OODA LOOP

Frans Osinga argues that Boyd's concept of an OODA loop is much deeper, richer, and more comprehensive than it is commonly viewed. The objective, according to Osinga, is to operate inside [the] adversary's observation-orientation-decision-action loops to enmesh [the] adversary in a world of uncertainty, doubt, mistrust, confusion, disorder, fear, panic, chaos . . . and/or fold the adversary back inside himself, so that he cannot cope with events/efforts as they unfold.[11]

There are two key concepts here. Let's deal with the first one before turning to the second. First, there is the concept of operating inside the opponent's OODA loop so that your side can act more effectively than can the opponent. We always want to do that—meaning that we react to opponents' actions more quickly than they can react to ours. But just how do you in practice do that? The cycle of CW deception by Libya and counterdeception by the United States and its allies throughout the 1980s and 1990s illustrates how the process works.

THE RABTA/TARHUNAH DECEPTION AND COUNTERDECEPTION

Beginning in 1984 the Libyan government began constructing a CW agent production plant near the city of Rabta, forty miles southwest of Tripoli. By late 1988, with extensive foreign assistance, Libya had completed construction and begun producing CW agents. During its three years of operation, the facility produced at least 100 metric tons of mustard gas and the nerve agent sarin.[12] To conceal the purpose of the plant, the Libyans set up an elaborate deception that failed because the Libyans presented an incongruent picture to Western intelligence, and because the United States and its allies were able to react to unfolding events more rapidly than the Libyans.

Rabta Deception—OODA Loop 1

Much of the resources needed to build the Rabta plant had to come from foreign companies. The Libyans set up a network of front companies, fake subsidiaries, and middlemen to hide their purchases. Considerable assistance in building the Rabta complex was provided by European and Japanese firms. The prime contractor at Rabta was Imhausen-Chemie, a West German chemical firm. Other supplies came from firms in Switzerland, Austria, and Hong Kong. Most of the equipment and supplies left European ports under false export documents. To circumvent export controls, the Libyans relied on a complex commercial network involving front companies that transferred goods through ports in the Far East. Libyan government officials publicly claimed that the Rabta facility was a pharmaceutical plant, and designated it Pharma-150. Construction at Rabta was carried out by 1,300 low-wage laborers imported from Thailand under tight security conditions.

The complexity of the deception made incongruences likely; any single inconsistency or failure in the chain of commercial transactions would be likely to alert Western intelligence. And in fact a number of incongruences did exist; they are discussed in Chapter 11. As a result of these incongruences, throughout the

(Continued)

(Continued)

mid-1980s US intelligence followed the developments at Rabta with increasing interest, relying heavily on IMINT. By the time the plant began production, the US government had enough evidence to go public and expose the deception.

Rabta Deception—OODA Loop 2

On September 14, 1988, the State Department went public with the following state-ment: "The U.S. now believes Libya has established a CW production capability and is on the verge of full-scale production of these weapons." CIA director William Webster provided further details in a speech on October 25, 1988, claiming that the Libyan plant was the largest chemical weapons facility the agency had detected anywhere in the developing world.[13] The announcement triggered a second Libyan deception and another circuit around the OODA loop.

The Libyans apparently recognized that IMINT was the source of the US assess-ment. They responded with an elaborate deception operation to counter imagery analysis, fabricating evidence of a fire on March 13, 1990, to make the Rabta facil-ity appear to be damaged and possibly inoperative.[14] The fabrication reportedly involved painting burn marks on buildings and burning stacks of tires to create the perception of a fire for imagery collectors. They also rushed ambulances to the area to make it appear that the plant had suffered severe fire damage and casualties—probably targeting HUMINT channels.[15] When the French commercial Earth-resources satellite SPOT 1 photographed the Rabta facility on March 18, however, it looked to be intact.

The second round of Libyan deception also was a failure, again due to the incon-gruent picture that the Libyans presented to Western intelligence. By mid-1990 the United States and its allies had again operated inside the Libyan OODA loop. In August 1990 the US intelligence community deduced that large-scale produc-tion of chemical agents at Rabta had begun after a photoreconnaissance satellite observed specialized trucks, designed to transport CW agents, picking up barrels of the suspected agent at the plant. In 1992 a US intelligence official stated publicly that the Rabta facility had produced and stockpiled more than 100 metric tons of mustard gas and the nerve agent sarin.[16]

The Tarhunah Deception—OODA Loop 3

Libya subsequently moved to another round of deception, relying heavily on denial. The Libyans closed the Rabta plant later in 1990 after it became clear that the sec-ond deception had failed. To replace the facility, they began constructing a large underground CW plant near Tarhunah, a mountainous region about sixty kilome-ters southeast of Tripoli. Putting the facility underground masked its activities and increased its survivability in case of an attack.[17] Libyan press releases claimed that the plant had a civilian purpose—petrochemical production in one case, and part of a Libyan plan to funnel water from its southern aquifers to its coastal cities in another.

In February 1996 then–director of central intelligence John Deutch accused Libya of "building the world's largest underground chemical weapons plant" near Tarhunah. US State Department spokesman Glyn T. Davies in an April 4,

1996, news briefing subsequently described the Libyan deception concerning Tarhunah:

> Libya is constructing what would be the world's largest underground chemical plants near a place called Tarhunah, about 60 kilometers southeast of Tripoli. They began this work, we think, in about 1992, and we know that their chemical weapons production facility at Rabta has been inactive since it was exposed in the late 1980s, partly as a result of our efforts. Tripoli, the government of Libya, still insists that the chemical plant at Rabta was designed to produce just pharmaceuticals. It claims that this new site, Tarhunah, is a training site for Libyan workers of the much publicized civilian great man-made river project, which is ongoing there. But our indication is that Tarhunah will be a reconfigured version of the plant at Rabta, and that it will, if it moves forward, be used to produce blister agents such as mustard gas and perhaps nerve agents as well.[18]

Once again, the United States and its allies had operated inside Libya's OODA loop by revealing the deception before the plant could produce CW agents. Outmaneuvered and again frustrated, Libya subsequently stopped construction at Tarhunah. Many of the chemical weapons caches from the Rabta plant were later destroyed under supervision of the Organization for the Prohibition of Chemical Weapons after an agreement was reached with Muammar Gaddafi's regime. The destruction reportedly was completed in 2014.

The preceding discussion was focused on making your side's OODA loop work faster and more effectively than the opponent's. An alternative to making your loop work faster is to slow down the opponent's OODA loop, and there are ways to do that. They involve applying Osinga's second concept: choosing to confuse or overload the target's intelligence apparatus and to introduce ambiguity or the "uncertainty, doubt, mistrust, confusion, disorder, fear, panic, chaos, . . ." that he refers to. In the terms of Chapter 1, that is an "A"-type deception.

"A"-type deceptions, or inducing uncertainty, can lead to unpredictable outcomes, which is not desirable in deceptions where the goal is to persuade a specific decision maker to take a specific action. But sometimes (especially in strategic matters) creating uncertainty is the goal—where the objective is to make an opponent hesitate to act. As one of Thaddeus Holt's deception commandments introduced in Chapter 1 asserts, non-action is a decision. Sometimes, the preferred purpose of a deception is simply to promote uncertainty. It's a common goal at the national strategy level. The United States has long left uncertain its threshold for military action in a number of situations, including the employment of nuclear weapons. That uncertainty gives opponents pause and leaves the US government more freedom of action.

Again, however, the objective in planning many deceptions, especially in military operations, usually is the opposite: *not* to leave the opponent uncertain and confused. The problem is that one can seldom predict what an opponent's resulting actions will be. The goal in these situations is to have a predicable outcome.

ATTENDING TO DETAILS AND TIMING

Successful deceptions are the ones where exceptional care is taken with the myriad attending details during each phase. Deceivers who do not properly handle each detail will find their operation exposed. The Indian nuclear test deception, introduced in Chapter 1 and returned to throughout the book, is notable precisely because of the great care that was taken to conceal preparations at the test site. At the other extreme, the 1990 Libyan deception projecting a fire at Rabta was just sloppy.

Attention to detail during execution has become even more important in conducting deception against technical collection channels such as CYBER, IMINT, and MASINT because of their sophistication. IMINT and MASINT sensors have become more sensitive and their resolution has improved steadily. Deceptions targeting these channels have to withstand closer inspection than in previous decades. Dummy tanks and missile launchers, for example, must look like the real thing at close range to fool current imagery sensors.

In executing deception, time can be a critical factor. The deceiver has to consider the speed of decision making. Sometimes it is desirable to time the arrival of deceptive information so that an opponent is forced to make fast, poor decisions on incomplete information. The opponent should have as little time as possible to see through the deception. The branch-point scenario discussed in Chapter 6 deals effectively with timing during execution. Attention to detail and good use of timing were keys to the success of the Argo deception.

ARGO REVISITED

Chapter 5 introduced the Argo deception, which resulted in the exfiltration of six US embassy employees from Iran. A highly risky operation, it succeeded because of attention to very minor details and good use of timing.

A cover legend and airline tickets showed the six studio executives arriving in Tehran from Hong Kong at approximately the same hour that the actual exfiltration team arrived from Zurich. So passengers disembarking from either flight would have been processed by the same immigration officers. Consequently, the Iranian entry cachets stamped in team passports could be duplicated and used to create fake passports with the same entry cachets for the six. If the team had used the entry stamps of someone who hadn't been on duty that day, it could have been spotted and blown the entire operation. The deception was in some ways a model for how to attend to such details. For example,

- In a cross-check of the documentation, a Canadian embassy official noted that the visas were incorrectly dated: the Iranian year begins at the vernal equinox, not on January 1. The CIA exfiltration team had brought extra passports, so they were able to put in correctly dated visa stamps.

- There was extensive backup in Los Angeles: An office for Studio Six was set up on Sunset Boulevard with a makeup artist, a film producer, and a receptionist; a film party was held in an LA nightclub; advertisements were posted in Hollywood magazines; and bogus business cards were printed.

- The exfiltration team arrived in Tehran with a set of storyboard drawings and production notes to show the Iranians.

- Prior to the day of departure, the exfiltration team conducted rigorous mock interrogations of the six embassy employees, in the event that any of them were detained for questioning at the airport.

The team also made smart use of timing in choosing their departure. The Swissair flight departed Tehran at 7:30 a.m. The team arrived at the airport at 5 a.m., when the airport was relatively quiet; the officials manning the exit gates were sleepy; and the Revolutionary Guards were mostly still asleep at home. A 2012 movie about the rescue, also titled *Argo*, depicts the Swissair flight departure as an exciting event, with Revolutionary Guards pursuing the departing aircraft down the runway. That depiction is pure Hollywood. Thanks to careful planning, the actual departure was uneventful.

MANAGING THE DEVELOPING SCENARIO

The final step in the execution process is responding to unfolding events in the opponent's OODA loop. Those executing the deception have to look for and monitor the leading indicators that would indicate which of the scenarios—or which combination of scenarios—is actually taking place. As Babson College professor Liam Fahey points out, indicators will also give important insights into what scenarios are *not* taking place.[19]

What this means, to begin with, is that the team must identify feedback channels. A channel is needed that will confirm whether the deception information has reached its intended target (the decider). Another channel may be needed to identify the actions that the target is taking based on that information. Feedback allows a determination as to whether the deception plan is believed and, what is more important, being acted upon. As Godson and Wirtz describe it,

A successful D&D campaign benefits from feedback mechanisms to collect data about the target's behavior. Discovering the way the target has interpreted the received data is especially important. A deception campaign is a dynamic enterprise: cover stories, communication channels, and specific initiatives require fine tuning to take advantage of unforeseen opportunities or problems. Knowing that a deception campaign is succeeding also can be crucial to the achievement of grand strategic objectives. To pursue a course of action that relied on deception if the target failed to "take the bait" would be foolhardy. Alternatively, if an initial deception plan failed, the feedback mechanism could activate backup D&D campaigns.[20]

The monitoring job may involve watching trends. The intelligence team, for example, might monitor demographic and economic trends or decreases in the number of terrorist cells. A political or economic analyst might look at the questions that opponents ask and the positions they take in negotiations. A military intelligence analyst might monitor troop movements and radio traffic for signals as to which scenario is developing.

Indicators such as these suggest movement toward a particular scenario.[21] They provide a means to decide which options should be the focus of the next set of decisions. Specifically, they help identify which outcomes should be prepared for, possibly by use of some of the instruments of national power, and which potential outcomes can be disregarded.

The US intelligence community has developed a formal methodology for monitoring these indicators, or what it terms "indicators or signposts of change." The methodology is described in the CIA's tradecraft manual as "[p]eriodically review a list of observable events or trends to track events, monitor targets, spot emerging trends, and warn of unanticipated change."[22] It depends on the analyst's identifying and listing the observable events that would indicate that a particular scenario is becoming more or less likely, regularly reviewing all of the lists (one for each scenario) against incoming intelligence, and selecting the scenario that appears most likely to be developing—preferably, the desired outcome scenario.

OPERATION MINCEMEAT REVISITED

Chapter 2 described the successful use of deception in Operation Mincemeat to draw German forces away from Sicily prior to the 1943 invasion. The British had two channels for obtaining indicators that the operation was succeeding. One confirmed that the information had reached its intended target, and the other confirmed that the information was believed and being acted upon:

- A British agent in the Spanish Navy reported that the documents on Major Martin's corpse had been opened, copied, and resealed before being turned over to the British embassy in Madrid; and that the Germans had been provided copies of the documents.

- By May 12, 1943, Ultra intercepts confirmed that German intelligence had accepted the documents as genuine and identified Sardinia and Greece as the invasion targets.[23]

Few deceptions will have the excellent channels available to monitor indicators that Operation Mincemeat had. More commonly, the indicators must rely on indirect evidence such as troop movements or public statements.

NOTES

1. "Red Teaming and Alternative Analysis," *Red Team Journal,* http://redteamjournal.com/about/red-teaming-and-alternative-analysis/.

2. CIA Directorate of Intelligence, "A Compendium of Analytic Tradecraft Notes," February 1997, http://www.oss.net/dynamaster/file_archive/040319/cb27cc09c84d056b66616b4da5c02a4d/OSS2000-01-23.pdf.

3. Ibid.

4. Raymond L. Garthoff, "Polyakov's Run," *Bulletin of the Atomic Scientists* 56, no. 5 (September–October 2000): 37–40.

5. Ibid.

6. Ibid.

7. Ibid.

8. Ibid.

9. Scott Gerwehr and Russell W. Glenn. *The Art of Darkness: Deception and Urban Operations* (Santa Monica, CA: RAND, 1999), http://www.rand.org/publications/MR/MR1132, p. 35.

10. Ibid.

11. Frans P. B. Osinga, *Science, Strategy and War: The Strategic Theory of John Boyd* (London: Routledge, 2007), 186.

12. US Congress, Office of Technology Assessment, *Technologies Underlying Weapons of Mass Destruction,* OTA-BP-ISC-115 (Washington, DC: US Government Printing Office, December 1993), 41-43.

13. Ibid.

14. Ibid.

15. Ibid.

16. US Department of Defense, "Proliferation: Threat and Response," April 1996, https://www2.gwu.edu/~nsarchiv/NSAEBB/NSAEBB372/docs/Document09.pdf.

17. Ibid.

18. State Department Daily News Briefing, April 4, 1996, http://www.hri.org/news/usa/std/1996/96-04.std.html.

19. Liam Fahey, *Competitors* (New York: Wiley, 1999), 415.

20. Roy Godson and James J. Wirtz, "Strategic Denial and Deception," *International Journal of Intelligence and Counterlntelligence* 13 (2000): 427.

21. Andrew Sleigh, ed., *Project Insight* (Farnborough, UK: Centre for Defence Analysis, Defence Evaluation and Research Agency, 1996), 13.

22. CIA, *A Tradecraft Primer: Structured Analytic Techniques for Improving Intelligence Analysis* (Washington, DC: Author, 2009), 12.

23. Thaddeus Holt, *The Deceivers: Allied Military Deception in the Second World War* (New York: Skyhorse Publishing, 2007), 378.

PREPARING TO COUNTER DECEPTION

The previous chapters described how to plan for and conduct a deception. They provided the essential background on how to detect deception when it is conducted against your side. This chapter is therefore addressed to the intelligence team that will in most cases have the job of identifying deception.

> According to Edward Waltz, the purpose of counterdeception is to find the answers to two fundamental and highly interdependent questions. First, counterdeception must make it possible for analysts and decision-makers to penetrate through deception to discern the adversary's real capabilities and intentions, in other words, to answer the question: What is real? Simultaneously, analysts and decision-makers must determine what the adversary is trying to make them believe in order to consider the second question: What does the adversary want you to do?[1]

The procedures for detecting a deception are relatively easy to grasp. The real challenge lies in establishing an intelligence-driven framework that organizes all of the participants in your OODA loop to provide deception warning and to answer the questions that Waltz poses. This chapter describes a methodology for doing that.

There are three steps to take toward countering deception. Two are preconditions; that is, they need to be done *before* the deception may be occurring. In advance, a vulnerability assessment must be conducted. That means identifying channels where your side is vulnerable to deception—usually the elements of your OODA loop that the opponent is familiar with. Then follow up with the next step—a continuing assessment of possible threats. Completing these two tasks requires that several principles of counterdeception be followed (equally critical in conducting deception, of course):

- *Know yourself*—a sound understanding of the cognitive vulnerabilities in your side's analysis and decision processes

- *Know your channels*—an understanding of your collection disciplines— their capabilities, their limitations, and their vulnerabilities to deception

- *Know your decision maker*

- *Know your situation*

- *Know your adversary*—an understanding and consideration of the means, motives, and culture of your adversaries.

Once a specific threat has been identified, it is time to execute the third step: using all of your channels to identify deception when it occurs. The remainder of this chapter describes how the first two steps are best handled. Chapter 11 addresses the third step.

ASSESSING VULNERABILITY

Preceding chapters have made clear that if you can't assess the opponent's OODA loop, deception is unlikely to succeed. The opponent has the same problem. To the extent that opponents can't figure out your side's loop, they are unlikely to attempt any deception. And any deception they do attempt should be easy to identify and counter.

Therefore, it is important to know what your OODA loop is, then make it strong and secure. This is in part about security: the protection of sources and methods, or the "OO" part of the loop. But it is much more than that. The decision/action part has to be secured as much as possible, and that can be very difficult. Let's start with the observation process.

Observation (Collection)

When collection becomes too predictable, and the opponent understands the observation part of the loop, tactics for countering denial and deception stop working. If opponents can understand your collection process, they can defeat it, as the examples throughout this text illustrate. There is a tendency to believe that IMINT and COMINT are less vulnerable to deception. But deception can succeed against both IMINT and COMINT if the opponent knows enough about the collection system. The effectiveness of deception is a direct reflection of the predictability of collection. So the first line of defense is to keep all potential opponents uncertain about your collection channels.

How to do that? Wherever possible, use deception to protect your collection channels. Military tacticians claim that the best weapon against a tank is another tank; and the best weapon against a submarine is another submarine. Likewise, the best weapon against deception is to mislead or confuse opponents about your intelligence capabilities. In the 1972 Soviet wheat purchase case discussed in Chapter 3, the deception succeeded because the Soviets knew that the United States had only one channel for gathering intelligence about crops (HUMINT by US agricultural attachés), and the Soviets controlled that channel. Realizing its vulnerability to such deceptions afterward, the United States developed alternate channels. Subsequently, satellite imagery from Landsat and other sources provided an alternate and more accurate channel for estimating crop yields. Post-1972, another such deception would be unlikely to succeed. Chapter 3 also detailed the extensive deception operations the British employed to protect the Ultra COMINT channel from being found out. Recall that before using any piece of intelligence from Ultra, the British made it appear to the Germans that information had been collected from non-COMINT channels, some real and some fictional. The Indian nuclear test deception, described in Chapter 1, illustrates the opposite outcome: The deception succeeded because the United States had shared with India both the details of its overhead imagery capability and the methods for analyzing the imagery, in an attempt to prevent an earlier test. Armed with that knowledge, and with knowledge of the importance that the United States placed on monitoring ballistic missile tests, the Indians were able to execute a near-perfect deception.

The case of Igloo White, which occurred during the Vietnam War, illustrates how deception can work at the tactical level, but also how defensive deception can be effective when the opponent knows too much about your collection sensors.

TECHNICAL DECEPTION: IGLOO WHITE

During the Vietnam War, the North Vietnamese supplied their forces in the South via a network of trails and roads running through Laos known as the Ho Chi Minh Trail. One US effort to degrade this supply route was known as Operation Igloo White. Between 1967 and 1972, American aircraft dropped over 20,000 battery-powered sensors along parts of the trail. Some sensors hung from trees, detecting the sounds of voices or truck engines. Some buried themselves in the ground on impact; these were designed to look like plants and to detect human urine or the seismic disturbances created by foot traffic and vehicles.

The sensors transmitted their readings to a control center in Thailand via airborne relay aircraft. The readings then were displayed on monitors that tracked movements of troops and equipment along the Ho Chi Minh Trail. The center then passed the movement data to US strike aircraft in the area so that the enemy units could be attacked.[2] Initially, the operation was a success, costing the North Vietnamese heavily in trucks and supplies destroyed.

(Continued)

(Continued)

However, the success was short lived and finally illusory, the result of an effective counterdeception campaign. Over time, the North Vietnamese were able to pick up and analyze an abundance of sensors, identify their purpose, and figure out how to counter them. Armed with this knowledge, North Vietnamese troops began dropping bags of urine near the urine sensors and playing recordings of truck engines near the acoustic sensors. In consequence, later inquiries found that many US attacks hit empty jungle.

Viewed in retrospect, the collection plan had a major vulnerability that the North Vietnamese could and did exploit. They could easily obtain copies of all the sensors used on the trail and assess how the sensors operated. Once that was done, a deception effort was no great challenge. It well illustrates the principle that knowledge of the opponent's channels makes deception relatively straightforward. Modern air-dropped sensors such as the US Steel Eagle devices are still easy to acquire but more difficult to deceive, because the new sensors have high resolution and are able to detect fine details in an audio signature.

Orientation (Analysis)

Orientation, or analysis, is the phase during which your side is most likely to catch deception. It is a simple tenet: All available channels have to be cross-checked during analysis. An opponent can deceive one channel, but it's difficult to deceive them all at once and present a consistent story.

There are no "best" channels for detecting deception. There is a well-known inclination of any collection agency to overvalue its own channels in preference to others.[3] It's natural for collectors to do this. In a counterdeception effort, the intelligence team has to help guard against this perception. It's true that some channels—HUMINT and OSINT, specifically—are used to project deception more often than others, and these can also be common ones for detecting deception. However, the focus must be kept broad.

There is no such thing as a *secure* channel—one that can be excluded when considering the possibility of deception. One side's cryptanalysts might break an opponent's encryption system, for example, and consider the intelligence garnered from that channel to be valid. In fact, encrypted communications repeatedly have been used to deceive, where the one side had reason to believe that the opponent had broken a cipher system. Returning to the Ultra deception, described in Chapter 3, when the British had exhausted alternate channels to use for deception, remember that they created a fictional spy as the source. As was noted in the case and again in Chapter 7, the British validated the spy's authenticity for the Germans by sending him a congratulatory note over radio COMINT using a cipher they knew the Germans could break. The British used this same technique successfully throughout World War II with the Japanese as well, as noted in Chapter 7. Today, in the cyber realm, the same concept is applied using cyber deception, where the intelligence product derived from a

CNE appears to be authentic when instead, as described in Chapter 8, it is the product of a decoy system.

Analysis is a team process. It is greatly enhanced if the whole network is collaborating. That means that analysts, collectors, operations staff, leadership, and their advisors all need to work together to identify deception. Typically, it is an analyst who makes the connections, simply by virtue of having ties to all parts of the network. Well before a threat develops, these connections have to be developed and nurtured.

A strong feedback system must exist between analysts and collectors, in particular. The link has to work both ways. Collectors need to see clearly how their reporting is being used in the final analytic product and have a chance to comment.

Collectors also should be able to easily share the false signals that they detect—something that is often not done in large intelligence organizations. The natural tendency is to move the material into a counterintelligence unit, compartment it, and not share with the all-source analysts who have access to the other channels and are better positioned to identify deception.

Be aware also of the speed of information flow through the channels, and shorten it where possible using the close ties with collectors and decision makers. Some channels naturally have to operate more slowly than others. An IMINT channel can provide real-time reporting. Clandestine HUMINT sources may have to report only periodically. And collection agencies usually want to analyze the material that they collect before publishing it. There are valid reasons for this, but the result can be that your side's OODA loop operates more slowly than the opponent's—resulting in the needed warning of deception arriving at the decision maker after it is too late. A competent deceiver will time the arrival of information to do exactly that, as the allies did in Operation Quicksilver when agent Garbo sent the urgent message to his handler that an invasion of Normandy was imminent—the day before the invasion.

An important element of a strong network is having competent people in each part. People with long experience in dealing with the current opponent are especially needed. The experience of collectors and analysts in dealing with the USSR turned out to be critical in identifying the deception that led up to the Cuban Missile Crisis.

THE CUBAN MISSILE CRISIS REVISITED

Chapter 3 outlined everything that the Soviets did right in their deception effort in support of the emplacement of strategic ballistic missiles in Cuba. However, the deception was not perfect. There were some incongruences—one of which exposed the deception:

- The Soviets used the freighter *Poltava* to carry missiles. Some US experts speculated that the ship might be carrying ballistic missiles, because the Soviets typically used large-hatch ships such as the *Poltava* to deliver such missiles.

(Continued)

(Continued)

- The Soviet Union was not an automobile exporter at the time. Yet the captains were instructed that if their vessel experienced mechanical failure, any ships offering assistance should be told that they were exporting automobiles. Though this did not occur, it would have been an easy tipoff to analysts that something was amiss.

- In Cuba, the Soviet missile units began to deploy using the standard operating procedures that they had used in the USSR. In doing so, they created characteristic imagery signatures that quickly drew the attention of US intelligence. In September 1962, imagery analysts noticed that Cuban surface-to-air missile sites were arranged in patterns similar to those used by the Soviet Union to protect its ballistic missile bases. The United States accordingly resumed reconnaissance flights that had been suspended. On October 14, a U-2 flight discovered SS-4 missile units at San Cristobal, Cuba, leading to the Cuban missile crisis.[4]

Finally, remember that the decision maker is part of this network. Some channels usually exist outside the intelligence organization that can be used to convey deceptive information. These typically are channels that intersect with the operations team and with leadership. But they usually won't be available unless the analyst expends some effort to make it so. It bears repeating that access to incoming information from all channels that might carry deceptive information is critical, including collectors, operations, leadership, their advisors, and decision makers.

One last caution about the orientation phase: A serious cognitive vulnerability is associated with being aware of possible deception. Veteran CIA analyst and writer on intelligence Richards Heuer has noted the paradox that the more alert we are to deception, the more likely we are to be deceived. As Heuer explains it, our sensitivity to deception can influence our openness to new information.[5] When there is an existing belief about a given situation, and new evidence challenges that belief, we have a natural tendency to find some reason to discount the new evidence. This is one reason that it is so desirable for the deceiver to time the arrival of deceptive information so that an opponent is forced to make fast, poor decisions on incomplete information. The opponent should have as little time as possible to see through the deception. In counterdeception, information that arrives through any channel just before a decision must be made is especially suspect for that reason. This leads to a conundrum concerning new information:

- It may be the result of a deliberate deception; or

- It may be the first sign that existing belief is the result of a deception.

The solution to this conundrum and to Heuer's paradox is to follow a basic rule for evaluating raw intelligence: When new evidence doesn't fit with or contradicts what is already known, that is a signal to carefully evaluate anew *all* evidence—not just the new material. Chapter 11 describes a formal process for doing that.

Decision/Action (The Decision Maker)

In considering vulnerability to deception, historically the weakest link in the OODA chain has been the decision/action part. The opponent, after all, is targeting the decision maker. If the opponent can manipulate the channels, and if ties between the intelligence team and the decision maker are not as well developed as they should be, then deception is far more likely to succeed.

Former RAND senior staff member and counterdeception authority William Harris has noted that "those in positions of power must recognize the abundant opportunities for their victimization. Only then will they share information on top-level negotiations."[6] Getting to that point is very difficult. Decision makers— national leaders and military commanders—are typically more comfortable receiving information than sharing it. They sometimes believe things because they wish them to be so. Dictators such as Hitler, Stalin, and Saddam Hussein were vulnerable to deception for this reason. National leaders are sometimes vulnerable to surprises because they simply don't want to face the prospect of a war. Stalin didn't want to do so when faced with reports of a pending German attack in 1941. Neville Chamberlain wanted to believe that Hitler could be satisfied with the acquisition of part of Czechoslovakia in 1938. UK leaders during the 1982 Falklands crisis didn't want to face the consequences of a war, so they discounted mounting evidence that an invasion was imminent.

Lucky intelligence teams don't have to deal with leaders like these. Unlucky teams should at least get ready for the deceptions that are coming their way. But opponents who can't have confidence in the likely decision your leader will make when faced with a story should hesitate to use deception. A decision maker usually needs help to understand that.

Assessing vulnerabilities here requires doing something that isn't normally taught in intelligence courses: assessing one's own leadership. Reconsider the points made in Chapter 4 about evaluating the opponent's leadership. In counterdeception, you have to look at your own leadership as the opponent might.

Those who have completely rational decision makers are on fairly good ground. Even better are decision makers who follow the thirty-six stratagems described in Chapter 1. Leaders whose decisions appear to be unpredictable are a double-edged sword: They may cause difficulties for your own operations, but they also play havoc with an opponent's deception planners.

In defending against deception, the problem posed by new and contradictory intelligence, described earlier, can be made better or worse depending on the decision maker. He or she may need to be persuaded not to react too quickly and instead to wait for follow-up analysis to check for deception. With previously established close ties to the decision maker, the intelligence team's job here will be easier—though it never is easy. Identifying deception as it occurs, which requires operating inside the opponent's OODA loop, involves a tradeoff between speed and accuracy.

ASSESSING THE THREAT

The intelligence branch has the responsibility for understanding the adversary's observation and orientation capabilities when supporting a deception. It also is responsible (for the same reasons) for creating a shared situational understanding of the adversary's capability and/or intention to execute a deception and for identifying adversarial deception plans at the strategic or operational level. This begins with an assessment of the threat in the broadest terms, starting with an assessment of the situation.

Recognize that the threat of deception can come from an opponent, an ally, or a neutral power. The deception that preceded the Indian nuclear test, for example, was conducted by India against the United States while the two countries were on reasonably friendly terms. So when the term *adversary* or *opponent* is used in this chapter, it includes *anyone* who might use deception against your side's interests, including neutrals and allies.

Assess the Situation

Be alert for cues that indicate the situation is ripe for deception. These include high-stakes situations, events, or developments in the world that threaten security or provide opportunity for an adversary, such as the following:

- Asymmetric power relationships between participants (deception is often the equalizer in these situations)

- Changes among opponents, neutrals, or allies in leadership, motives, political goals, military doctrine, or technology (for example, the 2014 leadership change in Ukraine ousting Ukrainian president Viktor Yanukovych that preceded Putin's seizure of Crimea)

- Potential for surprise and risk as part of a high-risk/high-gain strategy (for example, the Cuban missile crisis deception)

Assess the Adversary's History, Capability, and Motivations

When the situation is ripe for deception by a specific adversary, the analysis effort should focus on that individual or organization. This can require answering questions such as: What is the opponent's desired end-state scenario? What do they want? What do they fear? If the intelligence team is able to assess the opponent's desired outcome scenario(s), it is possible to identify early warning indicators of deception that can be established and controlled to specifically support deception detection.

Does the adversary have a past history of engaging in deception? If so, what kind? Opponents have a preference for using the methods that have worked in the past. Remember that a stratagem is not invalid or unlikely just because it's old. The betting parlor trick in *The Sting* was old, but it continues to work today, just in updated settings. Confidence scams such as Ponzi schemes in general are old but continue to separate people from their money. So, next, consider the following questions:

- Do the current circumstances fit the pattern that preceded past deceptions?

- If not, are there other historical precedents?

- If not, are there changes that would explain the use of a specific type of deception at this time?

Work backward from the answers to these questions to identify situations in which deception might be occurring. In a sequel to the document binder deception described in Chapter 6, one Russian did exactly that and identified a likely deception. Unfortunately for the Russians, his associate ignored his advice.

THE DOCUMENT BINDER DECEPTION REDUX

The document binder deception described the use of bugged binders to identify Evgeny Buryakov as a spy for Russia. In building their case against Buryakov, the FBI conducted another deception to incriminate him in an act of espionage. They recruited an Atlantic City businessman who approached Buryakov with a proposal: The businessman had a client in the gaming business who wanted to open casinos in Russia.[7]

As noted in Chapter 6, Russian intelligence operatives are suspicious of persons who contact them; they prefer to initiate contact, probably based on past experience in dealing with US and British intelligence. His handler, Sporyshev, told Buryakov that the contact seemed like "some sort of setup. Some sort of trap."[8]

That was good advice, but Buryakov apparently ignored it and fell into the trap. The businessman, at Buryakov's request, provided him with government documents marked "Internal Treasury Use Only" and "For Official Use Only." The documents were subsequently used to convict Buryakov.[9]

Assess the Adversary's Understanding of Your OODA Loop

Like deception, countering deception often is a network management process that requires a good understanding of how the adversary sees your side, or the third OODA perspective presented in Chapter 2. It is a reflexive perspective that involves identifying the opponent's understanding of exploitable channels in terms of your platforms and sensors. Your intelligence team also has to understand how your opponent views your side's decision-making process. Finally, what are the limitations as well as the capabilities of the potential deceiver? What channels is he or she likely to be unaware of, or misinformed about the capabilities of? These channels often are the result of conducting your own deception, as noted earlier in this chapter, in the section on assessing vulnerabilities.

The preceding principles and steps are preparation for dealing with deception when the material for the opponent's story arrives in your side's channels. Your intelligence network should be especially alert to deception in the following situations:

- A potential deceiver has a history of conducting deception

- Key information is received at a critical time or from a source whose bona fides are questionable

- Analysis hinges on a single critical piece of information or reporting

- New information would require analysts to alter a key assumption or key judgment

- Accepting new information would cause the decision maker to expend or divert significant resources

- A potential deceiver may have a feedback channel to check on the success of deception

NOTES

1. M. Bennett and E. Waltz, *Counterdeception: Principles and Applications for National Security* (Boston: Artech House, 2007), 143.

2. Brian Bergstein, "The Problem with Our Data Obsession," *MIT Technology Review*, February 20, 2013, http://www.technologyreview.com/review/511176/the-problem-with-our-data-obsession/.

3. William R. Harris, "Counter-Deception Planning," in *The Art and Science of Military Deception*, ed. Hy Rothstein and Barton Whaley (Boston: Artech House, 2013), 566.

4. James H. Hansen, "Soviet Deception in the Cuban Missile Crisis," *CIA: Studies in Intelligence* 46, no. 1 (2002), http://www.cia.gov/csi/studies/vol46no1/article06.html.

5. Richards J. Heuer Jr., "Cognitive Factors in Deception and Counterdeception," *Multidisciplinary Perspectives in Military Deception* (May 1980): 45–101.

6. Harris, "Counter-Deception Planning," 565.

7. Garrett M. Graff, "The Spy Who Added Me on LinkedIn," *BloombergBusinessweek*, November 15, 2016, http://www.bloomberg.com/news/articles/2016-11-15/the-spy-who-added-me-on-linkedin.

8. Ibid.

9. Ibid.

IDENTIFYING DECEPTION

O nce the detection preparation work has been done, the next task is to identify when deception is actually occurring. This is about monitoring your channels for indicators. And that requires some sort of channel management plan.

DECEPTION DETECTION VIA CHANNEL MANAGEMENT

Chapter 9 discussed the use of channel management when conducting deception. This same channel management framework can be used to identify abnormalities or incongruences in collected information that could indicate an adversarial deception. This means that the initial steps of sensor mapping your own organization and your adversary's organization are still required in order to establish a picture of existing channels between both parties, as shown in Figure 11-1 (replicated here from Figure 9-2 for convenience).

In managing channels, the most difficult may be the one represented by "other" in Figure 11-1. This includes all non-intelligence channels, usually ones that are managed by operations, through liaison, or directly to your leadership.

Let's go through an admittedly simple example of using channels to detect deception. Chapter 9 presented an example of using channels to conduct a deception about a pending amphibious assault. The assault was expected to occur on either X beach or Y beach.

FIGURE 11-1 ■ Channel Management for Deception Detection

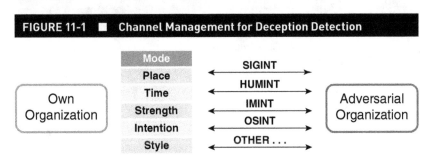

In contrast to deception projection, in counterdeception the intelligence team is looking at incoming channels instead of shaping outgoing channels. That is, incoming information must be examined to identify abnormal congruence or incongruence in the indicators of place, time, strength, intention, or style, or various combinations of those. In Figure 11-2 the same amphibious assault example is used, but here it is framed from a deception detection perspective. The notes in the figure illustrate some abnormal congruences or incongruences in reporting on an assault, suggesting a deception story that the assault will hit Y beach, when X beach is the actual target.

FIGURE 11-2   ■   Deception Detection

Task: Estimate whether your adversary will launch an amphibious assault on X beach or Y beach.

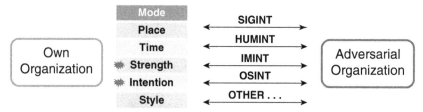

Are there abnormal congruences in reporting vs. Y assault?
Yes, increased HUMINT reporting on strength buildup near Y at the same time SIGINT intercepts increase with abnormal correlation to HUMINT content.
Are there abnormal congruences in reporting vs. X assault?
No
Are there abnormal incongruences in reporting vs. Y assault?
No
Are there abnormal incongruences in reporting vs. X assault?
Yes, regarding intention: MASINT indicates more submarine sonar activity in vicinity of X beach vs. Y beach.

To illustrate how this works in practice, let's revisit the Rabta deception from a counterdeception perspective.

RABTA COUNTERDECEPTION

Chapter 9 showed the deception/counterdeception OODA loops for the Rabta CW plant. The Rabta case illustrates the importance of using as many channels as possible to detect deception: COMINT, IMINT, and technical channels in addition to traditional OSINT and HUMINT channels. There were a number of incongruences in the channels, as discussed below.

During the mid-1980s, satellites and high-altitude reconnaissance aircraft provided imagery that followed the progress of construction at the Rabta site. By

1988 the imagery suggested that the facility, which sprawled over several acres, was nearing completion. Yet the factory was unusually large by the standards of the pharmaceutical industry and was ringed by high fences and forty-foot sand revetments—seemingly excessive security for an ordinary chemical plant. Also, the imposition of tight security on imported laborers for a "pharmaceutical plant" was suspicious.

Since the production facility was completely enclosed inside a warehouse-like structure, overhead photography revealed nothing about the process equipment inside, but the plant's oversized air-filtration system suggested an intention to produce toxic chemicals.

Once the overhead imagery had aroused suspicions, Western countries sought to develop new sources of information among the foreign technicians and construction workers from more than a dozen European, Asian, and Middle East countries employed at the Rabta facility. These sources described plant equipment layout, and supplies, providing additional clues that the site might be intended for CW production.

Intelligence analysts assessed that the complex comprised a large chemical agent production plant, a chemical arms storage building, and a metalworking plant built by Japan Steel Works. The latter facility contained Japanese-made machine tools, officially intended for the production of irrigation pumps but also suitable for the production of artillery shells and gas canisters. And delivery to the plant of special steels used in bomb casings suggested to US and British intelligence that Libya was actually manufacturing chemical munitions.

The United States also made use of HUMINT (the liaison channel). The West German government obtained construction blueprints of the Rabta plant from the engineering firm Salzgitter. These plans revealed some anomalous features suggestive of CW agent production. According to a German government report, "The joint planning of chemical plants and the metal processing plant as well as security facilities not usually found in a pharmaceutical facility (airtight windows and doors, gas-tight walls between the production and the control unit, burn-off unit, corrosion-proof lining on pipes, and escape routes) made it possible to draw the conclusion that 'Pharma 150' is a chemical weapon plant."[1]

It was not until August 1988, however, that the CIA obtained more solid evidence that the Rabta plant was engaged in CW agent production. Following a partial test run of the production process, an accidental spill occurred as highly toxic wastes were being transferred for disposal outside the plant. The resulting cloud of fumes killed a pack of wild desert dogs in the vicinity of the plant. Their bodies, detected by satellite, indicated that the plant was producing chemicals of warfare toxicity.

Conclusive evidence of the plant's purpose reportedly came from communications intercepts after the accidental spill. Panicked Libyan officials called the plant's designers at Imhausen-Chemie for emergency advice. Western intelligence was able to intercept the international telephone conversation. According to an account in *Time* magazine, "in a frantic effort to get advice on cleaning up and repairing the plant, Libyan officials spoke at length with Imhausen-Chemie personnel. Those conversations left no doubt that employees of the West German firm were just as aware as the Libyans that the plant was being used to produce toxic gas."[2]

In managing the channels, intelligence analysts have to evaluate the source, the channel itself, and the evidence that the channel provides.

EVALUATING THE SOURCE

As explained in Chapter 7, the channels provide two basic types of intelligence: literal (in the form that humans use for communication) and nonliteral (material, usually of a technical nature, that requires technical processing to be understood). They have to be treated differently, as the next two sections explain.

Literal Sources

Much deception is conveyed in literal form, with HUMINT and OSINT being primary channels. But COMINT and CYBER channels are increasingly used to deceive. And in communication, people can be misinformed or they lie to each other. So even if the product is not a deliberate deception, the outcome can be much the same. Given those parameters, consider these counterdeception source evaluation tenets:

Accept nothing at face value. Evaluate the source of evidence carefully and beware of the source's motives for providing the information. Evaluating the literal source involves answering these questions:

- Is the source competent (knowledgeable about the information being given)? It is easy, in a raw intelligence report, to accept not only the observations of a source but also the inferences that the source has drawn. Always ask: What was the basis for this conclusion? If no satisfactory answer is forthcoming, use the source's conclusions with caution or not at all.

- Did the source have the access needed to get the information? Was the access direct or indirect? The issue of source access typically does not arise because it is assumed that the source had access. When there is reason to be suspicious about the source, however, check whether the source might not have had the claimed access. Be suspicious of sources when it is unclear how they obtained the information.

- Does the source have a vested interest or bias? Sources may deliberately distort or misinform because they want to influence policy or increase their value to the collector. Moreover, reports do not contain the nonverbal details of the conversation—the setting, the context, facial and body expressions—to aid judgment. Be suspicious of sources who have not been interviewed by a trusted partner. Failure to shorten this part of the reporting chain had severe consequences in the case of Curveball's reporting on Iraqi biological weapons programs discussed later in this chapter. US intelligence officers were not able to directly interrogate Curveball and observe his demeanor during interrogation. Had they been allowed to do so, quite different conclusions about the validity of his reporting might have been reached.

In the HUMINT business, this is called determining *bona fides* for human sources. Even when not dealing with HUMINT, one must ask these questions. They are useful not only for identifying state-sponsored or organization-sponsored deception but also for catching attempts by individuals (such as Curveball) to deceive for their own purposes.

OSINT

OSINT has to be vetted and analyzed very carefully. Two standard checks done in validation of material are to examine

- *Accuracy.* It's often necessary to cross-check against known valid sources, especially against existing finished intelligence.

- *Credibility and authenticity.* This has always been an issue with OSINT. It is even more important with cyber material, but there are additional ways to check cyber sources:

  o Check the URL. What type of domain is it, for example, .com, .org, .edu, .gov, .mil, or a country code?

  o Check that it's an appropriate source for the material presented.

  o Check to see if it's a personal page. Independently search on the author's name (sometimes embedded in the website's source code).

  o Check who owns the host server and where it appears to be located. Cross-check to see if the author is located physically near the server.

  o Find out who links to the site. See if the site is in reliable web directories.

Note that a failure to pass validity checks does not mean that the information is useless. Material having questionable validity may have intelligence value. Deception attempts may not pass validity checks, but the fact that an attempt was made can tell you much about an opponent's intent.

COMINT

As with the other literal channels, identifying COMINT deception relies heavily on understanding your own OODA loop, how the opponent views it, and the difference between the two views. If the opponent is aware that you have broken an encryption system or that you search for certain key words, for example, then intelligence based on those channels should be vetted carefully. COMINT derived from push-to-talk radios (which indeed still exist in use) or high-frequency (HF) communications also should be looked at closely, because such communications are easily intercepted.

Having the best possible talent on the COMINT analysis team makes a big difference, as does having team members with long experience on their assigned targets. The clues to detecting deception in COMINT are usually subtle, and experienced analysts are best positioned to spot inconsistencies that tip off deception.

HUMINT

Countering HUMINT operations falls into the broad category of counter-espionage. This field of deception and counterdeception is the subject of many books. Counterespionage is touched on here only lightly, with the mention of double agents, moles, and dangles.

Double Agents

A major tool of offensive counterespionage is the double agent. A double agent can be a spy who becomes an employee or agent of the target intelligence service or an agent who is turned as a result of discovery and threats (usually of execution) for noncooperation. Double agents are often used to transmit disinformation or to identify other agents as part of counterespionage operations. Their success depends on trust by the organization that they are working against; the organization that has doubled them helps build that trust by providing true, but low value, information to pass along.

The objective of using double agents usually is to control the operations of the foreign intelligence service. One of the best known examples is the success that Cuban intelligence had in discovering and doubling the CIA's agents in Cuba—many, if not all, of whom in the 1970s and 1980s may have been turned into double agents.

Moles

The great fear of any intelligence service is a specific type of double agent: the mole, a trusted insider who provides information to an opposing service. On the flip side, the holy grail of HUMINT is a penetration of a foreign intelligence service—ideally, a double agent who works in the counterintelligence component. The Ames and Hanssen cases, described in Chapter 6, illustrate the extensive damage that such moles can cause.

Dangles

A dangle is a seemingly attractive potential recruit intentionally placed in front of a targeted intelligence service. The idea is for the targeted service to initiate contact and thus believe it has spotted, developed, and recruited an agent. If the target service swallows the bait and accepts the agent, then the dangle's parent service may learn the identities and vulnerabilities of some of the target's officers, its collection requirements, and tradecraft.[3] Dangles can also be used to pass misinformation to the recruiting organization.

To counter the possibility of recruiting a dangle, most clandestine services conduct some form of vetting. This vetting is primarily concerned with testing the agent's veracity. Some countries rely on the polygraph in questioning agents about lifestyle, contacts, access to information, and past history, searching for signs of deception in the responses. Many other countries still use techniques that predate the polygraph for vetting.

Questions specific to HUMINT include the following:

- What is the basis for judging the source to be reliable? Seek and heed the opinions of those closest to the reporting. Is the source vulnerable to control or manipulation by the potential deceiver?

- Is the true identity of the source an issue? Identity intelligence (biometrics, for example) can be used to validate or authenticate an identity. Biographic (public and private records) and behavioral data (travel, consumer patterns, Internet and other communications activity) can be used to check on human sources.

- How good is the source's track record of reporting? Check all instances in which a source's reports that initially appeared correct later turned out to be wrong—and yet the source always seemed to offer a good explanation for the discrepancy. Before and during the Quicksilver deception, Juan Pujol Garcia (Garbo) repeatedly was able to deceive the Germans because of his skill at explaining discrepancies.

In detecting deception in HUMINT, two reminders are especially useful:

- *Avoid over-reliance on a single source of information.* The deception succeeded in the 1972 US–USSR wheat deal because the United States had only one source—an agricultural liaison. Do not rely exclusively on what one person says.

- *Always look for material evidence* (documents, pictures, addresses or a phone number that can be confirmed). Take care, though, to look closely at how the evidence was obtained, if there is reason for suspicion. A deceptive technique that continues to succeed after long use is known as the "haversack ruse." Although it predates his use, the haversack ruse is generally credited to British colonel Richard Meinertzhagen. During the Sinai and Palestine campaign of World War I, Meinertzhagen allowed a haversack containing false British battle plans to fall into

Ottoman military hands. The result of the deception was a British victory in the Battles of Beersheba and Gaza. Operation Mincemeat was one of several variations on the haversack ruse that the British used during World War II.

The importance of feedback was noted in Chapter 10. It can be a challenge in HUMINT. A key component in the failure to correctly identify Iraq's WMD program status in 2002 was that critical feedback among collectors and analysts didn't happen. That miscall contributed substantially to a subsequent reshaping of the US intelligence community.

THE IRAQI WMD MISCALL

In October 2002, at the request of members of Congress, the US National Intelligence Council produced a national intelligence estimate (NIE) on the Iraqi WMD program. Many of the key conclusions of that estimate were wrong because of poor source evaluation or poor communication across the network—that is, inadequate or missing feedback.

The analysts who prepared the estimate readily accepted any evidence that supported the theory that Iraq had stockpiles and was developing weapons programs, and they explained away or disregarded evidence that pointed in other directions. Two of the most egregious examples were the evaluation of a key HUMINT source on Iraq's biological weapons program and of HUMINT and IMINT sources on Iraq's chemical weapons program.

The conclusions about Iraqi biological weapons relied heavily on a single source, an Iraqi chemical engineer nicknamed Curveball. This source claimed that Iraq had several mobile units for producing biological weapons agents. The evidence presented by Curveball fell short of being credible, according to several criteria discussed in this chapter:

- *Competence.* Curveball was variously described as a drinker, unstable, difficult to manage, "out of control," and exhibiting behavior that is typical of fabricators.[4]

- *Access.* There was no evidence of access to biological weapons laboratories. Corroborating evidence only established that Curveball had been to a particular location, not that he had any knowledge of biological weapons activities being conducted there.[5]

- *Vested interest or bias.* Curveball had a motivation to provide interesting intelligence to obtain resettlement assistance and permanent asylum.[6]

- *Communications channel.* The reporting was through liaison with the German intelligence service, and US intelligence officials were not provided direct access to Curveball. The communications channel between Curveball and the WMD analysts therefore had many intermediate nodes, with consequent possibilities for the analysts to get a distorted message.

Analysts evaluating Curveball's information were aware of some of these problems yet judged his reporting reliable and continued to make it the basis for the NIE judgment and subsequent judgments about Iraq's biological weapons program. They dismissed imagery reporting that indicated inconsistencies in Curveball's account as being due to Iraqi denial and deception against overhead imagery.[7] That Curveball was a fabricator was subsequently confirmed.

The NIE also erroneously concluded that Iraq had restarted chemical weapons production and increased its chemical weapons stockpiles, based on poor evaluation of both IMINT and HUMINT:

- Analysts relied heavily on imagery showing the presence of "Samarra-type" tanker trucks at suspect chemical weapons facilities. These distinctive trucks had been associated with chemical weapons shipments in the 1980s and during the Gulf War. Analysts also believed that they were seeing increased Samarra truck activity at suspect chemical weapons sites in imagery. They apparently did not consider an alternative hypothesis—that the trucks might be used for other purposes, as turned out to be the case. And they failed to recognize that the more frequent observed activity of the trucks was an artifact of increased imagery collection.[8] The trucks were simply observed more often because of more imagery reporting.

- One of the human sources, an Iraqi chemist, provided extensive reporting, about half of which defied reason. Despite evidence that he might not be a credible source, analysts used his reporting that Iraq had successfully stabilized the nerve agent VX in the NIE because it fit their existing mindset.[9] Another source reported that Iraq was producing mustard and binary chemical agents. But he also reported on Iraq's missile, nuclear, and biological programs. Given Iraq's known use of compartmentation to protect sensitive weapons programs, analysts should have recognized that the source was unlikely to have access to all these programs.[10]

Nonliteral Sources

Nonliteral intelligence channels include IMINT, SIGINT other than COMINT (that is, ELINT and FISINT), and MASINT. These channels, especially IMINT, are used to deceive. The wide use of dummy tanks and landing barges to deceive imagery collection during World War II has already been noted. The Serbs used IMINT deception frequently during the Kosovo conflict described in Chapter 3.

Nonliteral channels are generally more difficult to use for conducting deception, but they can be effective in defeating it—especially when combined with the product of literal sources. Collating information from all channels usually results in a more complete picture of the situation.

Countering Visible Imagery Deception

Three techniques that rely on imaging are often used, individually or in combination, to defeat visible imagery deception. Infrared, spectral, and radar imagery of a given target area can be combined to produce unique insights about the target that are not possible with any one imagery type alone. The combination can be a powerful tool for defeating deception. From a deceiver's point of view, it can make conducting imagery deception an especially difficult task.

Countering Infrared Imaging

Imagers operating in the infrared part of the optical spectrum can sometimes defeat denial techniques, either by sensing hot features or by distinguishing camouflage from surrounding vegetation. An infrared imager operating in the right optical bands could have sensed that the Al Kibar structure, discussed in Chapter 7, was not what it seemed had the reactor begun operation, as it would have produced heat. Whether it could have done so during the construction phase depends on the infrared imaging quality.

Countering Spectral Imaging

Spectral imaging—taking many images of an area simultaneously in different optical bands—offers more insights about a target than does infrared imaging alone. It enables the creation of a composite picture of the target area. These composite images allow an analyst to identify targets of interest and to characterize those targets based on measurements of the energy received from them.

Spectral imagers have substantial advantages because they make an opponent's denial and deception (using camouflage, for example) very difficult. Buried roadside bombs and tunnel entrances are more readily detected using spectral imagery. It is highly desirable in detecting deception to be able to determine the materials that a target is made of, detect degradation of the surface, resolve anomalies, and classify and identify the target. Spectral imaging has demonstrated the ability to do all of these things.[11]

Countering Radar Imaging

Radar imagery today relies mostly on either airborne or spaceborne synthetic aperture radars (SARs). A SAR is one of the most complex imaging systems to build and operate. But it is an important one for detecting deception. SAR imagers have a number of advantages when compared to optical imagers. They can

- Provide high-resolution images at night and under most weather and cloud conditions.

- Acquire their images by observing sideways from the SAR platform; this means they can look into openings in buildings, sheds, and tunnels.

- Penetrate numerous materials or surfaces that would normally hide equipment or facilities (for example, canvas tents and most wooden sheds become transparent to radar).

- Permit imagery analysts to characterize the ground texture, vegetation, sea surface, snow, and ice in detail, and to identify slight changes in these over time.

SAR imagery presents an entirely new set of challenges to the deceiver. It is difficult to create decoys that accurately resemble a radar image of the real thing. And conventional shielding under camouflage netting or nonmetal structures doesn't work—radar can penetrate these. (Admittedly, metal shielding can be effective.)

Following are some of the important applications of SARs that are used to counter deception:

- *Terrain mapping and characterization.* Optical imagers can provide maps, but because they do not measure range to the target, they don't do well at determining terrain elevation. SARs do measure range, so they can provide precise topography of the target area. Furthermore, SARs can characterize terrain, identifying soil and moisture changes that often accompany attempts at visible imagery deception.

- *Change detection.* One of the major advantages of SAR is its ability to detect changes in a scene over time. Change detection is an application to which SAR is particularly well suited. Examples of surface changes that can be observed include vehicle tracks, crops growing or being harvested, and soil excavation. Changes in the terrain surface due to underground construction also can be observed by change detection. The underground excavation results in both vertical settlement and a horizontal straining that is detectable.[12]

- *Foliage and camouflage penetration.* An application of SAR that has obvious counterdeception uses is foliage penetration. SARS can be built to operate in the low-frequency bands known as VHF and UHF bands. At these lower frequencies SARs can effectively image objects concealed in dense foliage, even objects located underneath the forest canopy.[13] They also penetrate into dry earth for short distances to detect buried objects such as land mines.[14]

- *Identifying targets.* SARs can identify and classify targets of intelligence interest—ships, aircraft, and military vehicles—and collect details that would identify visible imagery deception.[15] The higher the SAR's resolution, the more detail it can obtain about a target.

- *Monitoring moving targets.* SARs also have the capability to detect target motion. This capability can be used to create an image that highlights moving targets in an area. It is possible to detect aircraft, helicopter, or ship movements, as well as ground vehicular movement.[16]

Countering Technical Collection Deception

Technical collection is of particular value for countering both denial and deception because a typical target has multiple signatures, and it is difficult to hide or simulate them all. The fact that some techniques are poorly understood by foreign intelligence services helps as well.

Deception that targets technical collection can be defeated, if your side can conceal the details about the performance of your collection sensors. If your technical collection system is more sophisticated than the opponent thinks it is—can measure signatures to a finer level of detail, for example—then your intelligence network can probably spot the deception. It is difficult, for example, to simulate exactly all of the acoustic signatures created by submarines, because there are so many of them. Machinery vibration, water flow over the vessel's hull, propeller rotation or cavitation, and crew activity all generate acoustic signatures. If the opponent misses just one of these, and your system collects it, then you can readily identify the deception. Furthermore, sensors that measure signatures such as sound or radar emissions are continually improving in resolution and in the details they measure. A misstep here by the deceiver in underestimating performance of the opponent's sensor can be fatal to the deception effort.

EVALUATING THE CHANNEL

In detecting deception, it is important to understand the channel through which raw intelligence flows, and make it as effective as possible. In a large intelligence system, collection requirements must move through a bureaucracy to a requirements officer, from there to a country desk, a field requirements officer, a SIGINT collector or a HUMINT case officer (for instance), then to an agent in the case of HUMINT; and the response then goes back through the reports chain. In the process, what HUMINT operatives call "operational information"—details about the source or collection methods—are stripped. As a result, critical clues that can identify deception can disappear. A somewhat different process leads to a similar result in COMINT and IMINT reporting. In those cases, things that don't make sense to the COMINT or IMINT analyst often are omitted in the published report. But the items that don't make sense can be critical in identifying deception.

So a counterdeception team needs to both understand its own channels and be close to the people who handle the information in those channels. Ask them questions such as: What was the channel? Is this information being provided intentionally? If so, what part of it is true? Could it be deception or the sending of a message or signal? If it is a message or signal, what is the message, and what is the reason for it? How accurate is the source's reporting? Has the whole chain of evidence including translations been checked? Does the critical evidence check out? Did it depend on translation or interpretation, for example, by a COMINT or OSINT analyst? If the analyst drew conclusions based on the material, check the validity of the conclusions.

The intelligence team should also consider the level of the opponent's understanding of each channel. In crafting the 1955 Moscow Air Show deception, the Soviets took advantage of their intimate knowledge of attaché collection. They even knew exactly where the attachés would stand to observe the flyby, so the Bison racetrack flight pattern was designed to follow a path that the attachés could not observe. And they knew that two passes by the same number of bombers would be likely to arouse suspicion, so they increased the number of bombers in the second pass. As another example, in deceiving IMINT during preparations for their nuclear test, the Indian government took advantage of their knowledge of US imagery quality and of the details that imagery analysts were relying on.

In looking at the channel, a sub-source or ancillary source can be more critical than the primary source, as the next example illustrates.

OPERATION MINCEMEAT REVISITED

The World War II deception known as Operation Mincemeat was introduced in Chapter 2 and has been returned to throughout this book. Although the plan was successful, it had a number of potentially serious flaws. The body was released in a coastal area known to have strong pro-Axis sentiments, but the documents wound up in the control of the Spanish Navy—the least pro-Axis of possible recipients. Furthermore, a large number of people knew of the operation (apparently including the Soviets), increasing the chances of a leak.

The major flaw, though, could have been caught if Spanish and German intelligence had shortened the channel by going back to an ancillary but critical source. The Spanish coroner who examined the body was, contrary to British expectation, an expert pathologist who had long experience in examining drowning victims. He noticed several incongruences in his examination. No fish or crab bites, shiny instead of dull hair, and clothing that wasn't shapeless, all of which indicated that the body had not been in the water as long as the briefcase's documents indicated; but the state of decay indicated that the body had been in the water longer than the documents indicated.[17]

The deception succeeded despite these flaws until Italian intelligence services identified Sicily as the likely target just prior to the invasion, based in part on identifying the movement of airborne forces to their assembly areas.[18]

The point is that complex deception efforts are very difficult to pull off, even with a good model of the opposing services such as the British had. In the end, the success of the British effort depended on a few lucky breaks—the biggest one being the failure of their opponents to manage their own intelligence channels.

EVALUATING THE EVIDENCE

Finally, your side needs to step back and look at the whole picture—the story that emerges from all of the evidence in all channels. The data from different collection sources are most valuable when used together. The synergistic effect of combining data from many sources both strengthens the conclusions and increases confidence in them. It also allows a counterdeception intelligence team to identify deception.

- Determine whether or not you have a complete picture. An incomplete picture can mislead as much as an outright lie, and deception requires concealing part of the true picture.

- Look for incongruences—items that don't fit into the story, or things that are expected to match or tie together, but don't. Inconsistencies should always be a flag to look closely at the evidence. For example, does evidence from one source of reporting (for example, HUMINT) conflict with another source (SIGINT or OSINT)? Is evidence one would expect to see noteworthy by its absence?

- Do other sources of information provide corroborating evidence? Is there an unusual abundance of corroborating evidence? Here, look for too much congruity—a story that ties together too neatly.

In terms of the 1955 Moscow Air Show case, there had been many flyovers before. The established pattern was for aircraft of one type to fly by in a single formation. Two flybys by the same aircraft type was an incongruity that should have received some attention.

Traps to Avoid in Evaluating Evidence

In evaluating evidence, there are many pitfalls or traps to avoid, yet we fall into them repeatedly. The sections that follow describe a few that we encounter in identifying deception. More detail is contained in Clark's *Intelligence Analysis: A Target-Centric Approach.*[19]

Vividness Weighting

In general, the channel for communication of intelligence should be as short as possible; but when could a short channel become a problem? If the channel is too short, the result is *vividness weighting*—in which evidence that is experienced directly is strongest ("seeing is believing"). Decision makers place the most weight on evidence that they obtain directly—a dangerous pitfall that executives fall into repeatedly and that makes them vulnerable to deception. Strong and dynamic leaders are particularly vulnerable: Franklin Roosevelt, Winston Churchill, and Henry Kissinger are examples of statesmen who occasionally did their own collection and analysis, sometimes with unfortunate results.

Source Preferences

One of the most difficult traps to avoid is that of weighing evidence based on its source. HUMINT operatives repeatedly value information gained from clandestine sources—the classic spy—above that from refugees, émigrés, and defectors. COMINT gained from an expensive emplaced telephone tap is valued (and protected from disclosure) above that gleaned from high-frequency radio communications (which almost anyone can monitor). The most common pitfall, however, is to devalue the significance of OSINT; being the most readily available, it is often deemed to be the least valuable. Using open sources well is a demanding analytic skill, and it can pay high dividends to those who have the patience to master it. Collectors may understandably make the mistake of equating source with importance. Having spent a sizable portion of their organization's budget in collecting the material, they may believe that its value can be measured by the cost of collecting it. No competent analyst should ever make such a mistake.

Favoring Recent Evidence

It's natural to give the most recently acquired evidence the most weight. The freshest intelligence—crisp, clear, and the focus of attention—often gets more weight than the fuzzy and half-remembered (but possibly more important) information that was acquired and recorded or reported on some time ago. It is important to remember this tendency and compensate for it. It's worth the time to go back to the original (older) intelligence and reread it to bring it more freshly to mind.

Premature Closure

The opposite of favoring recent evidence, *premature closure* also has been described as "affirming conclusions," based on the observation that people are inclined to verify or affirm their existing beliefs rather than modify or discredit those beliefs when presented with new information. It has been observed that "once the Intelligence Community becomes entrenched in its chosen frame, its conclusions are destined to be uncritically confirmed."[20]

The primary danger of premature closure is not that the analyst might make a bad assessment because the evidence is incomplete. Rather, the danger is that when a situation is changing quickly or when a major, unprecedented event occurs, the analyst will become trapped by the judgments already made. The chances of missing indications of change increase, and it becomes harder to revise an initial estimate.

Evaluating Alternative Hypotheses

It is important to evaluate a full set of plausible hypotheses—including a deception hypothesis, using other channels where possible. The deception conducted at the 1955 Moscow Air Show illustrates the consequences of a failure to consider alternative hypotheses. It also illustrates the value of having or opening new channels to check on deception, as discussed next.

MOSCOW AIR SHOW: EVALUATING EVIDENCE

As described in Chapter 9 and earlier in this chapter, the deception at the 1955 Moscow Air Show involved the Soviets presenting the impression of a larger fleet of Bison bombers than they actually had by flying the same aircraft over the air show observer area twice. The deception succeeded because of failures in evaluating the evidence, specifically:

- *Mindset.* Western defense analysts expected a bomber buildup and were predisposed to believe that the USSR had a large bomber fleet. Consequently, they were prepared to accept evidence that supported that assumption.

- *Failure to consider alternative hypotheses.* When reviewing the observer reports, they didn't consider alternative hypotheses. Had alternative hypotheses been considered, measuring the length of time between passes would have indicated that the flyovers could have resulted from the flights making a racetrack maneuver.

- *Failure to consider motivation.* Analysis of political motivations could have shown that the Soviets had a need to project strength against the United States, and deception at the air show was a logical way to do so. Moscow's military demonstrations were known to have the purpose of projecting strength.

The deception eventually was exposed when US intelligence developed alternative channels that the Soviets did not anticipate. The Bisons were produced at the Fili Plant in Moscow. US defense attachés were able to obtain long-range photographs from sites near the plant, and subsequent analysis showed a discrepancy in the tail numbers of the Bisons being produced. Aircraft tail numbers typically follow a sequence. Bison tail numbers didn't do that. After a sequence of five tail numbers—ending in 10, 11, 12, 13, and 14, for example—the numbering sequence would jump to 20, 21, 22, 23, and 24, and then continue in the 30s. There were no tail numbers ending in 5, 6, 7, 8, or 9.[21] The conclusion was that the plant was producing fewer bombers than US intelligence had estimated, and the tail numbering was part of a deception. Later on, U-2 missions photographed all of the Soviet bomber bases and found that the bomber gap did not exist.

NOTES

1. *Report Submitted by the Government of the Federal Republic of Germany to the German Bundestag on 15 February 1989 concerning the Possible Involvement of Germans in the Establishment of a Chemical Weapons Facility in Libya* (English version provided by the Embassy of the Federal Republic of Germany to the United States, 1989), p. 9.

2. William R. Doerner, "On Second Thought," *Time,* January 23, 1989, 31.

3. John Ehrman, "What Are We Talking about When We Talk about Counterintelligence?" Center for the Study of Intelligence, *Studies in Intelligence* 53, no. 2 (2009): 18, https://www.cia.gov/library/center-for-the-study-of-intelligence/csi-publications/csi-studies/studies/vol53no2/toward-a-theory-of-ci.html.

4. *Report of the Commission on the Intelligence Capabilities of the United States Regarding Weapons of Mass Destruction,* March 31, 2005, 91, 97.

5. Ibid., 113.

6. Ibid., 96.

7. Ibid., 92.

8. Ibid., 122, 125.

9. Ibid., 127.

10. Ibid., 128.

11. John A. Adam, "Peacekeeping by Technical Means," *IEEE Spectrum* (July 1986): 42–80.

12. J. Happer, "Characterization of Underground Facilities," JASON Report JSR-97-155 (April 1999), http://www.gwu.edu/~nsarchiv/NSAEBB/NSAEBB372/docs/Underground-JASON.pdf.

13. Merrill Skolnik, ed., *Radar Handbook*, 3rd ed. (New York: McGraw-Hill, 2008), 17.33–17.34.

14. L. Carin, R. Kapoor, and C. E. Baum, "Polarimetric SAR Imaging of Buried Landmines," *IEEE Transactions on Geoscience and Remote Sensing* 36, no. 6 (November 1998): 1985–1988; David J. Daniels, *Ground Penetrating Radar* (London: Institution of Engineering and Technology, 2004), 5.

15. Dai Dahai, Wang Xuesong, Xiao Shunping, Wu Xiaofang, and Chen Siwei, "Development Trends of PolSAR System and Technology," *Heifei Leida Kexue Yu Jishu,* February 1, 2008, 15.

16. Zhou Hong, Huang Xiaotao, Chang Yulin, and Zhou Zhimin, "Ground Moving Target Detection in Single-Channel UWB SAR Using Change Detection Based on Sub-Aperture Images," *Heifei Leida Kexue Yu Jishu,* February 1, 2008, 23.

17. Ben Macintyre, *Operation Mincemeat* (New York: Harmony Books, 2010), 201–202.

18. Thaddeus Holt, *The Deceivers: Allied Military Deception in the Second World War* (New York: Skyhorse Publishing, 2007), 379.

19. The material in this section was taken from Robert M. Clark, *Intelligence Analysis: A Target-Centric Approach*, 5th ed. (2016) and modified.

20. Matthew Herbert, "The Intelligence Analyst as Epistemologist," *International Journal of Intelligence and Counterintelligence* 19 (2006): 678.

21. CIA, *Penetrating the Iron Curtain: Resolving the Missile Gap with Technology* (Washington, DC: US Government Printing Office, 2014), 43–45.

EXERCISES

PART TWO

SENSOR MAPPING AND CHANNEL TRACKING EXERCISES

In earlier chapters we discussed the inverse OODA loop for deception planning, and the concepts of sensor mapping and channel management. In this chapter, some very basic scenarios are presented in order to allow students to work with both of these concepts using raw intelligence. The scenarios are short and the intelligence, especially where it concerns sensor mapping, is intentionally direct with very little "noise" in order to allow students to quickly grasp the theory to practice conversion of the concepts. The channel management exercises are somewhat more challenging; they require story telling via channels, and therefore require some critical and creative thinking.

SENSOR MAPPING EXERCISES

In Chapter 6, the concept of sensor mapping was introduced in order to provide a common reference concept for understanding one's own and an adversary's "observe" part of the OODA loop. Building an understanding of how an adversary observes his or her operational environment is essential to having some basis for how a deception should be projected. Embedded in the intelligence reports you receive are both obvious and subtle clues about an adversary's collection (observational) capability. The short fictional exercises in this chapter are intended only to provide students an opportunity to connect the sensor mapping concept to practice in fictional settings.

Use the following example as a model for how to format final products for the following three sensor mapping exercises.

Example Exercise in Sensor Modeling: Pirating in the North Sea

The purpose of this example exercise is to create a sensor model from an intelligence roll-up. This exercise uses a fictional scenario set in Scotland, as illustrated in Figure 12-1.

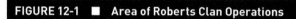

FIGURE 12-1 ■   Area of Roberts Clan Operations

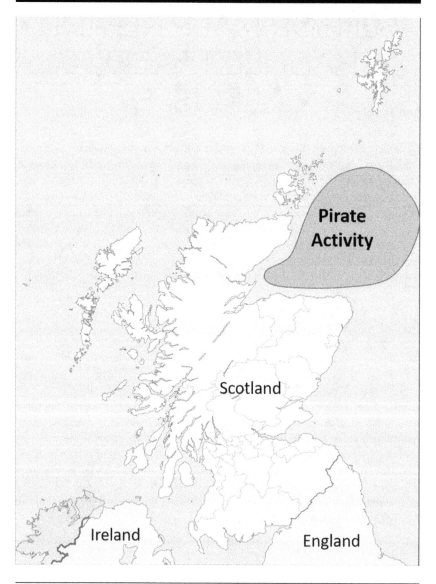

Source: Derived from a file licensed under Creative Commons License. https://commons.wikimedia .org/wiki/File:Scotland_location_map.svg.

Since the closure of most of the oil fields in the North Sea due to their depletion and also the falling demand for oil, there has been an increase in the pirating of regular transport and fishing vessels rather than of tankers in order to ransom the crew members. Pirating incidents usually occur within the 200 kilometer (km) limit of the Scottish east coast, and a great many of the pirate boardings of vessels are done at night. Investigations done by cooperating authorities have determined that the pirating along the east coast of Scotland is dominated by a large clan, the Roberts Clan. Despite analysts for the coast guard and navy providing some good pattern of life (PoL) information, the pirates manage to maintain a steady level of activity along the coast. The Scottish government has worked to improve coordination between sea, land, air, and cyber assets. However, the pirates seem always to be one step ahead. It is becoming clear that the Roberts Clan has an effective intelligence collection capability. Table 12-1 illustrates a sensor mapping of the clan in roll-up form.

A reminder: The rating schema in the roll-ups in this chapter and the following ones uses the source evaluation and rating schema introduced in Table 6-2. The numbers in HUMINT reporting (for example, 023) refer to specific sources.

From the intelligence provided and with a focus on identifying the sensors/sources used by the Roberts Clan to observe their environment, we are able to build a model of how the Roberts Clan observes the operational environment that they use for pirating (see Figure 12-2).

TABLE 12-1 ■ Roberts Clan Roll-Up		
REP #	**DTG**	**TEXT**
R1	1 MAY 2017	**HUMINT-023-C-3:** It is reported that many of the harbor masters along the east coast of Scotland are in the pocket of the Roberts Clan.
R2	1 MAY 2017	**SIGINT:** Analysis indicates that registered trawlers X, Y, and Z conduct satellite phone reporting on the presence of coast guard patrols along the east coast of Scotland.
R3	2 MAY 2017	**PB (patrol boat) *HMS Spike* Report:** Interviews with crew of ship where a hijacking attempt failed indicate that the ship was scouted by small surface vessels within 60 minutes prior to the actual hijack attempt.
R4	3 MAY 2017	**HUMINT-005-F-6:** The Roberts Clan recently gained access to longer range radars that enable them to enlarge their "security bubble" and has led to a significant increase in the hijacking success rate.
R5	3 MAY 2017	**ELINT:** Naval ELINT reporting and analysis from the last 2 months indicates that unidentified tactical radar emissions are occurring frequently within an X × Y box area off the east coast of Scotland.

(Continued)

TABLE 12-1 ■ (Continued)		
R6	4 MAY 2017	**HUMINT-005-F-6:** The Roberts Clan reportedly has a source inside the operational planning center of the coast guard.
R7	5 MAY 2017	**CYBER:** Known pirating suspects of the Roberts Clan make use of false profiles to follow the Facebook and Twitter profiles of several shipping firms, including some of the ship profiles or crews.
R8	6 MAY 2017	**TEAR LINE:**[1] Suspected pirates of the Roberts Clan receive VHF reports of ship names and types leaving and arriving in seven harbors along the east coast.
R9	6 MAY 2017	**OSINT:** Analysis suggests that suspected members of the Roberts Clan regularly attend marine technology conferences.
R10	7 MAY 2017	**PB** *HMS Springer* **Report:** Ships in the area are reporting being overflown by a small unmanned aerial vehicle (UAV) equipped with a video camera.

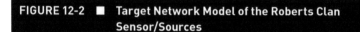

FIGURE 12-2 ■ Target Network Model of the Roberts Clan Sensor/Sources

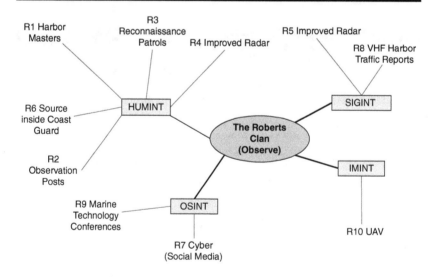

Suggestion for class use: In each of the following three exercises, read the short scenario and, individually or in teams, use the accompanying raw intelligence to develop your own sensor map understanding of the target organization. Follow the format in Figure 12-2. Participants should then present, discuss, and compare their sensor maps with those developed by other students or teams.

List and discuss some of the challenges with identification of possible sensors from raw intelligence. Discuss what is just "noise" and what is useful. Discuss how training could be conducted in your organization to ensure that adversarial sensors are identified from raw intelligence.

Sensor Mapping Exercise 12.1: The Red 5th Battalion

Sensor mapping is essential to all levels of deception planning. On the tactical level in a land operation battlespace, component commands are responsible for understanding the OODA loops of their immediate adversaries in the same battlespace. If deception is to be successfully conducted within their battlespace, they must understand how the adversary observes and orients information. This short sensor mapping exercise provides practice in doing that.

Scenario

You or your team are part of the 10th Blue Battalion's S2 (intelligence section) and are preparing to support deception planning. The Blue Battalion has been assigned a geographic area, their battlespace, called Krag Valley West. Opposing you in your battlespace is an adversarial Red 5th Battalion.

Task

Use the intelligence provided in Table 12-2 to construct a simple sensor map/ model of the enemy Red 5th Battalion. Use Figure 12-2 as a model template. How many different types of INTs do they have?

TABLE 12-2 ■ The Red 5th Battalion Intell Roll-Up		
REP #	DTG	TEXT
R1	19 JUNE 2017	**INTSUM:** Red 5th Battalion requested 2 weeks provisions from their task force headquarters (HQ).
R2	20 JUNE 2017	**INTSUM:** Recent enemy propaganda originating from the Red 5th Battalion information operations units indicate knowledge collected from monitoring 10th Blue Battalion's VHF communications.
R3	20 JUNE 2017	**A Company Patrol Report:** Enemy units belonging to the Red 5th Battalion continued probing north of the Tigress River, resulting in several short skirmishes. It is assessed that they will continue to probe for possible weakness in our defensive lines.

(Continued)

TABLE 12-2 ■ (Continued)		
R4	20 JUNE 2017	**B Company Patrol Report:** Outpost "Eyes Front" bravo 24 reported several Piranhas equipped for VHF COMINT collection moving up hill 49.
R5	20 JUNE 2017	**C Company Patrol Report:** COMINT reports the enemy discussed ordering a "green eyes fly over" this evening "if there was one available."
R6	20 JUNE 2017	**D Company Patrol Report:** All quiet in our sector and along the perimeter of our area of responsibility (AoR).
R7	24 JUNE 2017	**INTSUM (Intelligence Summary):** There are indications from spectral analysis that new positions have been established further upriver around 10 km from the nearest bridge. It is unclear as to the intended purposes of these positions.
R8	26 JUNE 2017	**INTREP (Intelligence Report):** Walk-in local "smith" from village of Granary reports that soldiers from the 5th battalion were trying to look like tourists on mountain bikes while riding around the village of Granary earlier this week.
R9	3 JULY 2017	**INTSUM:** Several intelligence threads indicate that the Red 5th Battalion will attempt to resupply their prepositioned fires (artillery and mortar) positions with an augmentation of 50 rounds per piece, within the next 10 days.
R10	3 JULY 2017	**SUPINTREP (Supplementary Intelligence Report):** It is likely the Red 5th Battalion has IMINT support available every day from 1300 to 1400 hrs and 0100 to 0200 hrs.
R11	4 JULY 2017	**HUMINT-005-F-6:** The commander of the Red 5th Battalion has no combat experience.
R12	5 JULY 2017	**CYBER:** IP mapping of the Red 5th Battalion indicates that several members of their 2nd company log on to private Internet services when they can. Two social media profiles are already being monitored.
R13	6 JULY 2017	**TEARLINE:** The Red 5th Battalion are monitoring the communications of our reconnaissance platoon.
R14	6 JULY 2017	**SIGINT:** The Red 5th Battalion commander has requested a new staff car because of the current vehicle's poor suspension.
R15	7 JULY 2017	**INTSUM:** There are several streams of reporting suggesting that some local farmers within our battlespace count the number of vehicles that enter and exit the HQ.

Sensor Mapping Exercise 12.2: Hells Cross Motorcycle Gang

Sensor mapping is not restricted to military environments. This sensor mapping assignment takes place in a fictional civilian environment common to most nations where there is a constant struggle between authorities and organized crime.

Scenario

In this fictional scenario, you or your team are part of the Copenhagen Police District specialists in a new operational-level intelligence section that has been created to help the police gain the initiative against the most powerful organized crime gang in the city. The gang is known as the Hells Cross Motorcycle Club (Hells Cross MC). A key figure in the gang is named Bo Sondergaard, but it is not clear exactly what role he has.

Task

The first order of business for your intelligence section is to produce an easily communicable model of how the Hells Cross MC collects and orients information for use in their illicit activities as part of understanding their overarching OODA loop. Use the provided intelligence reporting in Table 12-3 to construct a visual model that depicts how you as the subject matter expert (SME) believe the gang observes and orients intelligence in the Copenhagen Police District. Use Figure 12-2 as a model template.

TABLE 12-3 ■ Hells Cross Intell Roll-Up		
REP #	DTG	TEXT
R1	2 FEB 2016	**HUMINT-003-C-2:** Court tactics, techniques, and procedures (TTPs). Anne-Marie Koldby, senior lawyer for the Hells Cross MC from Koldby Legal Offices, briefs Bo Sondergaard at his residence on police TTPs used in cases against MC members. Her briefs are based on post-case debriefings from the junior lawyers who conducted the defense.
R2	8 FEB 2016	**SIGINT:** Local MC support. 5 FEB 2016 intercept from Mob. 8767 5432 belonging to Frederick Olsen, local leader of Hells Cross MC support group in West Copenhagen. An unknown (UNK) person is ordered to organize a "police" picket (observers) at three intersections that cover the access to a local restaurant "The Black Pot" while the "warning" is being delivered. (*Comment:* Drive-by shooting at The Black Pot reported on evening of 6 FEB 2016.)
R3	15 FEB 2016	**CYBER:** Known Hells Cross MC local support group has several online profiles being run by Patrick Muller, known local support group member. The objective of these profiles is believed to be befriending various local police members via their private online profiles.
R4	17 FEB 2016	**HUMINT-025-B-3:** Lars Johannsen, a Hells Cross MC member convicted of arson and currently imprisoned for 3 years, is responsible for debriefing new prisoners on police TTPs used in their investigations and reporting them to Bo Sondergaard.

(Continued)

TABLE 12-3 ■ (Continued)		
R5	22 FEB 2016	**HUMINT-003-C-2:** For each case at court against Hells Cross MC members, one or more members are assigned to identify witnesses and testifying police officers on their way in and out of court. The information is passed on to Bo Sondergaard, who briefs Frederick Olsen, the suspected current Head of Hells Cross MC.
R6	3 MAR 2016	**CYBER:** Several IP addresses belonging to known Hells Cross MC members are used for monitoring OSINT sources on police activity, with special focus on tip-offs provided to police over social media.
R7	7 MAR 2016	**SIGINT:** Exploitation of hidden cell phone found in Lars Johansson's cell. SMS sent to Bo Sondergaard containing names of prison guards and where possible their social insurance numbers.
R8	8 MAR 2016	**CYBER:** Chat activity between several Hells Cross MC members indicates a monitoring capability against police radio frequencies to provide early warning of police operations.
R9	10 MAR 2016	**SIGINT:** Legacy monitoring of known Hells Cross MC support members' communication indicates an operational command relationship with Hells Cross MC, and members often receive orders approved by "Fred."
R10	14 MAR 2016	**INTREP:** A collation of reports from witnesses involved in cases against Hells Cross MC indicates that Hells Cross MC systematically identifies and intimidates police witnesses.
R11	20 MAR 2016	**HUMINT-025-B-3:** Lars Johannsen was overheard bragging about the ability of Hells Cross MC to bribe prison guards he identifies as being weak or easily corrupted. He currently has a list of 15 out of the 87 guards working at the prison who fit that profile.
R12	24 MAR 2016	**CYBER:** Exploitation of confiscated external hard drives indicates there is a well-organized and systematic process for identifying persons of interest to the Hells Cross MC.
R13	2 APR 2016	**SUPINTREP:** All-source analysis suggests there is a Hells Cross MC network at the court that has the objective of identifying undercover police officers called in to testify in cases.

| R14 | 6 APR 2016 | **HUMINT-003-C-2:** Junior lawyer from Koldby Legal is heard discussing the collection of geographic locations related to Hells Cross MC activities known to the police and sending them to Anne-Marie Koldby. The junior lawyer stated, "It's a dirty job, but someone has to do it for the money they are offering, so it might as well be me." |
| R15 | 9 APR 2016 | **SIGINT:** Exploitation of a second mobile phone found hidden in Lars Johannsen's cell. Text messaging indicates a network of at least four other prisoners at the same prison who contribute to Lars Johannsen's collection of police TTPs. |

Sensor Mapping Exercise 12.3: People's Party Militia Wing

Sensor mapping to support a coming strategic campaign is no different from sensor mapping at other levels. It will quickly involve tactical considerations as to how whole organizations observe and orient in the expected theater of operations. Intelligence collection assets and platforms can be tactical in their performance but strategic in their effects. Sensor mapping to support a strategic campaign still encompasses the same methodological approach as the two previous exercises.

Scenario

In this fictitious scenario, the Russian Federation is concerned about possible unconventional warfare activities being directed by North Korea against the Russian Federation. In the far east of the Russian Federation along the border with North Korea, a local insurgency is being conducted by a group calling themselves the People's Party Militia Wing (PPMW). The group has established shadow governance in the cities of Bamburovo, Bezverkhovo, and Narva, and currently threatens Primorsky. Moscow has established a fusion analysis cell consisting of members from the Foreign Intelligence Service (FIS), Federal Security Service (FSS), and the Main Intelligence Directorate (GRU) and sent them to Primorsky in order to assess the PPMW.

Task

Your team is tasked to sensor map the PPMW in order to understand how they collect intelligence. You have three weeks before counterinsurgency operational planning begins. Use the provided intelligence reporting in Table 12-4 to construct your sensor map, and use Figure 12-2 as a model template.

TABLE 12-4 ■ People's Party Militia Wing Intell Roll-Up		
REP #	DTG	TEXT
R1	23 SEPT 2017	**INTREP:** The PPMW have internal security teams (ISTs) present in Bamburovo, Bezverkhovo, and Narva. They live in the cities, are not armed, and act as handlers for informers among the local population. The ISTs run a systematic collection and reporting operation.
R2	23 SEPT 2017	**INTREP:** Over the past 3 months there have been several raids on military and police installations in Bamburovo, Bezverkhovo, and Narva. Along with a wide variety of weapons and ammunition, the list of equipment stolen includes VHF monitoring systems, night-vision equipment, computers, servers, files on servers, and one mobile radar unit. No sensitive SATCOM equipment has been stolen.
R3	24 SEPT 2017	**HUMINT-048-D-2**: Semyonova Raina Denisovna is a PPMW member and meets often with market shop owners and bus drivers in Bamburovo and Bezverkhovo. Yakimova Sara Dmitrievna is a PPMW member and meets with senior police officials and other government members in Narva.
R4	24 SEPT 2017	**HUMINT-051-A-4:** Friends of known hacker Khanilov Ivanovich have been heard talking about his big new contract with a rebel group. When one of the friends heard how much he was getting paid, he suggested there must be much larger backers than the "Wing."
R5	27 SEPT 2017	**OSINT:** The North Korea propaganda bureau has launched a news and social media campaign that promotes a narrative that supports the PPMW claims to territory near the North Korean border. North Korean spokesman Chil-Soon appears to be the front man for the regime's effort to legitimize the PPMW. *Note*—There were only 2 hours from the first reported PPMW attack in Narva back in June 2017 in Russian media, to the first Chil-Soon presentation in support of PPMW.
R6	2 OCT 2017	**SUPINTREP:** A recently captured and interrogated PPMW member, Shubin Semyonovich, was recognized by FIS as having been in contact with Oh-Seong, a known agent of the North Korean Reconnaissance General Bureau (RGB) who works out of the North Korean Consulate in Vladivostok.
R7	3 OCT 2017	**CYBER:** Recent DDoS attacks on police servers in Primorsky are believed to be originating from North Korea. The attacks are focused on computers with files on known members of the PPMW. Several police files on PPMW members were copied by hackers on these same servers in July.

R8	4 OCT 2017	**SIGINT:** PPMW SATCOM activity includes requesting imaging information on Russian military and police installations in and around Narva from a closed North Korean network used primarily by their consulate in Vladivostok.
R9	4 OCT 2017	**SIGINT:** It is estimated that PPMW has local encrypted VHF and UHF intercept ability due to captured Russian communication equipment and material.
R10	8 OCT 2017	**OSINT:** Reaction time in PPMW counter-messaging in media and social media indicates the PPMW have an extensive media monitoring organization.
R11	10 OCT 2017	**CYBER:** Known hacker signatures attributed to the modus operandi of Khanilov Ivanovich have been augmented by hacker signatures previously attributed to Young-Ae, a known hacker in the service of the North Korean RGB.
R12	10 OCT 2017	**ELINT:** Since July there has been a significant increase in air defense radar emissions from the mountains surrounding the North Korean border town of Hanyopyonhri. It is estimated that early warning coverage of Vladivostok has improved 300%. This can only be accomplished by the addition of significant men and materiel.
R13	11 OCT 2017	**CYBER:** Files copied from North Korean consulate servers in Vladivostok include requests by Oh-Seong to the RGB for satellite imagery of military installations in Primorsky.
R14	11 OCT 2017	**MASINT:** Significant increases in sonar activity around Zarubino naval station are attributed to a North Korean mini-sub type known to be used for littoral (near-shoreline) reconnaissance along the shorelines.
R15	13 OCT 2017	**SIGINT:** Intercepted text messaging from a cell phone belonging to a Trans-Narva bus line includes grid references of police checkpoints on the route from Narva to Primorsky. Messaging is sent to various mobiles, never the same one, but all are registered on a network in Bamburovo.

CHANNEL MANAGEMENT EXERCISES—DECEPTION PROJECTION

Chapter 9 introduced the concept of channel management, along with the concepts of congruence and incongruence. The following exercises allow readers to practice identifying possible abnormal congruences or incongruences within one's own organizational channels being used to plan and project a deception against a targeted adversary—in short, to better manage deception. The objective

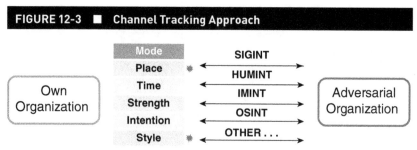

FIGURE 12-3 ■ Channel Tracking Approach

Are there abnormal congruences in the channel projection?
Are there abnormal incongruences in the channel projection?

in each exercise is to illustrate how channel management can improve deception planning and reduce abnormalities that might undermine the story line of the deception plan.

For each scenario you or your team are supporting an eventual deception through channel management. The task is to apply the abnormality detection framework found in Figure 12-3 and identify possible issues with the planned story-line projection that could undermine the deception.

Each exercise includes a brief summary of the proposed story line for the deception, as part of the situation description. The details of the story are contained in a channel table, based on your understanding of the adversary's sensors. So you do not need to develop a sensor map. The table includes a proposed timeline for the projection of the different elements of the deception.

The assignment (task statement) in each exercise is to (1) identify the abnormal elements in the table, using the deception projection data provided and the principles of channel tracking; and (2) deconflict friendly channels that are projecting the story line so that they do not undermine the planned deception.

Channel Management Exercise 12.1: Pick a Port

Scenario

The date is October 2016. You or your intelligence analysis team are in South America working for a EUROPOL counternarcotics task force, focusing on countering cocaine smuggling from South America to Europe. French Guiana has long been a favorite cocaine smuggling hub to Europe because of its departmental status in France. Cocaine is smuggled via private yachts over the Atlantic Ocean to Africa and eventually to Marseille in southern France. It is an important smuggling route, as 1 kilogram (kg) of raw cocaine from Guiana can be turned into as many as 10 kg for sale to users on the streets of Europe. Intelligence analysis to date has determined with high certainty that a large shipment of cocaine is being readied somewhere in the equatorial forests of French Guiana's interior. The shipment is expected to be sent overland to a port on the Guyanese coast, to be placed on waiting yachts, in

January 2017. The task force commander, recognizing the limited resources for coastal surveillance, has ordered your intelligence section to project a deception story via identified channels to the cartel, in order to convince the cartel to choose a specific port for an expected attempt to load the yachts. The purpose of the deception is to mitigate the lack of resources for monitoring the whole of Guiana's west coast and still intercept the shipment before the yachts depart. There are five possible ports for the delivery. They include Cayenne, Tonate, Kourou, Organabo, and Mana. The task is to project a story to convince the cartel to attempt to load the cocaine at Kourou. The cartel's window for delivery to the coast is January 5–13, 2017, so you have approximately two months to project the story.

Task

Compare and discuss abnormal congruences and incongruences between the channels presented in the draft story-line deception plan (see Table 12-5) of the counternarcotics task force.

Suggestion: Discuss in groups how you could improve the deception story projection by mitigating the identified abnormalities.

TABLE 12-5 ■ Pick a Port Deception Channel Tracker		
CH #	Targeted Cartel Channel (Description)	Planned Story Projection
1	Adversarial OSINT monitoring capability	15–30 NOV 2016: Leak to local and international media that the Guyanese government is increasing coast guard patrols outside of Mana and Organabo because of Surinamese overfishing in Guiana's territorial waters.
2	Adversarial HUMINT: confirmed corrupt port officials on the cartel's payroll in Cayenne	10 DEC 2016: Inform targeted officials in Cayenne to double their inspections because of an expected major cartel shipment within the next three months.
3	Adversarial CYBER: restricted social media monitoring	11–15 DEC 2016: Using own cyber capability, identify social media profiles of counternarcotics officials that have been penetrated by cartel hackers.
4	Adversarial OSINT monitoring capability	15–18 DEC 2016: Instigate several disruptions in Tele Guyane GSM service in and around Organabo. Plant a story in local media that mobile services in Organabo can be unstable over the next 6 weeks.
5	Adversarial SIGINT monitoring capability	19 DEC 2016 to 15 JAN 2017: Spoof (fake) increased coast guard patrol VHF traffic in and around Mana and Organabo.

(*Continued*)

TABLE 12-5 ■ (Continued)		
6	Adversarial HUMINT: confirmed corrupt official in the Ministry of Defense on cartel's payroll	20 DEC 2016: Inform targeted official of planning for special operations in and around the port of Tonate sometime in early JAN 2017. Have unit designations ready including a supporting "sniffer" dog section.
7	Adversarial HUMINT: confirmed corrupt Cayenne harbor officials	22 DEC 2016: Announce in-house an increase in local coast guard inspection personnel starting on 1 JAN 2017.
8	Adversarial OSINT: monitoring capability	23 DEC 2016: Have the Marine Travel Department issue a general warning for seafarers that the harbor radar station at Kourou is expected to be shut down 8–10 JAN 2017 for maintenance.
9	Adversarial HUMINT: confirmed corrupt harbor master in Mana	27 DEC 2016: Arrest corrupt Mana harbor master on suspicion of smuggling. Send a state investigator to Mana.
10	Adversarial CYBER: social media monitoring	30 DEC 2016: Use compromised profiles of counternarcotics officials on social media to post messages indicating they are being unexpectedly sent for 2 weeks to Cayenne.

Channel Management Exercise 12.2: Bangui Backroads

Scenario

The date is May 12, 2016. The Central African Republic has asked the United Nations for assistance in transporting a large amount of weapons-grade uranium out of the country to an undisclosed location in the United States. The move was prompted by the growing threat of radical insurgents in Bangui who have close ties with international terrorist networks. As the assigned joint task force J3 planner (operations), in close coordination with the intelligence section, you are to put together a deception plan to support the planned transport of the material from 1st Arrondissement in Bangui, approximately 8 km to the Bangui International Airport. Three possible routes have been put forward: Ave. de France, Ave. de Martyrs, and Route Nationale 2 (RN2). The route that will be used for the actual transport of the uranium is Ave. de Martyrs. The Central African government has already announced that the route will be closed to the public on the planned date for the delivery, October 4, 2016, due to the uranium transport. However, this could possibly play to your advantage in terms of planning a deception. The objective of the deception is to fix the insurgent focus and resources on Ave. de France and/or RN2. You have a timeline of approximately three months to work with.

Task

Compare and discuss abnormal congruences and incongruences between the channels presented in the draft story-line deception plan (Table 12-6) that could undermine the attempt to deceive the insurgents as to the route that will be used to transport the uranium to the airport.

Suggestion: Discuss in groups how you could improve the deception story projection by mitigating those identified abnormalities. Discuss if, and how, the announcement of the Central African government as to the planned route for uranium transport was exploited in the deception plan.

TABLE 12-6 ■ Bangui Backroads Deception Channel Tracker		
CH #	Targeted Insurgent Channel (Description)	Planned Story Projection
1	Adversarial HUMINT: local insurgent sympathizer surveillance	5 JUNE 2016: Initiate visible road improvement projects along Ave. de France between 1st Arrondissement and airport.
2	Adversarial HUMINT: local insurgent sympathizer surveillance	6 JULY 2016: US Special Operations Forces (SOF) team supporting the operation will conduct a visible route inspection on Ave. de France.
3	Adversarial HUMINT: confirmed insurgent sympathizer in the Ministry of Interior	18 JULY 2016: Plant rumors that the official transport plan is a deception.
4	Adversarial OSINT: local media monitoring	25 JULY 2016: Announce the establishment of two new police checkpoints along Ave. de France between 1st Arrondissement and Airport.
5	Adversarial OSINT: local media monitoring	13 AUG 2016: Plant public complaints over closing of Ave. de Martyrs.
6	Adversarial OSINT: local media monitoring	14 AUG 2016: Plant government response that they will reconsider the route choice.
7	Adversarial HUMINT: local insurgent sympathizer surveillance	1 SEPT–1 OCT 2016: Increase Foreign Legion reconnaissance company patrols on Ave. de France.
8	Adversarial SIGINT: basic VHF monitoring capability	15–30 SEPT 2016: Increase military/police VHF patrol traffic along RN2. Content should focus on training convoy support—with references to locations on Ave. de France.

(Continued)

TABLE 12-6 ■ (Continued)		
9	Adversarial HUMINT: local insurgent sympathizer surveillance	25–30 SEPT 2016: Practice flying surveillance drones over Ave. de France.
10	Adversarial HUMINT: confirmed insurgent sympathizers in the local police	3 OCT 2016: In-call local police and inform them to be ready to support a convoy on Ave. de France.

NOTE

1. A tear line is a short intelligence report that does not name a specific source in order to protect the collection method.

13

GENERAL DECEPTION PLANNING EXERCISES

This chapter contains exercises that require the participant to do deception planning. Some exercises call for two or three separate deception plans. These provide an option for a class to divide into teams, with each team developing and briefing one plan. Alternatively, each participant can develop all of the plans.

The exercises are designed to illustrate the use of deception in a wide range of transnational issues. Military operations are a part of some exercises, but the emphasis is on aspects other than traditional force-on-force operations. Chapter 14 covers purely military exercises.

Although the details presented vary from plan to plan, each deception plan should describe at least the following:

- Desired outcome

- Target(s)

- Story

- Channels to be used

- Timing of information

- Deconfliction analysis

EXERCISE 1: DERAILING A TRADE NEGOTIATION

You are the special assistant to the minister of industry and trade (MIT) in the country of Monopolitania. The ministry recently received a classified report from the country's intelligence service, the Monopolitania Intelligence Bureau (MIB). The report indicates that secret multilateral trade negotiations are under way involving the Philippines, Thailand, Vietnam, and Indonesia. The objective of the negotiations is to establish a free trade zone among these four countries for iron and steel products, computers and electronics, and chemical products.

Monopolitania is a major exporter of all these products to the four countries. The Philippines is a major importer of iron and steel products and chemicals. Thailand imports electronic integrated circuits, computers, and parts. Indonesia imports iron and steel. Vietnam imports steel products and electronics. The minister has concluded that the trade agreement, if signed, would severely impact all of these Monopolitanian export industries. He wants to ensure that the negotiations do not succeed, and has assigned you the task of ensuring that they fail.

Key Participants

The trade negotiations are taking place in Bangkok and are hosted by the Thai government. The key participants are listed below. The comments about their positions in the negotiations were made by a clandestine MIB source who acts as secretary to one of the ministers participating in the trade talks.

- Thailand's minister of trade recently took office and initiated the negotiations. He previously ran an industrial combine in Thailand and is known to be hostile to Monopolitania because of what he considers its unfair trade practices. He is reportedly dictatorial and arbitrary. The ministry employees reportedly detest him, and several senior ministry officials have recently transferred or retired. The minister is an avid user of Facebook and Twitter, and regularly posts pictures of himself and his family on his personal Facebook page.

- The Philippines' trade minister has no quarrel with Monopolitania; he simply is interested in getting the best deal for his country. A technocrat, he relies heavily on econometric models in making decisions. He recently acquired a trade model from a US source and is having it validated. Once he is satisfied that it is valid, he plans to run the simulation model, use the results to assess the economic impact on his country of the proposed agreement, and make his decisions accordingly.

- The Vietnamese minister is concerned about the likely impact of an agreement on his country's exports to Monopolitania. He has expressed a concern at the negotiations that Monopolitania could retaliate by blocking imports from the four countries when the agreement is announced but has seemed to accept the assurances from the other members that any such retaliation would hurt Monopolitania more than it would hurt Vietnam or the other participants.

- The Indonesian minister has insisted that the negotiations be kept secret until he has assessed the likely effect of an agreement on his economy. He is concerned that, if the agreement becomes public, he will be pressed to provide an impact statement that he does not have and will have to deal with internal opposition.

The MIB has a cyber operations branch that targets Internet servers and government computer installations in Thailand and the Philippines. It has a number of successful intrusion operations that could assist in targeting the negotiating teams. The MIB cyber branch

- has obtained access to the econometric model that the Philippine minister is currently validating,

- can access the Thai minister's personal Facebook and Twitter accounts,

- has succeeded in planting a Trojan in the Vietnamese minister's laptop that sends a copy of his outgoing emails to the MIB cyber operations branch (the minister uses the laptop only for personal emails, however).

Guidance

Your assignment is to prepare a deception operation, targeting each individual minister, that will cause the negotiations to collapse. Remember: Monopolitania is *not* the United States. Therefore, there are no restrictions on lying to the press and no concerns about unethical conduct. Because negotiations are ongoing, you have two days to craft the plan.

EXERCISE 2: PROTECTING DRUG CARTEL SHIPMENTS

This exercise requires the development of two deception plans to divert US attention away from a drug cartel's proposed novel methods for shipping drugs into the United States and exfiltrating profits. Though based loosely on factual information, the exercise scenario is notional.

You are employed as the intelligence officer for Carlos "el Chacal" Gutiérrez, the head of the Sinaloa drug cartel. El Chacal is desperately trying to find a way to deal with declining cartel revenues and has turned to you for help.

His cartel has long been a leader in the distribution of Colombian cocaine, Mexican marijuana, methamphetamine, and Mexican and Southeast Asian heroin into the United States. In its early years, the cartel relied on automobiles, buses, tractor trailers, and rail cars for bulk delivery. As those channels were methodically shut down by US drug enforcement actions, the cartel switched to airborne, seaborne, and even subterranean delivery. Small aircraft, flying low to avoid US radar coverage, delivered drugs to airports in the South and Southwest. "Go-fast" boats and small submarines (semi-submersibles) moved drugs via the sea route from Colombia to Mexico and from there into California. Tunnels—some as long as 700 meters and as deep as 30 meters—were dug beneath the US–Mexican border near Tijuana and used to move both bulk drugs and illegal immigrants into the United States.

In the last two years, though, these channels for delivery have been severely restricted and losses of drugs in transit have increased dramatically. Tunnels beneath the border near Tijuana are being discovered quickly, in some cases during their first use. The US Navy and US Coast Guard are routinely intercepting the cartel's sea shipments, with consequent loss of cargo and crew. It has become harder to find crews willing to attempt the sea delivery route. The airborne delivery route has been basically shut down. Radar detection and interception of aircraft (including unmanned aerial vehicles) now is routine. Other cartels are having the same problem. The result is that the wholesale price of cocaine has skyrocketed in the last year. Gutiérrez is dealing with the most lucrative market the drug trade has ever seen, but he needs to be able to deliver drugs in bulk to meet the demand.

Gutiérrez can afford to lose 75 percent of his drug shipments—the loss rate up until two years ago—and still make a substantial profit. But his current loss rate is approaching 90 percent, and the resulting low profit margin is unacceptable over the long term. Furthermore, the cartel is suffering substantial losses in its attempts to move the profits back across the border into Mexico. Gutiérrez can launder the funds once they are in Mexico, but the US Drug Enforcement Administration (DEA) increasingly has had success in intercepting the profits before they can be exfiltrated.

Gutiérrez believes that he has the solution to both problems, in the form of a new way to clandestinely move goods in both directions across the border. He has two options for increasing the quantities of drugs delivered. One option makes use of an unmanned underwater vehicle (UUV). The other option relies on two unmanned aerial vehicles (UAVs). Both options result in about the same delivery rate—about 400 kg/day. The current street prices are $110/gram for cocaine and $245/gram for heroin. Either option would generate income for the cartel, at the current street prices, of between $44 million and $98 million per day.

Gutiérrez can afford to pursue one of the two options—to acquire one UUV or to acquire two UAVs. The problem is that increased quantities of drugs available on US streets will be quickly noticed by the US DEA, and the agency will make a determined effort to find out how the drugs are entering the country. The deception needs to keep the DEA and its partner agencies looking in the wrong places for entry routes. El Chacal wants a detailed deception plan to protect each of his proposed options.

Sea Delivery Option

This option calls for a UUV to onload cargo from a ship off the Costa Rican or Mexican coasts, then submerge and travel autonomously to a predesignated point off California or Oregon, and rendezvous just offshore with a pleasure boat. The boat crew would offload narcotics cargo and onload drug profits for the return trip. The UUV would then make the return trip to its departure point for maintenance, fresh fuel cells, and a new cargo load. The UUV would therefore stay continuously in the water.

The UUV is a modified copy of the Talisman UUV design first produced by the Underwater Systems Division of BAE Systems. It features an innovatively shaped carbon fiber composite hull, with internal pressure vessels containing the electronics systems and payload. The hull was designed to be stealthy against both passive and active sonar. The vehicle weighs approximately 2,000 kg without cargo and is approximately 6 meters long by 2.5 meters wide. Once loading is completed, it dives to a depth of 200 meters and stays submerged until reaching its destination.

The primary concern is detection en route. If the United States suspects that a UUV is being used, and has a general idea of the delivery route, then the UUV is likely to be intercepted and captured or sunk. Although it is silent and stealthy during normal operation, some acoustic techniques (discussed later) make detection likely if a thorough search is made for it.

Airborne Delivery Option

Airborne delivery relies on two UAVs purchased from Iran. They are Iranian copies of a US RQ-170 UAV, which was brought down over Iran near the Afghan border in December 2011. The Iranians later reverse-engineered the drone. The UAVs feature a stealth design that is difficult for conventional radar to detect. The drones are about 3 meters long with a 20 meter wingspan. They can carry an 800 kg payload.

The operational plan calls for the drone to be launched from a different Mexican airfield on each mission, to avoid creating a noticeable pattern. The drone would fly nighttime missions to one of six small airfields (having sod runways) located in Arizona or New Mexico, well away from the Mexican border. There the drug payload would be offloaded, drug profits onloaded, and the drone refueled for a return mission the next night. At all times when on the ground, the drone would be concealed in a barn at both ends of the flight route.

Cartel OODA

HUMINT: You believe that the DEA has recruited one of the cartel's enforcers in Tijuana as a source for reporting on cartel activities. Gutiérrez wants to eliminate him but on your recommendation has reluctantly agreed to keep the man alive—for now—so that you can use him as an unwitting channel for passing misleading information to the DEA. You do not know how credible the source is in the DEA's eyes.

SIGINT: You have a network in place for monitoring DEA radio communications in the Southwest. The communications are encrypted, but you have mapped the DEA network and have been able to conduct traffic analysis on it. You are often able to identify the location and nature of DEA tactical operations using traffic analysis.

OSINT: You have two staffers who monitor news wires and Internet accounts of "drug busts" in the United States. These accounts have provided valuable insights into DEA, Border Patrol, and Coast Guard methods for identifying and intercepting drug shipments.

US OODA

Although your title is "intelligence officer," most of your work to date has been counterintelligence, that is, assessing and countering official US and Mexican governmental intelligence efforts to target the cartel. The primary threat, the United States, has deployed a number of sensors to monitor drug trafficking from Mexico and Central America. You have developed threat analyses on the following intelligence sources and sensors.

HUMINT

Although you are aware of one DEA HUMINT source in your organization, you suspect that the Mexican government or the DEA has at least one other source that you have not yet identified.

OTH Radars

Two US Navy high-frequency (HF) over-the-horizon (OTH) radars known as ROTHR (Relocatable Over-the-Horizon Radar) are operated at Corpus Christi, Texas, and Chesapeake, Virginia. The two radars provide coverage of the Caribbean Sea and portions of the Atlantic Ocean and the Gulf of Mexico. The radars are operated full time in a counternarcotics surveillance role. They can detect small aircraft flying at any altitude. However, you have consulted with radar experts who believe that the UAV is not detectable by these radars—or, at the most, is detectable only intermittently. Although the present ROTHR coverage does not include the likely flight routes for cartel UAVs, the DEA could have the radars reaimed to cover those routes if they suspect the existence of UAV flights.

Aerostats

The US Tethered Aerostat Radar System (TARS) is designed to detect low-level air, maritime, and surface smugglers and narcotics traffickers. TARS provides coverage of the US–Mexico border, the Florida Straits, and the Northern Caribbean. These aerostats resemble blimps but are raised and lowered by tether to adjust to weather conditions and for maintenance. The sensor suite is known to include a radar that can detect small aircraft and small boats. You suspect that it also has SIGINT equipment that is used to monitor communications. Six aerostats are deployed at Yuma and Fort Huachuca, Arizona; at Deming, New Mexico; and at Marfa, Eagle Pass, and Rio Grande City, Texas.

After talking with technical experts, you have concluded that the stealth UAV probably could not be detected by the TARS radars operating in normal mode, unless the UAV comes within 18 miles (30 km) of a radar. But your expert has advised that, if the *Yanquis* suspect that stealth aircraft are being used, they probably could network the radars using a technique called "bistatic radar" (using one TARS transmitter in conjunction with the receiver on another TARS) to detect the UAV.

Tunnel Detection Technologies

The US Department of Homeland Security (DHS) has developed sensors that make use of seismic and infrared technology to detect tunnels. One such method reportedly uses buried fiber optic cables to sense the vibrations associated with tunnel excavation. You do not know the extent of deployment of these sensors but have concluded that they are deployed and effective, based on the rate of tunnel discovery.

Sea Surveillance: P-3 Aircraft

Drug shipments via ships and mini-submersibles are typically detected by US Navy P-3 aircraft. The P-3 carries a radar that can identify both surface ships and semi-submersibles (when surfaced) at ranges of more than 60 miles (100 km). The P-3 crews conduct patrols over the Caribbean and eastern Pacific that total about 6,000 patrol hours annually.

All P-3 flights are intelligence driven and planned by a joint task force. A typical flight is designed to conduct surveillance of a designated search area. If the P-3 spots a suspect craft, the aircraft will typically stay out of the ship's visual range, taking pictures of the vessel and its cargo. The P-3 usually continues to monitor the suspect craft until a US Coast Guard or US Navy ship interdicts the craft. If interdiction is not possible, the P-3 will overfly the boat at close range, usually resulting in the crew tossing the drugs overboard.

Cyber Operations

A DEA cyber operations team is believed to be responsible for some recent diversions of cartel funds into accounts that may have been DEA controlled. The team is also suspected of identifying cartel funds-laundering efforts.

Undersea Acoustic Sensing

The US Coast Guard and US Navy have acoustic sensor systems that may be capable of detecting a UUV. You are aware of two such sensors that pose a threat:

- The US Coast Guard Underwater Imaging System is an active (transmit and receive) 3-D sonar system designed for use in maritime security, port and harbor maintenance, search and recovery, and detecting and classifying intruders along the US coastline.

- The SURTASS (Surveillance Towed-Array Sensor System) is a US Navy long-range sonar system. It features an array of hydrophones that are towed behind a ship. The sonar array can operate in either passive or active mode. The active mode is used when passive detection performance is insufficient. You suspect that SURTASS has been used in the past to detect the cartel's semi-submersibles and identify them for interception, but you cannot prove that.

SIGINT

The TARS aerostats are believed to carry SIGINT equipment that can detect and track radars operating in their areas of coverage. They also likely collect COMINT from cell phones and push-to-talk radios. The DEA also has intercept stations at several locations in California, New Mexico, Arizona, and Texas. These stations are believed to monitor the cartel's cell phone traffic.

Guidance

You are to develop two detailed deception plans—one for each drug transport and funds recovery option. The deception must lead US enforcement teams away from the actual method and route used. Gutiérrez will choose which new transport to engage with based on the deception plan that he believes is most likely to succeed.

EXERCISE 3: TAKING DOWN THE FORDOW URANIUM ENRICHMENT FACILITY

This exercise involves deception planning by Israel's Mossad to protect the source of a cyber attack against a clandestine uranium enrichment operation at Fordow, Iran. Though based loosely on factual information, the exercise scenario is notional. You are the Mossad agent in charge of planning the deception.

Fordow Background

The Fordow fuel enrichment facility is located 20 miles (32 km) northeast of the Iranian city of Qom, near the village of Fordow. Iran secretly began construction of the facility in 2006. In September 2009, US, French, and British officials notified the International Atomic Energy Agency (IAEA) that Fordow was a uranium enrichment facility and presented evidence to support their claim. Fordow at that time was Iran's second uranium enrichment facility, the other one being located at Natanz.

Fordow is considered to be a hardened facility, designed to withstand conventional airstrikes. The original uranium enrichment area at Fordow is buried in tunnels within a mountain. Satellite imagery has established that construction began between June 2006 and July 2007. Iran had originally planned to install highly efficient advanced centrifuges at Fordow. But after the plant's existence was disclosed to the IAEA, Iran announced that it instead would install the older and less efficient IR-1 centrifuges. In January 2012 Iran said it had begun uranium enrichment at Fordow, producing 20-percent enriched uranium. Under an interim nuclear deal with Iran concluded in November 2013, production of enriched uranium supposedly ceased at Fordow, and Iran agreed to turn its stockpile of enriched uranium there into a form that is less of a proliferation risk.[1]

Under the Joint Comprehensive Plan of Action (JCPOA) agreement signed in July 2015, Iran agreed to eliminate its stockpile of medium-enriched uranium (20-percent enriched), cut its stockpile of low-enriched uranium, and reduce by about two-thirds the number of its gas centrifuges for the next 13 years. The agreement specifies that no enrichment is permitted at Fordow for 15 years. The facility instead is to be converted into a nuclear research center. The facility was designed to hold 3,000 centrifuges. Under the agreement, the site is limited to a total of 1,044 centrifuges. The agreement specifies that the purpose of centrifuges installed at the site is to produce radioisotopes for nonmilitary use.

Recent Events

Mossad intelligence has determined that Iran is working to evade restrictions and produce enough fissile material for at least one nuclear warhead. The Iranians have expanded the underground facility and installed approximately 6,000 of the newest and most efficient centrifuges for uranium enrichment, with the goal of producing sufficient 90-percent enriched U-235 for a nuclear weapon. The facility began operation 2 months ago.

The primary source of Mossad's intelligence is an agent in the facility. "Rafael" (his Mossad codename) is a 28-year-old Iranian physicist who joined the Fordow team 2 years ago. Six months ago, at a scientific conference in Cairo, he was approached in a "false flag" operation, ostensibly by Saudi intelligence, and was offered a substantial sum to report on activities at Fordow. He agreed, indicating as a reason for cooperating that he opposed the idea of developing nuclear weapons that he fears would be used against innocent people. He considers himself a moderate Muslim and secretly opposes the Ayatollah-dominated government of Iran.

Since his recruitment, Rafael has provided plans of the facility, details on the progress of enriched U-235 production, and details about the computers and software that operate the centrifuges. The centrifuge control system is on a separate intranet accessible only by four key people at the facility (see "Key Personnel at the Fordow Facility" section). This intranet is protected by a firewall from the main Fordow network (which has no physical connection to the outside world). Because the plant's main network is not connected to the outside, the only way to introduce malware is by an insider with access to the computer network. Rafael has access to the main network but not to the centrifuge control intranet.

Based on information provided by Rafael, the Israelis have produced a malware package, similar to Stuxnet, but tailored to function with the Fordow plant's computers and software. Rafael has agreed to download the malware onto a thumb drive at an Internet café in Qom, then introduce it into one of the computers that connect to the main network. All electronic storage media brought into the facility are required to be virus checked before being accessed by the network, but Rafael believes that he can easily skip the checking process.

The malware makes use of what is called a VPN pivot. Once introduced into the main network, the malware "pivots" to bypass the centrifuge intranet firewall. It then infects the centrifuge control system and eliminates all evidence of its existence in both networks. It is designed to disrupt production by causing the centrifuges to spin out of control and self-destruct. The trigger date and time for the disruption is to be set by Rafael after he loads the malware into the main network.

Israeli scientists expect the resulting damage to include explosions, fires, and the release of enriched U-235 gases. Due to the facility's subterranean location, they do not know whether evidence of an explosion or fire will reach the surface. They do expect the gaseous component to eventually escape into the atmosphere. They also expect a number of casualties among workers at the plant. The malware is designed to erase any evidence of its presence after it has done its work—in case the computing facility survives.

Rafael has agreed to introduce the malware only if he can be assured that the resulting investigation will not center on him. He also does not want to be in the facility when the malware is triggered because of uncertainty about the possible collateral damage, but has agreed to report on the result later.

Mossad's counterintelligence unit remains suspicious of Rafael. They argue that he was too readily recruited, the reason he gave for spying was suspect, and he has not been fully vetted by independent sources. They are concerned that he might be a double agent, actually working for Iranian intelligence. The Mossad commander of the operation has decided nevertheless to proceed, since all of Rafael's reporting to date appears to be authentic.

Key Personnel at the Fordow Facility

Rafael has identified four key persons at the Fordow facility who have access to the centrifuge control system: Dr. Ranjbar Saeed, director of the plant; his chief scientist, Dr. Mousavi Ali Hatef; chief of the computer center, Dr. Mehran Asgharian; and Hassan Gharmeei, the lead software engineer. The Mossad operational commander has indicated a preference that as many key people as possible be in the facility when the malware is triggered.

Ranjbar Saeed

Prior to his appointment as plant director at Fordow, Ranjbar Saeed was the chief scientist in charge of fuel enrichment at Natanz. Saeed is known to be a strong supporter of Iran's nuclear weapons program. IAEA files indicate that Saeed was the head of the Institute of Applied Physics, which acted as a cover for scientific work on a possible Iranian nuclear weapons program. He previously chaired the physics department at Tehran's Imam Hossein University, which is linked to the Iranian Revolutionary Guard Corps and to work on nuclear weaponization. Saeed has also reportedly worked at Shahid Beheshti University, sanctioned by the European Union for associations with Iran's missile and nuclear programs. His name has been associated with the Iranian Nuclear Society, which was previously called Iran's Coordination Committee for nuclear specialists, allegedly founded by the Ministry of Defense to employ university professors and scientists in defense projects. He was a deputy chair of that group.

Mousavi Ali Hatef

Mousavi Ali Hatef has previously been linked to Iran's efforts to develop a nuclear weapon. According to an expert close to the IAEA, he was a key scientist in the Iranian fuel enrichment program at Natanz. Hatef personally directed work on the design and operation of more advanced centrifuges, this expert added. Hatef is a devout Muslim, dedicated to the Iranian Revolution, and a friend of the Ayatollah.

Hatef was an early addition to the United Nations sanctions list under Security Council resolution 1747 in 2007 as a person "involved in nuclear or ballistic missile activities." These sanctions restrict his travel and impose an asset freeze on any international holdings. He was subsequently placed under European Union sanctions. Although the Security Council did not provide the exact reason for his being added to the sanctions list, according to the expert close to the IAEA, his involvement in the Iranian nuclear program led to his sanctioning.

Mehran Asgharian

Mehran Asgharian graduated from the Iran University of Science and Technology with a doctorate in computer engineering. He is currently the chief of the computing section at Fordow and oversees both the hardware and software operations at the facility. Rafael frequently visits Asgharian's office to discuss process details with him.

Hassan Gharmeei

Hassan Gharmeei also graduated from the Iran University of Science and Technology with a bachelor's degree in computer engineering. He is responsible for development and maintenance of the software that controls the centrifuge operation. Rafael has worked closely with Gharmeei on several occasions during the control software development process and considers Gharmeei a friend. Like Rafael, Gharmeei is a moderate Muslim.

Iranian OODA

The Ministry of Intelligence and Security (MOIS) employs all means at its disposal to protect the Islamic Revolution of Iran, utilizing such methods as infiltrating internal opposition groups, monitoring domestic threats and expatriate dissent, arresting alleged spies and dissidents, exposing conspiracies deemed threatening, and maintaining liaison with other foreign intelligence agencies as well as with organizations that protect the Islamic Republic's interests around the world.

All organizations must share information with the MOIS. The ministry oversees all covert operations. It usually executes internal operations itself, but the Quds Force of the Islamic Revolutionary Guards Corps for the most part handles extraterritorial operations such as sabotage, assassinations, and espionage. Although the Quds Force operates independently, it shares the information it collects with MOIS.

SIGINT: Iran's ability to collect SIGINT information from external sources is limited. Its signals intelligence capability represents only a limited threat because it is still under development.

CYBER: In the summer of 2011, Iran created a "cyber command" in order to block incoming cyber attacks and to carry out cyber attacks in reprisal. The MOIS Security Directorate would likely call on experts from its cyber command to help in an investigation of events at Fordow.

Counterintelligence: The Security Directorate has the assignment of uncovering conspiracy, subversion, espionage, sabotage, and sedition against the independence, security, and territorial integrity of the Islamic Republic of Iran. Its director, Mahmoud Rafipoor, graduated from the Qum-based Haghani School, a Shi'a school controlled by a group of hard-line right-wing clerics. He has a law degree and has served as a prosecutor before the Islamic Revolutionary Court. He is a cleric with a conservative political and religious ideology. In his role as head of the Security Directorate, he would be responsible for conducting an investigation and deciding whom to arrest for suspected sabotage at Fordow.

The ministry has a Department of Disinformation, which is in charge of creating and waging psychological warfare against the enemies of the Islamic Republic.

Israeli OODA

HUMINT: Mossad has no sources in Fordow other than Rafael. It has one source who frequently visits the city of Qom, where the key personnel live.

IMINT: Israel has a suite of imagery satellites, the Ofek (or Ofeq) suite. The following members of that suite provide imagery of Fordow on a regular basis:

- Ofek 5 and Ofek 7 are visible imagers offering better than one-half meter of image resolution.

- Ofek 9, launched in 2010, is a multispectral imager. Like Ofek 5 and Ofek 7, Ofek 9 offers a resolution that is substantially better than one-half meter.

- Ofek 10, also known as TecSAR, is a radar reconnaissance satellite. It is equipped with a high-resolution synthetic aperture radar that is capable of collecting imagery at night and through clouds.

SIGINT: Much of Israel's SIGINT collection is done by a group known as Unit 8200 at its Urim base in the Negev Desert. The base features a number of satellite communications intercept dishes. Urim's collection is focused on phone calls, emails, and financial transaction details originating in the Middle East and North Africa. Urim's computers perform automated searches on intercepted traffic to detect words, email addresses, and phone numbers of interest. The product is then transferred to Unit 8200's headquarters at Herzliya. From there, the information is translated and reported to the Israeli Defence Force (IDF) headquarters and to Mossad.

CYBER: In addition to its SIGINT operations, Unit 8200 also operates a cyber collection effort targeted on Arab countries and Iran. The unit targets Internet forums, blogs, and darknets. It also monitors Twitter and Facebook activity by key Iranian officials and defense-related scientists.

The IDF has several elite teams of cyber warriors who engage in both cyber offense and defense to support military operations. The teams target Iranian missile and nuclear-related establishments for cyber intrusion and intelligence collection as well. Over the last year, the teams have had several successes against military targets, but they report increasing difficulty in penetrating these targets as the Iranians have developed better cyber defenses.

OSINT: Mossad obtains news reporting from a wide range of sources, focusing on nearby countries that pose a threat to Israel. It closely monitors Iranian TV broadcasts and newspapers.

Guidance

The Mossad operations commander has directed you to prepare a deception plan, having three objectives:

1. Although the commander has concluded that Rafael probably is not a double agent, he nevertheless wants independent confirmation that the attack actually took place and what the outcome was, in as much detail as possible.

2. He wants to protect Rafael from discovery because he needs the follow-up report on the results of the cyber attack, and he wants Rafael to survive for future use in reporting on any subsequent attempts to reconstitute the facility.

3. If possible, he would like to have suspicion fall on one or more of the key scientists (listed previously), ideally to have them permanently removed from the facility and executed—assuming that they survive in the aftermath of the centrifuge destruction.

The commander is willing to have any modifications made to the malware that would help the deception to succeed before passing it on to Rafael.

EXERCISE 4: COUNTERING ISRAELI EFFORTS TO TAKE DOWN FORDOW

This exercise makes use of the facts in Exercise 3, "Taking Down the Fordow Uranium Enrichment Facility," with the modifications described here.

You are assigned to the Security Directorate of Iran's Ministry of Intelligence and Security (MOIS). Your directorate has a double agent named Jamal Farghadani who Israeli intelligence believes works at the Fordow facility. Six months ago the directorate offered Farghadani as bait and is pleased with the result to date. To establish Farghadani's credibility, he has been provided with chicken feed[2] to be passed to the Israelis, and four months ago he also provided them with an altered facility plan and false details of the computer hardware and software.

Farghadani has received from the Israelis a software file, with instructions to load it onto a thumb drive and insert it into the Fordow main computer system. The file contains malware that is designed to infect the plant's centrifuge control system. Your experts have reviewed the malware and believe that it would indeed cause the destruction of the plant centrifuges—if the details about the plant software that the Israelis received had been accurate.

The MOIS minister wants the Israelis to believe that their plan succeeded and that Fordow is out of operation for the foreseeable future. He has turned to you with instructions to make that happen.

Iranian OODA

This is your understanding of your own Iranian OODA—which differs from the Israeli view presented in Exercise 3. *Disregard the corresponding information from that exercise.*

HUMINT: You are aware that the Islamic Revolutionary Guard Corps—Quds Force has an officer clandestinely operating in Jerusalem who runs an agent network in the Israeli capital. You do not have any details about the available sources, but the director of the operation has agreed to use his sources, if they have the necessary access, to either pass information or to obtain information. Based on discussions with your friends in Quds Force, you suspect that the sources are low level, better positioned to carry out covert action than to collect intelligence or to feed misleading information to the Israelis.

IMINT: Iran relies primarily on purchases of commercial imagery for imagery-derived intelligence. It obtains imagery of Israeli targets from Russian imaging satellites.

SIGINT: Three clandestine SIGINT stations are located in the Al-Jazirah region in northern Syria and on the Golan Heights. The stations are operated jointly by Iranians and Hezbollah insurgents, and are targeted on Lebanon and Israel. They collect some cell phone traffic from Israel and Israeli military communications that use push-to-talk radios.

CYBER: In the aftermath of the Stuxnet debacle, Iran developed a cyber operations capability that rivals that of Russia and China. It has a capability to conduct information operations against a number of Israeli commercial websites and has had some success against government websites.

OSINT: MOIS routinely obtains and analyzes the content of Israeli newspapers and news websites.

Counterintelligence: Iran has developed a comprehensive counterintelligence system to protect its nuclear program. But Israel has occasionally succeeded in infiltrating the system, and on at least one occasion was able to put an agent into Iran's intelligence system.

Israeli OODA

This is Israel's OODA as viewed by the MOIS—which differs from the Israeli view presented in the previous exercise. *Disregard the corresponding information from that exercise.*

IMINT: Israel has a suite of imagery satellites, the Ofek (or Ofeq) suite. The satellites are believed to image government and defense installations in Iran on every pass:

- Ofek 5 and Ofek 7 are visible imagers reportedly offering better than one-half meter of image resolution.

- Ofek 9, launched in 2010, reportedly is a multispectral imager. Like Ofek 5 and Ofek 7, Ofek 9 offers a resolution that is substantially better than one-half meter.

- Ofek 10, also known as TecSAR, is a radar reconnaissance satellite. It is reportedly equipped with a high-resolution synthetic aperture radar that is capable of collecting imagery at night and through clouds.

SIGINT: Much of Israel's SIGINT collection is done by a group known as Unit 8200 at its Urim base in the Negev Desert. The focus of Urim's collection reportedly is phone calls, emails, and financial transaction details originating in the Middle East and North Africa. The base is believed to monitor satellite communications. Iranian intelligence assesses that Urim monitors all transmissions of the Iransat3 satellite. This geostationary satellite provides radio and television broadcasts of Iranian news and the Iranian viewpoint to listeners and viewers throughout the Middle East. It also carries domestic and international telecommunications and Internet services.

CYBER: In addition to its SIGINT operations, Unit 8200 also is believed to operate a cyber collection effort targeted on Arab countries and Iran. Iranian intelligence assesses that Unit 8200 targets Internet forums and blogs. Your cyber defense teams are reporting frequent attempts to hack into Iranian defense and intelligence networks, and are almost weekly discovering a successful intrusion into other government networks.

OSINT: Israel is believed to monitor Iranian TV and newspaper media routinely, including broadcasts from Iransat3.

Guidance

Your assignment is to develop a deception plan to convince the Israelis that their malware has successfully wrecked the centrifuges. Your plan must include some means to ensure that Israeli intelligence has bought in to the deception.

EXERCISE 5: SUPPORTING A NEO EVACUATION

This exercise features the development of a multi-INT deception plan to cover a noncombatant evacuation operation (NEO) in the city of Tripoli, Libya. It is fictional but is based loosely on real organizations.

Background

Two weeks ago, a Daesh contingent conducted a surprise attack on Tripoli from the sea, seizing much of Tripoli harbor. The attack was launched by Daesh units stationed in Sirte, Libya. The attackers had support from Daesh cells in Tripoli. The attack is being resisted by fighters from the pro-Islamist militias known collectively as Libya Dawn, who control most of the Tripoli area and serve as the military enforcement arm of the current Tripoli government.

During the last week, Daesh units have mounted a series of attacks in Tripoli from their harbor positions. They currently control the entirety of Tripoli harbor, as shown in Figure 13-1. Libya Dawn militias control the rest of the area shown, though their level of "control" is quite loose.

The city appears to be descending into chaos, and local residents are panicked. The government of Tripoli, the General National Congress (GNC), has fled the

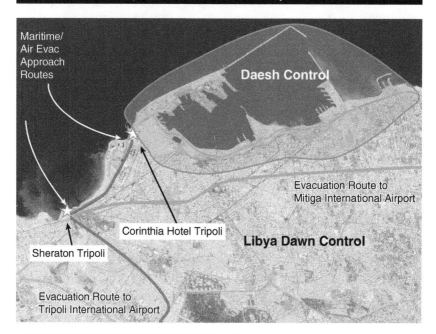

FIGURE 13-1 ■ Tripoli Areas of Control and Proposed Evacuation Routes

Source: Public Domain map, retrieved from https://commons.wikimedia.org/w/index.php?curid= 660014.

city in the face of Daesh advances. Libya Dawn forces remain in the city and outnumber the Daesh force, but Daesh is better organized and equipped.

Approximately 950 Westerners, including 134 American, 256 German, 158 French, and 312 British citizens, among others, have taken refuge in two hotels shown in the figure. Libya Dawn forces have refused to allow those trapped to leave either hotel, claiming that they cannot guarantee the safety of anyone found outside the hotels. Intelligence assessments have concluded that leaders of the various Libya Dawn factions are in disagreement about what to do with the trapped Westerners. Some factions want to use them as bargaining chips; others appear willing to let Daesh capture them, arguing that the result would be NATO action against Daesh in Libya.

A seaborne NATO joint task force (JTF) has been established and is currently en route to Tripoli, expected to arrive off the coast in two days. The JTF is charged with conducting a noncombatant evacuation operation (NEO) of foreigners trapped in the two hotels. The JTF commander has received three different proposals from his subordinate commanders on how to conduct the NEO. All proposals involve sending an advance special operations team into both hotels to protect civilians trapped there and to coordinate the evacuation.

- The US commander proposes a landing on the coast by contingents from Task Force 62, a US Marine Corps Expeditionary Unit (MEU), following the two routes shown in Figure 13-1. The marines would then clear a path to the hotels and conduct a seaborne evacuation of those trapped in the hotels. The commander notes that both hotels are very close to the beach and readily accessible for a landing party. Other JTF commanders object that Daesh units are well positioned to respond to any approach from the sea; Daesh snipers have a clear view of the Corinthia Hotel landing zone; and this will be a too-obvious evacuation route.

- The UK commander proposes using helicopters to conduct an evacuation from the hotel rooftops, using much the same approach routes as proposed for the MEU. Because of the number of evacuees, the objection is that this would take many flights over an extended period, likely alerting Daesh to attack the helicopters with man-portable air defense systems (MANPADS).

- The German commander proposes using German and British Special Forces units deployed from Malta to escort evacuees from the two hotels to Tripoli International Airport, either using civilian transportation in the hotel vicinity that has been requisitioned for the purpose, or using armored vehicles flown into the airport. An alternative evacuation route was considered, along the Al Amrus Highway to Tripoli's active civil airport: Mitiga International Airport, located about 5 miles (8 km) east of Tripoli's city center. The alternative was rejected because of the risks involved in transiting a route close to Daesh-held territory. The two proposed evacuation routes are shown in Figure 13-1. Planners are concerned that the evacuation aircraft landings at Tripoli International could be observed by Daesh and by Libya Dawn units, and that the land evacuation route could encounter resistance from Libya Dawn fighters.

The JTF commander has concluded that, no matter which option is selected, it will be essential to conduct a deception to misdirect Daesh and Libya Dawn forces away from the actual evacuation to improve the chances of success for the NEO. He has asked for a detailed and complete deception plan to support each of the three operations.

Daesh Background

The Daesh commander in Tripoli is Abdul Sa'ad al-Tajuri. He reportedly was the mastermind behind several attacks on government forces and civilians in the Sirte region. Associates describe him as brutal, short tempered, impulsive, and suspicious, bordering on paranoiac about both external and internal threats. As a unit commander in Sirte, he was responsible for numerous public beheadings and hanging men in orange jumpsuits from scaffolding in what he called "crucifixions" for alleged crimes including blasphemy, sorcery, and spying.

Tajuri appears determined not to allow Westerners trapped in the two hotels to escape, though his plans for them remain unknown. In Internet communications monitored by the NATO SIGINT units, Tajuri has ordered all units in the Tripoli area to be on alert for an airborne or seaborne attempt to rescue foreigners in the two hotels.

The areas of Daesh control are shown in Figure 13-1. Tajuri has positioned snipers close to the Corinthia Hotel, and Libya Dawn units near the hotel have taken some casualties from sniper fire.

Tajuri is intimately familiar with a previous NEO in Libya. It was a large-scale military operation for the evacuation of foreign nationals from Libya between February 26 and March 3, 2011. During that time a joint task force of the British and German military removed several hundred foreigners from the country. The German part of the operation, Operation Pegasus, used C-160 transport aircraft to evacuate 262 people, including 125 Germans, from the Nafurah airstrip in eastern Libya. Among those evacuated were the employees of the BASF subsidiary Wintershall, which operated oil production facilities in Libya. A British operation, nicknamed Operation Deference, used C-130 aircraft to evacuate some 300 British and other foreign oil workers from the eastern Libyan desert.

Daesh OODA

Daesh units now are well positioned to observe activity at the Corinthia Hotel Tripoli. Unconfirmed reports indicate that a Daesh cell also has the Sheraton Tripoli under observation. Daesh monitors CNN and Al-Jazeera broadcasts about the crisis.

Daesh SIGINT units in the area make use of commercially available French SIGINT equipment and captured Russian SIGINT equipment. They are believed to be able to monitor radio traffic from shipping in the area; hand-held two-way radio traffic; cell phones; and air-to-ground communications from commercial and military aircraft. Daesh also reportedly monitors Internet traffic to and from both hotels. The possibility exists that the SIGINT unit will be able to detect the approach of the JTF by monitoring the ship radar and ship-to-ship communications.

It is believed that Daesh SIGINT units also are able to monitor at least the Libya Dawn two-way radio traffic, and possibly their cell phone traffic as well.

Some Libya Dawn units in Tripoli probably have been infiltrated by Daesh agents, but there are no details on specific infiltrations.

Libya Dawn Background

Libya Dawn is a grouping of pro-Islamist militias that in summer 2014 attacked Tripoli International Airport and went on to seize large parts of the capital. The militia alliance can be viewed as the "armed forces" of the GNC, the former parliament that was reconvened in Tripoli as a rogue government. Libya Dawn controls most of Tripoli and the surrounding region. It comprises a number of small militias operating within their communities, able to police and defend their territory but poorly equipped for taking a broader offensive. Some militias, however, reportedly have acquired military aircraft and antiaircraft weaponry. Their position regarding the NEO is not known; but some militia leaders may resist attempts to evacuate foreign noncombatants, regarding them as bargaining chips for recognition of the GNC.

Libya Dawn OODA

The Libya Dawn forces are not known to use the Internet, but they coordinate operations using hand-held walkie-talkies and cell phones—both of which the coalition forces are able to monitor. Libya Dawn monitors CNN and Al-Jazeera broadcasts about the crisis.

Zintan Brigades

The powerful anti-Islamist Zintan militia or Zintan brigades support the internationally recognized government of Libya (the Government of National Accord, or GNA) and have clashed on numerous occasions with Libya Dawn. The group is equally hostile to Daesh but has not previously engaged Daesh units.

On July 14, 2014, Tripoli International Airport was the site of a fierce battle between Libya Dawn forces and the Zintan militia, leaving the airport facilities almost completely destroyed. The airport has been closed since then, but the runways remain operational. The Zintan militia currently has units in the region surrounding the airport; the units moved in after Libya Dawn militias moved back into the center of Tripoli to deal with the threat from Daesh.

Jilani Dahesh is the Zintan militia commander of forces at Tripoli International Airport. He reportedly is on good terms with many Libya Dawn commanders, arguing that an alliance is essential to overcoming the Daesh threat. He is willing to assist coalition forces in the NEO. He is accessible to NATO units via radio or cell phone contact, but it is likely that his communications are monitored by Libya Dawn and possibly by Daesh as well.

NATO Force

German units afloat include frigates *Brandenburg* and *Rheinland-Pfalz* as well as the task force supply ship *Berlin* and the fleet service boat *Oker*. The Germans have three C-160 aircraft (each with the capacity to carry 95 passengers) on standby in Malta that are available to support the NEO. A Bundeswehr Special Forces team (*Kommando Spezialkräfte*) of 400 troops is on standby in Malta.

British units include four C-130 aircraft (each with the capacity to carry 92 passengers) and a 500-man special operations contingent, also on Malta.

A US Navy strike group from the Sixth Fleet is the main force supporting the operation. It includes the following:

- The aircraft carrier USS *Harry S. Truman.*

- Task Force 61, comprised of approximately three amphibious ships and their embarked landing craft. From these ships, US Marine ground forces can move ashore by sea and air in amphibious assault or emergency evacuation missions.

- Task Force 62, a 1,900-man Marine Expeditionary Unit (MEU). The MEU is equipped with armor, artillery, and transport helicopters that enable it to conduct operations ashore, or evacuate civilians from troubled areas.

The JTF intelligence assessment is that both organized and impromptu resistance can be expected in the form of ambushes and attacks featuring small arms and RPG fire. The local civilian population is estimated to be on the order of one million, many of whom are in the process of fleeing the city. The JTF commander accordingly has imposed restrictive rules of engagement (ROE) to prevent excessive noncombatant casualties. The JTF commander has indicated that the option to conduct a sector-by-sector "clear and hold" approach is not feasible, given the size of his extraction force and the size of the built-up area. He prefers a quick penetration of lightly armed forces to both hotels, followed by a speedy withdrawal that both minimizes collateral damage and ensures the safety of both his forces and the evacuees.

NATO OODA

Cyber operations support is provided by the US Tenth Fleet (US Fleet Cyber Command). The NATO information operations team also has tapped into the Daesh intranet and is monitoring traffic between the leadership and individual units scattered around Tripoli.

The Joint Intelligence Center supporting the operation is routinely provided with visible and radar imagery from US, French, and German reconnaissance satellites, and Tripoli is being targeted for imagery collection on every satellite pass. The imagery includes visible, infrared, multispectral, and radar imagery of very good quality.

The JTF has access to sanitized HUMINT reporting from intelligence services of the participants. One source, JTF codenamed Tealeaf, reports on Daesh force deployments, but Tealeaf's reporting usually is delayed by 15 to 22 hours due to source protection concerns. A source codenamed Chairarm can provide near real-time reporting of Libya Dawn unit movements in the vicinity of the Sheraton

Tripoli. Occupants of both hotels are providing cell phone and Internet reporting of the situation immediately around the hotels, but the reporting has been subject to intermittent outages, and both Daesh and Libya Dawn are believed to be monitoring these communications.

Guidance

Your assignment as the lead planner is to develop and present a deception plan to support *one* of the three proposed evacuation options. (*Note for classroom use:* This assumes a class divided into three teams, each team taking a different option.) The JTF commander is amenable to modifying any of the three proposed evacuation plans or conducting demonstrations to support the deception. The plan must identify the information to be provided to each opposing or friendly force (Daesh, Libya Dawn, and the Zintan brigades), who provides it, and how and when to provide it. It must also identify and schedule information that is to be provided publicly (e.g., via press releases, or CNN or Al Jazeera broadcasts).

EXERCISE 6: DISRUPTING BOKO HARAM OPERATIONS

This exercise features a no-holds-barred PSYOPS deception plan to disrupt the terrorist group Boko Haram in North Africa. It is fictional but is based loosely on real organizations.

You are the commander of a clandestine joint Chad-Cameroon-Nigeria task force that has been set up with French support to develop and execute unconventional means to disrupt the terrorist group Boko Haram. Officially, you don't exist: You operate with no government attribution for your operations. You have the following operational guidance:

- Stop the recruiting of new fighters.

- Motivate existing fighters to defect.

- Encourage infighting among individual Boko Haram units and among their leadership.

- Disrupt funding and the ability of the group to acquire supplies.

There are no rules of engagement. Your job is to disrupt Boko Haram operations by any means possible. Your performance will be measured by operational successes, collateral damage notwithstanding. The roles of participating governments (Chad, Cameroon, Nigeria, and France) in your operations are not to be disclosed under any circumstances. So long as the involvement of these countries is protected and the operation succeeds, your methods will not be called into question.

You are currently planning a series of deception operations to carry out your mission. Following are details about your opponent and the resources available to you. Military leaders in Chad, Cameroon, and Nigeria have agreed to conduct operations to assist in the execution of your overall deception plan, so long as it does not unduly interfere with their normal operations.

Boko Haram Background

Boko Haram is an Islamic extremist group based in northeastern Nigeria, and active in Chad, Niger, and northern Cameroon.

Boko Haram initially relied on donations from members. Its links with al-Qaeda in the Islamic Maghreb opened it up to funding from groups in Saudi Arabia and the United Kingdom. But it also gets funding from bank robberies and kidnapping for ransom. Boko Haram also occasionally has been connected in media reports with cocaine trafficking. The group cloaks its sources of finance through the use of a highly decentralized distribution network. The group employs an Islamic model of money transfer called *hawala*, which is based on an honor system and a global network of agents that makes the financing difficult to track.

Although Boko Haram is organized in a hierarchical structure with one overall leader, the group also operates as a clandestine cell system using a network structure, with units having between 300 and 500 fighters each.

Boko Haram's loyalty pledge has so far mostly been a branding exercise designed to boost its international jihadi credentials, attract recruits, and appeal to the Daesh leadership for assistance.

Despite suffering a series of setbacks, Boko Haram remains lethal. It launched its deadliest raid in over a year in June 2016, killing 30 soldiers and forcing 50,000 people to flee when it took over the Niger town of Bosso.

There have been periodic reports of cooperation between Boko Haram and the Libyan branch of Daesh. In April 2016, OSINT reported that an arms convoy believed bound for Boko Haram from Libya was intercepted in Chad, providing one of the first concrete examples of cooperation. Evidence shows that Boko Haram cooperation with the Daesh Libya branch has increased since then. Boko Haram fighters travel to Libya to fight for Daesh. In turn, Daesh sends arms and supplies to Boko Haram via convoys through Chad.

Boko Haram's practice of informing on rival factions to security forces and their past negotiations over hostages with the Nigerian and Cameroonian governments suggest that Boko Haram is not as "faceless" as the Nigerian government portrays, and that it is possible to communicate with at least some Boko Haram leaders.

Boko Haram's operational areas in Nigeria are shown in Figure 13-2.

Key Officers

Abubakar Shekau, Mamman Nur, and an unidentified leader of the Ansaru splinter group, are the three most influential leaders in Boko Haram's network.

FIGURE 13-2   ■   Area of Boko Haram Operations in Nigeria

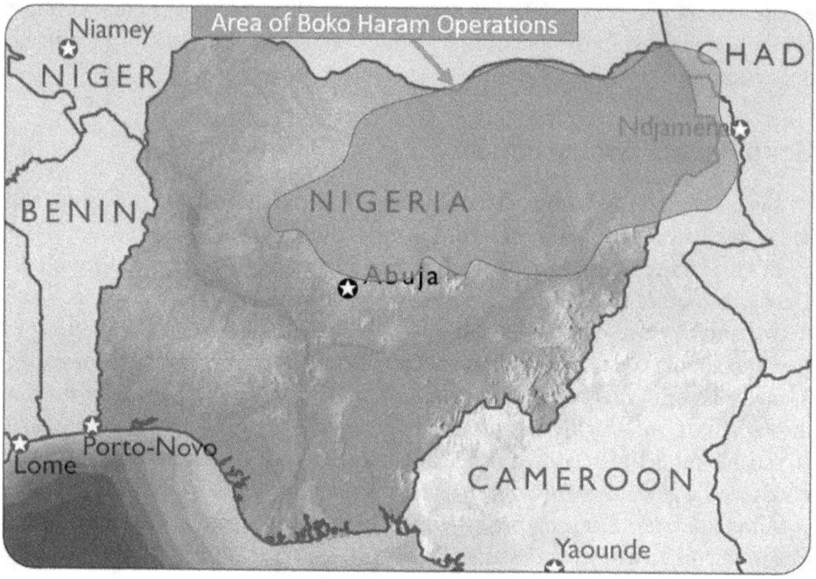

Source: Public domain image modified by author from https://www.usaid.gov/political-transition-initiatives/where-we-work/nigeria.

Shekau is the network's most visible leader, but the other two leaders wield power in the network and have a complex relationship with Shekau.

Abubakar Muhammad Shekau

Boko Haram's current leader was born in Shekau village in Nigeria's northeastern state of Yobe. He is said to be a fearless loner, a complex, paradoxical man—part theologian, part gangster. He is known for his intense ideological commitment and ruthlessness. He reportedly said, "I enjoy killing anyone that God commands me to kill—the way I enjoy killing chickens and rams."[3] Shekau is fluent in Hausa and Arabic as well as his native Kanuri language. He is believed to be in his late thirties to mid-forties. Shekau does not communicate directly with his troops. He wields power through a few select subcommanders, but even with them contact is minimal. He remains firmly opposed to any negotiations or reconciliation with the Nigerian government.

Shekau is a divisive leader but has legitimacy because he was deputy to Boko Haram founder Muhammad Yusuf and remained close to grassroots followers in Borno State. He retains a core group of loyalists because many militants who opposed him have defected or were killed by Boko Haram's more ruthless and indoctrinated militants. The loyalty of these militants to Shekau remains high, though some reportedly oppose his decision to align closely with Daesh.

Mamman Nur

Mamman Nur is connected to al-Qaeda affiliates in Africa and is both an operational and ideological leader. Nur reportedly bases his operations in Kano and has little or no network presence in Borno. His fighters are former followers of Boko Haram founder Muhammad Yusuf, with whom Nur was closely allied. They tend to have an international outlook. Nur occasionally cooperates with Ansaru militants. He has ideological disagreements with Shekau because of Shekau's leadership style and close relations with Daesh.

Ansaru

Ansaru is an Islamist jihadist militant organization based in the northeast of Nigeria. It is a Boko Haram splinter group, founded in January 2012. Ansaru was headed by Khalid al-Barnawi until his capture in April 2016. Al-Barnawi has been replaced, but his replacement has not been identified in press releases.

The group has its home base in Kano State in north-central Nigeria. It coordinates its operations with al-Qaeda in the Islamic Maghreb (AQIM), based in northern Mali. Many of its members were trained in AQIM camps in Algeria.

On the local level, Ansaru's mid-level commanders cooperate with Shekau and Boko Haram. But while it maintains links to Boko Haram, Ansaru members oppose Boko Haram's internal orientation and tactics such as indiscriminate killing. In contrast to Boko Haram's focus on Nigeria and neighboring countries, Ansaru has an international perspective. It includes many Western-educated Boko Haram members. The Ansaru tactics emphasize capturing high-profile foreign targets and attacking Western interests.

Ansaru, with its most recent operations in Niger, Cameroon, and possibly Central African Republic, now functions like an "external operations unit" in its self-declared area of operations in "Black Africa" in a way that separates Ansaru from Boko Haram in Borno and avoids conflict with the group.

Your Resources

French Cyber Unit

France has set up a special cyber unit that is available to assist in the execution of your deception plan. It monitors the Boko Haram social networks used for recruiting and radicalizing terrorists. It routinely monitors the al-Urhwa al-Wutqha Twitter account used by Boko Haram to threaten attacks and to communicate with supporters and hawala funding sources. The cyber unit has email addresses of Mamman Nur and some Ansaru officers. It has managed to put a backdoor in Mamman Nur's personal computer, for intelligence value. The unit keeps track of Internet news feeds and television broadcasts that the terrorists monitor. The unit reports that Boko Haram monitors Nigerian newspapers for intelligence about Nigerian force deployments, for attack targeting, and to observe popular reactions to Boko Haram attacks.

Special Operations Unit

Under your command is a special combat unit trained in unconventional warfare. The unit was formed from Chadian and Nigerian volunteers who lost family members in Boko Haram attacks and includes fighters who were forced into Boko Haram service and later escaped. The unit has recently finished combat training, is equipped with Boko Haram uniforms and weaponry, and is trained in Boko Haram combat tactics.

Channels

Your special operations unit has acquired two Boko Haram short-range communications transceivers and can use them to monitor Boko Haram communications in a local area or to communicate with Boko Haram officers.

Boko Haram has increasingly used videos for online recruiting and for indoctrinating new recruits. It has incorporated into its recruiting strategy the same message that Daesh has used successfully: that it is steadily winning and controls territory that constitutes a state. These videos are produced by Daesh operatives outside the region and transmitted via a dark web connection that the French cyber unit monitors. The videos include several Daesh-produced manuals on weapons manufacturing and training.

Guidance

Your assignment is to develop and execute a plan having several separate deception operations to help carry out the operational missions set forth at the beginning of this exercise.

NOTES

1. The Institute for Science and International Security, "Nuclear Sites: Fordow Fuel Enrichment Plant (FFEP)," http://www.isisnucleariran.org/sites/detail/fordow/.

2. The term *chicken feed* refers to true material of low intelligence value that a double agent provides to an opposing intelligence service to lead it to accept him or her as a credible source.

3. Jacob Zenn, "Leadership Analysis of Boko Haram and Ansaru in Nigeria," West Point Combating Terrorism Center, February 24, 2014, https://www.ctc.usma.edu/posts/leadership-analysis-of-boko-haram-and-ansaru-in-nigeria.

MILITARY DECEPTION PLANNING EXERCISES

For the following military deception (MILDEC) exercises, participants should use the information and intelligence provided to generate a basic MILDEC concept of operations (CONOP). These are meant to be simple scenarios for training in the basics of MILDEC CONOPs and for applying some of the methods and techniques illustrated in this book. They are by no means intended to make one into a CONOP expert, or to challenge more experienced CONOP planners. Instead, the goal is to provide an opportunity for demystifying the CONOP process by practicing some of the fundamental principles. Formatting is elementary, and the first CONOP, Operation Bulldozer, is provided as a generic model. Instructors may adjust product formatting as desired according to experience levels. For the remainder of the CONOP exercises, only the beginning scenario and intelligence roll-ups are provided. All cases are fictional.

It is recommended that participants work in groups on their CONOPs and that time be taken for comparative study of end products between groups. It is highly unlikely that two resulting deception plans will be exactly the same, leaving a lot of space for discussion. For example, substantial differences are probable in terms of estimating first-, second-, or third-order effects within the deception plan. Use the following Operation Bulldozer CONOP for inspiration on how to format final products for the exercises.

MILDEC CONOP EXAMPLE: OPERATION BULLDOZER

Situation

It is the summer of 2012. The country of Chad has been locked in civil war for the better part of two years. The conflict is between pro-Western government troops and a radical tribe called the Zagaweri, which has control of the second largest city, Abeche. Since the militants have been in control of Abeche, they have reinforced all perimeter defenses with deep trenches, improvised explosive device (IED) belts, and tunnels.

The Chadian government has determined that Abeche must be taken in the spring of 2013, and essentially they wish to do it from the inside out in a plan called OP Termite Junction to avoid the perimeter defenses. While the Chadian military is busy with covert training and infiltration operations supported by Western special operations forces (SOFs), they have asked African Union (AU) contingent operational planners to design and execute a deception plan in support of an uprising being planned by anti-Zagaweri tribes inside the defensive perimeter.

Based on intelligence reporting, the Zagaweri have very limited intelligence, surveillance, target acquisition, and reconnaissance (ISTAR) capability. They rely heavily on HUMINT and OSINT collection for tracking national and international events, and on HUMINT and COMINT for monitoring activity within 30 km of their defensive perimeters. They are active on social media and have a limited analytic capability with regard to social media. The Zagaweri sensor situation is summarized in Figure 14-1.

Four main channels are identified for deception projection for this operation, summarized in Figure 14-2.

FIGURE 14-1 ■ Zagaweri Sensor Map

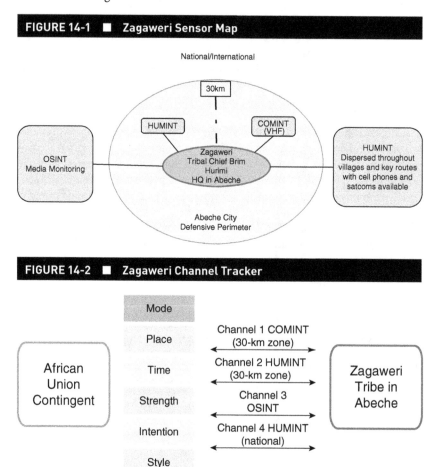

FIGURE 14-2 ■ Zagaweri Channel Tracker

Basic CONOP Format

A CONOP has many formats depending on the organization, its doctrine, and the CONOP's state of development. It is often confusing or hard to decipher generally because of the bureaucracy and organization surrounding it. But a CONOP in its most basic draft form at start-up is literally no more than a planner's sketch on a white board, or on a paper napkin at a café—reportedly the case for US Army General Franks prior to Operation Iraqi Freedom. Three fundamental elements are usually present from the start in any CONOP, regardless of the format:

1. A proposed mission statement. (What does the operation need to accomplish? What are the desired effects of the operation?)

2. A rough outline of the actual execution of the CONOP over time and space. (Who does what, when, where, how, and why?)

3. A clear conditions-based statement as to when the operation ends.

There is no difference between CONOPs and deception CONOPs in terms of these elements; therefore, all MILDEC CONOPs should include all three. The following is an example of a written description of MILDEC CONOP Bulldozer; a visual representation of the MILDEC CONOP can be seen in Figure 14-3.

1. Proposed Mission Statement

MISSION: Project a deception that will continue to fix Zagaweri efforts on the perimeter defense of Abeche, up to the starting date of the uprising in OP Termite Junction, noted in all planning efforts hereafter as *D-Day*. The deception is to make the Zagaweri believe a large-scale land attack by AU/Chadian forces on the Abeche defensive perimeter will occur on D-Day, in order to fix Zagaweri focus on defensive efforts and resources on the perimeter of Abeche, and not on the internal security of the city.

2. Outline of the Execution

Note: This is where the rough outline of the actual CONOP is presented in written format. It should reflect the timing of specific actions relative to each other—but not actual dates. The description of the CONOP execution usually is broken down into sequential phases that delineate what conditions have to exist before switching focus and effort. For example, collecting information on a proposed target would be Phase 1, and Phase 2 would be taking action against the target. Obviously, Phase 2 will not happen before Phase 1 is determined to be completed.

FIGURE 14-3 ■ MILDEC CONOP Visualization

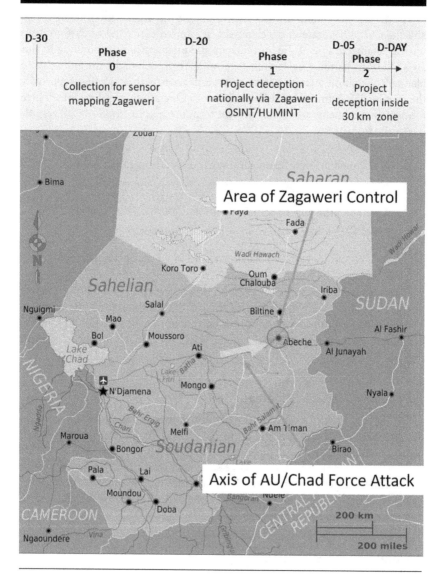

D-30		D-20		D-05	D-DAY
	Phase 0		Phase 1	Phase 2	
	Collection for sensor mapping Zagaweri		Project deception nationally via Zagaweri OSINT/HUMINT	Project deception inside 30 km zone	

Source: Modified by the authors from a map at https://commons.wikimedia.org/wiki/File:Chad_Regions_map.png. Image credit: burmesedays and the University of Texas Library Map Collection.

CONCEPT OF OPERATIONS: To achieve the stated mission, the J2 (intelligence section) of the AU will synchronize efforts to make the Zagaweri believe that a large-scale land attack will occur on D-Day. This operation will have three phases: Phase 0 will involve further intelligence collection to support a detailed mapping of Zagaweri national HUMINT channels. Based on Phase 0 results, Phase 1 will begin targeted shaping activities, exploiting Zagaweri OSINT and HUMINT in order to project an impending conventional land attack on Abeche. Based on the results of Phase 0 and Phase 1, Phase 2 will intensify targeted shaping activities inside the Abeche 30-km perimeter exploiting HUMINT and COMINT to project impending land attack on the Abeche perimeter. The deception operation ends on D-Day.

Phase 0 (D-30): The AU J2 will establish an intelligence collection plan and designate appropriate and available intelligence, surveillance, targeting, and reconnaissance (ISTAR) to further develop an understanding of the Zagaweri national HUMINT network and their OSINT capability in preparation for exploitation. The AU J2 will also define collectable measurements of effectiveness (MoEs) for the deception operation for running estimates. MoE activities should continue until D-1 and the final estimate of the deception effectiveness should be presented to the commander no less than one day before D-Day.

Phase 1 (D-20): The AU J2 will coordinate/synchronize message projection through identified Zagaweri HUMINT network sources suggesting an impending conventional land attack by AU/Chadian forces on the perimeter of Abeche. This should include the exploitation of double agents with direct messaging, or conducting visible AU ISTAR activities, clearly showing interest in the Abeche perimeter for the benefit of Zagaweri HUMINT collectors. The AU J2 will also synchronize messaging being projected through Zagaweri OSINT hubs (media/social media) of known interest in order to project the picture of an impending conventional land attack on the perimeter of Abeche. These activities will continue until D-Day.

Phase 2 (D-5): In close coordination with J3 (operations) the AU J2 will synchronize messaging/activities within the 30-km zone with regard to HUMINT and COMINT to project an impending land attack on the defensive perimeter of Abeche city on D-Day—including increasing communications traffic to suggest time, place, and strength of impending attack.

3. End-of-Operation Statement

MILDEC operations typically end after the real operation has begun. The condition for ending the deception is thus that the real operation has progressed to a point where adversaries can no longer be uncertain as to the intent of the real operation, are reacting to the real operation, or simply are ignoring the deception.

End of Operation (D+1): The deception operation will cease when intelligence estimates provide substantial indicators that the Zagaweri forces are no longer expecting an attack on the Abeche perimeter.

EXERCISE 1: OPERATION LIGHTS OUT

Scenario

Political

The country of Tyronika (TKA) has been in a state of civil war with the North Tyronika Region (NTR) since 2014, when NTR declared unilateral independence and named the second largest city in Tyronika, Bruks, as its capital. The TKA government reacted immediately, mobilizing the southern region, and developing a military campaign plan to reassert central control over NTR. By the end of 2016, despite TKA air superiority over NTR-held territory, a stalemate had developed with the NTR forces, called the Northern Rebel Defense Forces (NRDF), restricted to a pocket on both sides of the Frank River and backed onto the Northern Sea coast.

Key Infrastructure

The NTR pocket includes the city of Bruks and the strategically important Marble Dam power station that supplies the two million citizens of Bruks with electrical power. NTR also has access to a coal-fueled power station (Tetia) at the southern perimeter of the pocket near the town of Avalon. However, this station is not activated and it would require some effort to get it running; and being so close to the front lines, it would require considerable resources for protection. A TKA PMESII analysis of NTR infrastructure has identified NTR's electric power situation as a possible "center of gravity" for the strategic defeat of the NTR. TKA analysis has determined that life in the NTR city of Bruks is fully dependent on electricity from the Marble Dam, especially in order to survive the winters, and the loss of the dam would leave the NTR with only one option—to activate the coal power plant at Avalon. (See Figure 14-4.)

NRDF Military

Having lost air dominance over the North early in the conflict, militarily the NRDF has been focusing on strengthening its surface-to-air missile (SAM) defenses, holding Bruks and the Marble Dam in order to force concessions from TKA. At the same time, the NRDF has been making extensive preparations for the urban warfare defense of Bruks, including extensive mining, IEDs, tunneling, and concrete bunkers. NRDF air defense units include several units equipped with SA-15s (12-km range), SA-8s (10-km range), SA-6s (25-km range), and possibly some SA-11s (35-km range). These defenses have reduced TKA air effectiveness over the city of Bruks, while the Marble Dam itself is

FIGURE 14-4   ■   Situation as of May 2017

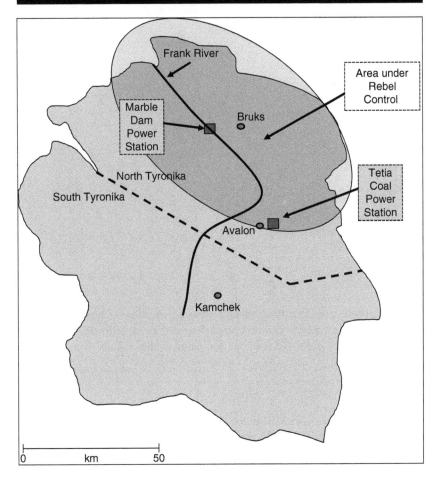

considered by TKA as a nonstrike target for many reasons, including the environment and humanitarian law, so the TKA air force does not fly missions near the dam. On land, the NRDF considers TKA freedom of movement for ground troops to be limited to the outskirts of the city of Avalon, approximately 50 km to the south of Bruks.

The NRDF has the bulk of its mobile reaction force in Bruks, including the 1st Motorized Rifle Division, consisting of approximately 12,000 men.

The 1st Motorized Rifle Division (see Table 14-1) is intended to be used as a reserve force to protect Bruks and the Marble Dam. It is severely restricted in venturing out of Bruks due to the reduced NRDF SAM defense coverage and risks being cut off from Bruks if it ventures too far south within the

TABLE 14-1   ■   NRDF 1st Mobile Rifle Division
Motorized Rifle Regiment 1
Motorized Rifle Regiment 2
Motorized Rifle Regiment 3
Tank Regiment
Artillery Regiment
Air Defense Regiment (SA-6 & SA-8)
Anti-Tank Battalion
Signal Company
Reconnaissance Company
Logistics Regiment

rebel-controlled area. The division represents an excellent bargaining chip so long as it creates a credible defensive capacity for the city of Bruks. Should the NRDF lose the division, NTR's hope for political concessions from the TKA will be diminished.

TKA Military

The TKA air force enjoys air superiority but is restricted by tight controls on targeting and by an NRDF SAM threat that increases as aircraft approach Bruks. However, the air force has restricted the NRDF's freedom of movement throughout their area of control. If substantial NRDF land units try to maneuver, they risk heavy losses from air attacks.

The TKA mobile land forces enjoy a substantial numerical advantage over the NRDF, but their edge is not sufficient to overwhelm defenses at Bruks, especially with the NRDF reaction force of 12,000 sitting in Bruks. The TKA land forces consist of two tank divisions (see Table 14-2) that are not well suited to urban warfare. To attack Bruks with these forces would also be very costly, especially without close air support. NRDF SAM defenses would in any circumstance have to be degraded to a sufficient level to allow for the level of close support necessary.

Tyronika also has a mobile amphibious force consisting of two marine brigades and one SEAL regiment (see Table 14-3).

TABLE 14-2 ■ TKA Mobile Land Forces	
Tank Division 1	**Tank Division 2**
Tank Regiment 1	Tank Regiment 1
Tank Regiment 2	Tank Regiment 2
Tank Regiment 3	Tank Regiment 3
Motorized Rifle Regiment	Motorized Rifle Regiment
Air Defense Regiment	Missile Brigade
Motorized Artillery Regiment	Air Defense Regiment
Logistics Regiment	Logistics Regiment

TABLE 14-3 ■ TKA Amphibious Force
Marine Brigade 1
Marine Brigade 2
SEAL Regiment 1

Situation

You work within Tyronikian Joint Operational Command (TKA JOC) as a future operations officer (J35). The date is June 2, 2017. To break the stalemate, the commander would like to develop a plan that would allow the majority of his mobile forces (land and/or amphibious) to engage and destroy the bulk of NRDF mobile forces outside the city of Bruks. The problem has been in getting the NRDF reaction force to come out of Bruks. Recently, however, TKA JOC J2 (intelligence) has suggested such an opportunity is likely to occur between November 4 and November 7.

TKA intelligence has been tracking the water levels at the Marble Dam through HUMINT and MASINT since the dry period started in May, and reports that the levels have been going down very fast—faster than usual. Specialists in the J2 have determined that when the water levels go below a certain level, the Marble Dam will stop producing electricity. At current rates, the expected date for the electricity to stop is on or around November 23, 2017. The only other source of electricity is the coal-fueled Tetia power station near Avalon that is not operational while the

Marble Dam is producing power. However, electricity is a strategic necessity for the city of Bruks over the winter, so the NTR will have to start up the Tetia power station and will send its mobile reaction force south to ensure the start-up is successful. It is assessed with a high level of confidence that NTR believes the falling water level is a secure secret.

Task

TKA JOC expects that NTR has no choice but to use the NRDF mobile force to help secure the Tetia power station near Avalon. In other words, the NTR will have to send the reaction force south to Avalon from Bruks. The TKA JOC has every intention of engaging the NRDF mobile force at or near Avalon and the Tetia power station and will dedicate 80 percent of its own mobile force to destroy the NRDF force. However, to improve the degree of surprise, reduce casualties, and increase the chance of success, the TKA JOC wants J2 and J3 to develop a MILDEC CONOP with the following objectives, in order of priority:

1. Deceive the NRDF into underestimating the number and type of TKA forces that will be available in the Avalon area during the period of November 4–7, 2017.

2. Fix as many of the NRDF mobile force air defense units as possible in or around Bruks during the period of November 4–7, 2017.

3. Fix as many of the NRDF mobile artillery units as possible in or around Bruks during the period November 4–7, 2017.

4. Fix as many of the NRDF anti-tank units as possible in or around Bruks during the period November 4–7, 2017.

The MILDEC CONOP can make use of 20 percent of all TKA mobile forces. The final configuration of the main fighting force will be established after the approval of the MILDEC CONOPs. The deception plan should be ready to set in motion no later than August 1, 2017, and continue until the main offensive begins on November 4, 2017.

The first step—for the J2 to sensor map the NRDF forces in order to identify channels for projecting a deception and tracking its progress—has already been executed. The sensor map in Figure 14-5 is provided for this purpose. Once a channel tracker has been established, you are to develop a MILDEC CONOP with a timeline and eventual phases to be presented to the commander.

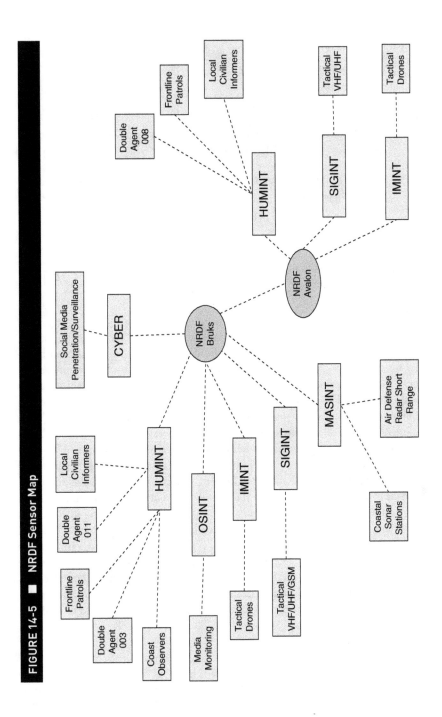

FIGURE 14-5 ■ NRDF Sensor Map

Guidance

1. Using the sensor map in Figure 14-5, establish a channel management framework for deception projection and eventual evaluation of the deception progress.

2. Prepare the first rough draft of the MILDEC CONOP for presentation, including timeline and phase breakdown, ideally on one presentation slide. (Use the CONOP format provided for Operation Bulldozer.)

3. List and discuss measurements of effectiveness (MoEs) and/or requests for information (RFIs) that can be collected during the deception projection to control for effectiveness.

EXERCISE 2: OPERATION TIMBER FLOAT

Scenario

This scenario begins with a campaign plan already in its early draft stages. An ethnic conflict on the Pastonian peninsula (see Figure 14-6) has been brewing for many years. The Niberian minority populations have been oppressed by local authorities who complain about the large percentage of organized crime being committed by ethnic Niberians. In the early spring of 2017, four Pastonian policemen were killed in a gunfight with narco-barons of Niberian descent. What followed was three months of escalating conflict between Pastonian and Niberian ethnic groups. Extremists on both sides sabotaged any attempts for conflict resolution. On July 4, 2017, the Pastonian government announced that all ethnic Niberians would have to report to "holding centers" once a day. Despite being warned by the Niberian government that any further action against ethnic Niberians would be a grave mistake, a week later Pastonia began rounding up all ethnic Niberians now registered via the holding centers, and placing them in internment camps spread throughout the peninsula. As a result, unknown to Pastonia, the Niberian Navy has been tasked by the Niberian government to prepare a surprise amphibious invasion of the Pastonian peninsula. The Pastonian Armed Forces (PAF) are completely unaware of the impending attack. PAF are relying on a political assessment: They believe that Niberia has not yet been pushed to its limits.

Pastonian Armed Forces

Pastonian military defenses were improved in 2015–2016, when Pastonia made some serious investment in coastal defenses on the peninsula. The improvements included what one senior official called an "impenetrable" minefield off West Bay,

FIGURE 14-6 ■ Pastonian Situation

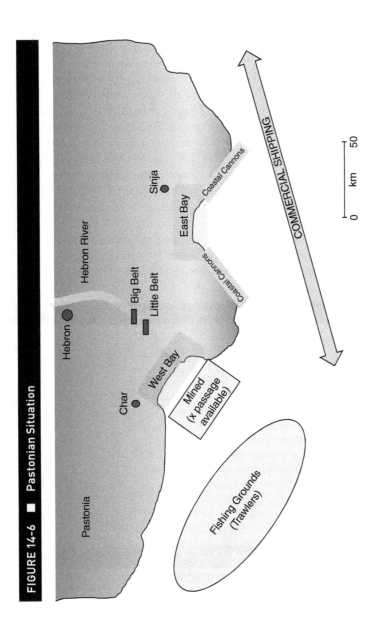

with a few passages known only to the PAF leadership and changed every four weeks. The coastal defenses at East Bay rely on land structures built with reinforced concrete, and PAF security assessments estimate that it would take at least three days of bombing to destroy them, limiting any chance of a surprise landing. The PAF have also increased their mobile armor reserve (see Table 14-4) in Hebron, which could quickly be put into action. However, in the case of war they expect their reserves to be restricted to either side of the Hebron River as there are only two bridges that can support armor, and they will most likely be taken out early in any conflict. The bridge to the north is called Big Belt, and the bridge to the south is called Little Belt.

The PAF Navy is under-equipped and poorly funded. It relies primarily on light coast guard patrol boats (PBs) responsible for border control, search and rescue, and fishing control. The PAF Navy has no submarines but does have a limited range coastal sonar station in East Bay. The PAF Air Force is extremely limited, with its few fighters being sent to patrol territorial water borders two or three times a month. The PAF does, however, have some SIGINT capability. To ensure a nonthreatening posture, Pastonia announces its territorial water patrols three days before they are conducted.

Outside of West Bay is an international fishing ground on the Grand Banks that lies just outside of Pastonian territorial waters. Here trawler fishing fleets from Pastonia and Niberia, nearly eighty trawlers in all, can be found on the Grand

TABLE 14-4 ■ PAF 1st Reserve Armor Division

Motorized Rifle Regiment 1
Motorized Rifle Regiment 2
Tank Regiment 1
Tank Regiment 2
Artillery Regiment
Anti-Tank Battalion
Signal Company
Logistics Regiment

TABLE 14-5 ■ Pastonian Coast Guard

West Bay	East Bay
PB Koplan	PB Levent
PB Narfish	PB Sodan
PB Letterik	PB Duke
	PB Wolfe

Banks at any time except in December, when a mutually agreed upon moratorium is respected. Outside of East Bay lie the internationally recognized commercial shipping lanes that are open to all traffic.

The Invasion Force

The Royal Niberian Armed Forces (RNAF) have two tank divisions at full strength to be used for the campaign. It is intended that Tank Division 1 will be the lead attacking division, while Tank Division 2 will follow as an occupying force. The difficulty, as always with amphibious landings, lies in getting enough capacity onto land before the defenders can achieve relative force superiority over the attackers. Using its amphibious and air assault capacity, the Royal Niberian Navy (RNN) has promised to deliver enough forces in good time.

The RNN has a small but well-equipped amphibious landing force consisting of two marine brigades and several landing ships. These are supported by an air assault ship, with twelve heavy-duty Chinook helicopters for troop transport and eight attack helicopters. In a joint operation these capabilities ideally would be synchronized to deliver the maximum effect in the shortest amount of time.

TABLE 14-6 ■ RNAF Mobile Land Forces

Tank Division 1	Tank Division 2
Tank Regiment 1	Tank Regiment 1
Tank Regiment 2	Tank Regiment 2
Tank Regiment 3	Tank Regiment 3
Tank Regiment 4	Motorized Rifle Regiment 1
Motorized Rifle Regiment	Motorized Rifle Regiment 2
Motorized Artillery Regiment	Motorized Artillery Regiment
Logistics Regiment	Logistics Regiment

TABLE 14-7 ■ RNN Amphibious Force

Marine Brigade 1
Marine Brigade 2
Marine Brigade 3
Marine Brigade 4
10 LKA (amphibious cargo ships)
50 LCMs (landing craft mechanized)
70 LCIs (landing craft infantry)

TABLE 14-8 ■ RNAF Air Assault Forces
1 air assault ship
12 Chinooks
8 attack helicopters

Task

The window for the amphibious landing is sometime between November 16 and November 30, 2017, so the deception should initially be phased from August 10, 2017, to November 15, 2017. Thanks to its national intelligence service, the RRN has the minefield passage data. The passage is small, but the RNN experts believe it can be widened very quickly by mine sweepers; therefore, it has been decided that the actual landing will be executed in West Bay. As the assigned J2 chief, you have the responsibility, in conjunction with the J3, to produce a first-draft deception CONOP to support the amphibious invasion. To improve the degree of surprise, reduce casualties, and increase the chance of success, the commander wants J2 and J3 to develop a MILDEC CONOP with the following objectives, listed in order of priority:

1. Maintain and promote strategic surprise within the political domain.

2. Direct the PAF's general focus toward East Bay.

3. Convince the PAF to commit reserve forces to the east side of the Hebron River shortly before D-Day.

Because surprise is important to the success of the campaign, the deception timeline will drive, as much as possible, the operational planning for the actual landing (D-Day). Therefore, planned deception projection activities must be sequenced (D-1, 2, 3, etc.). The commander has made 20 percent of the RNAF forces available for deception purposes. The first-draft CONOP should be ready for the commander's first decision brief in the form of one or two presentation slides.

Guidance

1. Using the given sensor map (Figure 14-7), establish a channel tracker for projection management and eventual evaluation of the deception progress.

2. Prepare the first rough draft of the MILDEC CONOP for presentation, including timeline and phase breakdown, ideally on one or two slides.

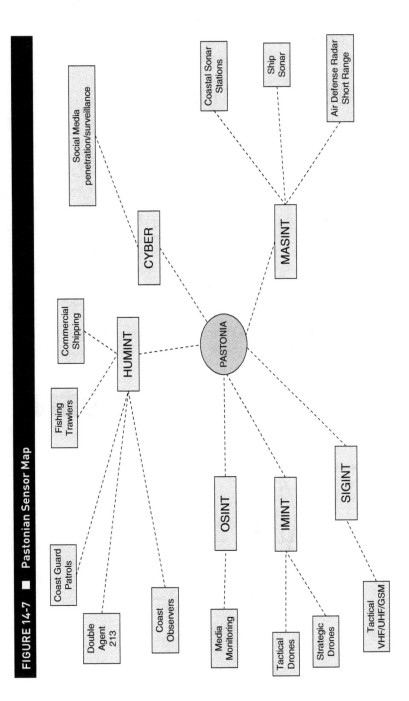

FIGURE 14-7 ■ Pastonian Sensor Map

3. List and discuss measurements of effectiveness (MoEs) and/or requests for information (RFIs) that can be collected during the deception projection to control for effectiveness.

EXERCISE 3: OPERATION CLOSING TIME

Scenario

The NATO Joint Task Force Land (JTFL) has been supporting the host country Taman in a war against radical religious insurgents for the better part of three years. The JTFL is responsible for defending a northern section of the Haldun River valley in a largely arid plateau surrounding a narrow irrigated strip known as the Green Zone. In early 2017 the JTFL established a string of patrol bases for Tamanian troops running east to west across the green zone and known as the Patrol Base Line (see Figure 14-8). It is June 12, 2017, and as part of the overall plan, the three-year-old Main Operations Base (MOB) Rhino will be closed on September 30, 2017. MOB Dragon in the south will remain operational for another six months as the Tamanian troops reestablish control of the valley.

The closing of MOB Rhino is a complicated affair requiring extensive manpower and a great deal of equipment to move from MOB Rhino to MOB Dragon.

FIGURE 14-8 ■ Green Zone Situation

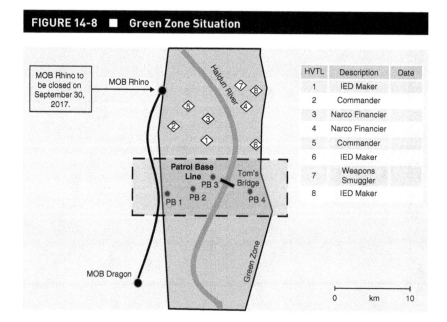

HVTL	Description	Date
1	IED Maker	
2	Commander	
3	Narco Financier	
4	Narco Financier	
5	Commander	
6	IED Maker	
7	Weapons Smuggler	
8	IED Maker	

The plan is to start very early on the morning of September 30 at MOB Rhino and return to MOB Dragon in the late afternoon with MOB Rhino closed. The relocation presents a very tempting target for the insurgents as defensive positions around MOB Rhino will not be operational during the process. At the same time, a special operations task group (SOTG) has one of its task forces operating in the battlespace, TF 222; their task is to capture or kill key members of the insurgent network operating in the northern Green Zone. This includes planning eight strike activities over the next three months based on the high-value target list (HVTL) provided (see Figure 14-8). TF 222 has yet to develop a timeline for the strikes. The strikes involve two complications: The SOTG has to make a land infiltration at night and, furthermore, the group can only be launched from a MOB or patrol base.

Task

As the TF 222 J2, you and your team have been ordered to coordinate support for the closing of MOB Rhino, relying on deliberate targeting activities to project a deception. The objective is to disrupt the insurgent's capability to mount a coordinated assault on MOB Rhino while it is being closed on September 30, 2017. To improve the degree of surprise, reduce casualties,

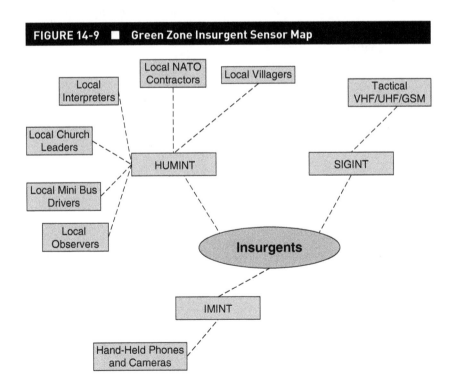

FIGURE 14-9 ■ Green Zone Insurgent Sensor Map

and increase the chance of success, you are to develop a first-draft deception CONOP to support the closing of MOB Rhino, with the following objectives, in order of priority:

1. Make the insurgents believe MOB Rhino is still operational on September 30, 2017.

2. All HVTL strikes must be executed by September 30, 2017.

Guidance

1. Using the given sensor map (Figure 14-9), establish a channel tracker for projection management and eventual evaluation of the deception progress.

2. Prepare the first rough draft of the MILDEC CONOP for presentation, including timeline and phase breakdown, ideally on one slide. It should also indicate a progression through the HVTL.

3. Compare and discuss differences in the prioritization of the HVTL; list and discuss measures of effectiveness (MoEs) and/or requests for information (RFIs) that can be collected during the deception projection to control for effectiveness.

DECEPTION DETECTION EXERCISES

The short exercises in this chapter give readers practice with methods for detecting deception. The ability to move between one or more of the three OODA perspectives in a situation is a fundamental skill set for deception projection. All three perspectives are inherently involved while working on deception detection. Keep this in mind when completing these exercises. In going through the exercises, participants should pose and discuss the following questions:

1. What are the adversary's observation and orientation capabilities to execute a deception?

2. What weaknesses in your own observation and orientation capabilities could facilitate the opponent's deception?

3. Could your adversary's observation and orientation capabilities identify and exploit those weaknesses?

Finally, these scenarios are based on limited information. It would be worthwhile to discuss what factors could further contribute to the deception detection (but are difficult to replicate through an exercise) in a real-life scenario.

EXERCISE 1: THE VALLEY OF DOUBT

Scenario

It is November 15, 2017. The Blue State is expecting a peace agreement between the Red and Blue States to collapse and a major Red State offensive to begin along the demarcation line between December 15 and 19, 2017. There are

FIGURE 15-1 ■ RED-BLUE Situation

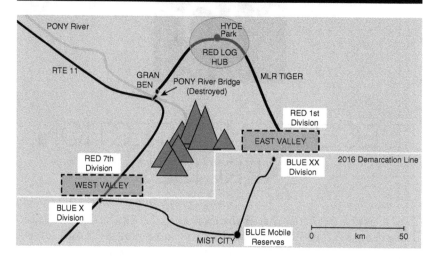

two avenues for a possible Red offensive: The most direct approach is along the 40-km Red main logistics route (MLR) Tiger, with an assault through the East Valley. This is the Blue XX Division's Area of Responsibility (AoR), and they have orders to retain and hold East Valley. (See Figure 15-1.)

The second option for the Red State offensive is attacking through West Valley. However, that option will require repairing or replacing the destroyed Pony River Bridge at Gran Ben; this option extends logistics lines supporting the assault through West Valley by 40 km to almost double that of an East Valley option. West Valley is the Blue X Division's AoR, and they have orders to retain and hold West Valley.

Situation

Though the Red State has more forces available, with a nearly three-to-one advantage, their forces are partially made up of conscripts and reservists. The Blue State has a professional defense force and a great deal more experience among the rank and file. The Red State will have to commit the majority of its assaulting forces to one avenue of advance in order to ensure relative numerical superiority for breaching the demarcation line. The Blue State is aware of this situation and has established a well-organized mobile reserve that should be sufficient to defeat any assault if they are in the right place at the right time. However, the Blue State must decide in which valley, East or West, to place its mobile reserve by December 15, 2017, in order to defeat the Red State's offensive. Essentially, each side has to commit a majority of its forces at the proper location to ensure a successful offense or defense. For the Red State to be successful, it must attack at a point where the Blue State mobile reserves are not committed. For the Blue State to be successful as the defending army, it must commit its mobile reserve to the location of the impending attack.

Task

As BLUE J2 chief you are responsible for providing an opinion as to which valley the BLUE mobile reserve must be positioned in before December 15, 2017. You expect the RED opponent to attempt to mislead your commander into committing his reserve forces in the wrong valley. Your analytic section has collated and produced a channel tracker to be used to identify adversarial indicators of a deception (see Table 15-1).

TABLE 15-1 ■ RED-BLUE Channel Tracker			
CH #	DTG	Channel	Story
1	07.2017–08.2017	OSINT Summary	Local media in Hyde Park have been interviewing RED military personnel (identified as being from two different tank divisions not normally stationed at Hyde Park). The interviewers asked the troops what they think of Hyde Park and its nightlife.
			A steady stream of media reports feature complaints about traffic jams on Route 11 due to the "recent" influx of military personnel. Another stream of reports suggest that Route 11 will be getting serious repair work in the fall.
			A separate stream of reporting indicates that work on the Pony River Bridge is expected to be finished by November 2017.
2	07.2017–08.2017	HUMINT Summary	**SOURCE 045 (B-3):** Reporting suggests there is an increase in RED HQ activities at Hyde Park with several senior RED officers working late at night. The group is led by General Mercant, known for his successful surprise attack against BLUE forces at the start of the previous conflict between the two states.
			SOURCE 011 (D-2): Reporting suggests several groups of special operations soldiers used for special reconnaissance missions have been sent to Gran Ben.

(Continued)

TABLE 15-1 ■ (Continued)			
3	07.2017–08.2017	IMINT	**HYDE PARK:** Imagery shows a buildup of military units, both operational and support, in the Hyde Park area. Of notable interest is that there seems to be almost double the number of tanks as there are tank transports.
			GRAN BEN: Light construction activity reported around the Pony River Bridge. Light construction activity reported on Route 11.
			EAST VALLEY: Routine maintenance of RED defensive lines noted.
			WEST VALLEY: Routine maintenance of RED defensive lines noted. Some light construction on Route 11 in the demarcation zone.
4	08.2017–09.2017	OSINT	National media in RED are suggesting that it might be possible to resolve the dispute with BLUE without further conflict. Several prominent politicians are suggesting compromise might be the best solution.
			There has been no reporting on RED military in Hyde Park by local media during this period.
			A stream of reporting features some RED locals from the area surrounding the East Valley demarcation zone complaining about money received for "temporary" land expropriations.
5	08.2017–09.2017	INTSUMs	**WEST VALLEY BLUE X Division:** A summary of all patrol reports from this period indicates an increase in RED reconnaissance activities. Frontline units also report being very entertained by RED engineers methodically testing the Pony River Bridge using a heavy bulldozer creeping meter by meter onto the bridge.
			EAST VALLEY BLUE XX Division: Situation normal—nothing to report.
6	09.2017–10.2017	IMINT	**HYDE PARK:** Imagery suggests there is a decrease in military activity at Hyde Park. The number of personnel and supporting units appears to have declined. Most of the tank transports are now gone from previous locations. There are some indications that police have established several new checkpoints around the outskirts of Hyde Park, particularly along the first part of MLR Tiger.

			GRAN BEN: Tank transports previously seen at Hyde Park are now encamped a short distance north of the Pony Bridge. It is estimated that at least half of the transports seen last month at Hyde Park are now placed in Gran Ben. What appears to be bridging equipment has been positioned south of Gran Ben and north of the Pony River Bridge. The Pony River Bridge is deemed operational, but the capacity is unknown.
			EAST VALLEY: Routine maintenance of RED defensive lines noted. Several new petrol bladders are positioned along MLR Tiger just north of the demarcation zone. Supply deliveries to frontline RED troops have increased by 10 percent over the last month—mostly ammunition trucks.
			WEST VALLEY: RED Reconnaissance units in the demarcation zone have established several new observation platforms overlooking the demarcation zone.
7	09.2017–10.2017	CYBER	**Social Media Penetration:** Known profiles of senior RED officers have been hacked. Online conversations with family members have a far more serious, somber, and dramatic tone. A few comments suggesting "things will be different" by "Xmas" or "next year" have been noted.
			Systems Penetration: Two systems hacked revealed that some reserves have been called into service as of December 1, 2017. Other files indicate that tank transport repairs in October were very high, with complaints as to why some of the "older transport" should have money wasted on them.
			CYBER: There were fifteen cyber reconnaissance incidents in October with the focus on systems and personnel related to BLUE X Division.
8	09.2017–10.2017	SIGINT	**COMINT:** Increased satellite communications activity observed in and around Gran Ben and the West Valley demarcation zone. Most content related to bridge repairs by contractors from Hyde Park.
			COMINT: Decrease in cell phone activity in RED East Valley. Increase in activity in RED West

(Continued)

TABLE 15-1 ■ (Continued)

			Valley. Limited intercepts indicate that personnel in either West or East Valley are there at least until the new year starts. RED personnel in both valleys appear to have no scheduled rotations for Christmas vacation.
			VHF/UHF: Routine communications activities are attributed to normal RED units in demarcation zones. Open transmissions by Hyde Park bridge contractors indicate the Pony River Bridge is operational. In one conversation the contractor jokes that the bridge is "strong enough for three MX-40s" (the RED army's heaviest tank).
9	10.2017–11.2017	OSINT	RED national media are reporting that senior RED politicians have put forward some new demands in order to restart the negotiation process. The reporting indicates a deadline for BLUE response of January 1, 2018, or the offer will be withdrawn.
			Local media in Hyde Park are reporting on everything but the military situation in the East Valley.
10	10.2017–11.2017	HUMINT	**SOURCE 045 (B-3):** General Mercant has moved his HQ staff to a villa in Gran Ben. Some of his staff were heard complaining not only about the move to Gran Ben but also that the loss of Christmas vacation has not helped with the officers' current marital issues. Sources providing bus services to Hyde Park have reported they have "all" been booked by the military from December 11 to 14, 2017.
			SOURCE 011 (D-2): RED planning surprise attack before Christmas on the West Valley frontline.

Guidance

1. Using the given channel tracker (see Table 15-1), identify abnormal congruences or incongruences.

2. List and discuss the merits of any deception hypotheses developed from the channel tracker.

3. Make a list of prioritized RFIs that could help confirm or deny any hypotheses developed.

EXERCISE 2: THE YUTA *GHOST*

Scenario

Since February 2017, the United Nations (UN) has been attempting to enforce an arms embargo on the country of Sladivista in order to stop the spiral of violence between the Sladivistian regime and several ethnic factions that live in the country. It has been difficult to enforce the embargo on land; the UN has relied primarily on neighboring states to enforce the embargo. In contrast, the UN has attempted to enforce the embargo at sea. However, many international criminal networks are ready to exploit every chance to make some money from weapons smuggling. And though both the rebels and the government are under the embargo, smuggling weapons by sea favors the Sladivistian regime and criminal networks with seafaring assets.

Situation

Intelligence reporting from the UN Southern Naval Command UNTF 91, charged with enforcing the arms embargo along the coast of Sladivista, suggests there will be an attempt by the international criminal organization YUTA to deliver a shipment of illegal weapons via mini-submarine on November 23, 2017. It is October 10, 2017. Your task group, UNTG 34, is responsible for intercepting the expected delivery. The challenge is that your resources cannot cover the whole of the coastal region at the same time, so it has been divided into three maritime patrol zones. However, you can cover only two of the zones at the same time. UNTG 34 has two medium-sized submarines available for patrol duty: the *UNS Gartner* and the *UNS Pike*.

YUTA has only one known mini-sub, but it is famous for its successful smuggling exploits; it has earned the appropriate call-sign *Ghost*. Furthermore, YUTA has two support ships available for the mini-sub: the *Shark* and the *Gamlin*. Either can be used to launch and recover the *Ghost*.

The actual coastline is also divided into areas of interest (AoIs) for UNTG 34 N2 (naval intelligence section) lead: They include Coast Zone Alpha with the main port of Bramaville; Coast Zone Bravo with the main port of Laurdal; and Coast Zone Charlie with the main port of Kipton. (See Figure 15-2.)

Task

As the UNTG J2, your section is responsible for providing an assessment to the commander as to which two maritime patrol zones she should place her two submarines on November 23, 2017, in order to interdict the *Ghost*. Your analysts have collated intelligence reporting and produced a channel tracker in order to identify possible deception indicators (see Table 15-2).

FIGURE 15-2 ■ YUTA *Ghost* Situation

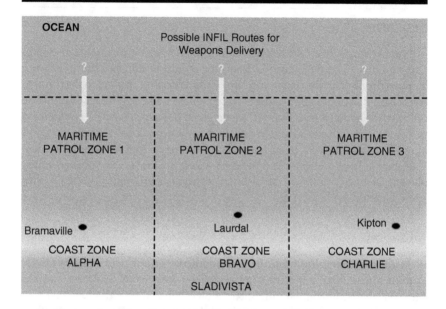

TABLE 15-2 ■ YUTA *Ghost* Channel Tracker

DTG	Channel	Story Coast Zone A (Bramaville)	Coast Zone B (Laurdal)	Coast Zone C (Kipton)
AUG 2017	HUMINT	**SOURCE 203 (B-1):** Two streams of reporting from the source indicate that local Bramaville authorities are running short of weapons and ammunition as the rebels have had several successes over the summer. They are actively looking for ways to get more weapons through the UN blockade.	**SOURCE 007 (A-2):** Unknown members of the Sladivista military met with John Tavish, the known head of maritime operations for YUTA on August 20, 2017, at a well-known Laurdal restaurant. **SOURCE 945 (F-6):** YUTA has	**SOURCE 556 (B-3):** Since the recent lull in fighting after July, Sladivistian military personnel in Kipton have been undergoing training on a new anti-tank missile system. Training is reportedly being conducted on virtual reality sets.

		SOURCE 011 (C-3): One of the known YUTA ships, the *Shark*, refueled several times in the harbor during the month, always between 2200 and 0200 hrs.	approximately twenty members living in Laurdal working for the local government as weapons instructors.	
			SOURCE 068 (B-2): Two Sladivistian army officers in Laurdal were overheard talking about the ammunition needing to last until November.	
AUG 2017	OSINT	The tightly controlled media continues its anti-UN messaging, and emphasizes the unfair treatment of UN-imposed sanctions on Sladivista.		
AUG 2017	MASINT	YUTA support ship *Shark* has made five entries into Zone 1 in August. The *Shark* used its active sonar and some hydrographic mapping equipment on all five visits. YUTA support ship *Gamlin* also made five entries into Zone 1 in August. It used its active sonar only, but it appeared to conduct a test of silent running equipment.	YUTA support ship *Shark* has made seven entries into Zone 2 in August. The *Shark* used its active sonar and some hydrographic mapping equipment on all seven visits. YUTA support ship *Gamlin* also made four entries into Zone 2 in August. It used	YUTA support ship *Shark* has made nine entries into Zone 3 in August. The *Shark* used its active sonar and some hydrographic mapping equipment on five of the nine visits. For three of the visits, it used only the hydrographic equipment. YUTA support ship *Gamlin* also

(Continued)

TABLE 15-2 ■ (Continued)

		Story		
DTG	Channel	Coast Zone A (Bramaville)	Coast Zone B (Laurdal)	Coast Zone C (Kipton)
			its active sonar all four times.	made two entries into Zone 3 in August. It used its active sonar both times.
AUG 2017	SIGINT	Diverse communications between Sladivistian officials and YUTA indicate a weapons delivery will be made to the coast on November 23, 2017, by the "most covert means available."		
AUG 2017	INTSUMs	**UNS Gartner:** Conducted six patrols in Zone 1 and had one possible contact with the *Ghost* around the edges of the coastal maritime zone. Moreover, observations of the *Shark* indicate it has an unusually large crew with several members rarely seen on deck. **UNS Pike:** Conducted eight patrols in Zone 1. Observed the *Gamlin* deliberately weaving through areas thick with fishing traps.	**UNS Gartner:** Conducted seven patrols in Zone 2. Nothing to report (NTR). **UNS Pike:** Conducted seven patrols in Zone 2. Observed the *Gamlin* deliberately weaving in and out between fishing traps. The same behavior observed in Zone 1.	**UNS Gartner:** Conducted eight patrols in Zone 3. On one occasion, the *Shark* appeared to be running courses to allow grid mapping of the seafloor with its hydrographic equipment in tow. **UNS Pike:** Conducted six patrols in Zone 3. NTR
SEPT 2017	HUMINT	**SOURCE 203 (B-1):** Preparations are being made for a new offensive	**SOURCE 007 (A-2):** YUTA Maritime Operations	**SOURCE 556 (B-3):** The Sladivistian army has recently

		against the rebels in Bramaville during December 2017. Discussions involve deployment of an anti-tank missile (ATM) system not yet owned or deployed by the Sladivistian military. **SOURCE 011 (C-3):** YUTA support ship *Shark* has been buying double its fuel capacity for several days now. When the harbor master asked about the constant need for the extra fuel, he was told in no uncertain terms to mind his own business.	Chief John Tavish has received a large bank deposit. He was told that the enormous sum, seven digits US, was only half of the final payment. The rest would be paid "by Xmas." **SOURCE 945 (F-6):** On November 23, YUTA plans to smuggle ATM systems to YUTA trainers in Laurdal by sea. John Tavish himself will be on the ship to bring the weapons ashore. **SOURCE 068 (B-2):** Several YUTA members in Laurdal were seen getting on buses late at night on September 26. They had their baggage with them.	established a new training site in Kipton with ranges that extend 2 km inland, and a variety of tank trails.
SEPT 2017	MASINT	YUTA support ship *Shark* has made eleven entries into Zone 1 in September. The	YUTA support ship *Shark* has made three entries into Zone 2 in	YUTA support ship Shark has made five entries into Zone 3 in September. The

(Continued)

TABLE 15-2 ■ (Continued)				
		Story		
DTG	**Channel**	**Coast Zone A (Bramaville)**	**Coast Zone B (Laurdal)**	**Coast Zone C (Kipton)**
		Shark used its active sonar and some hydrographic mapping equipment on all eleven visits. YUTA support ship *Gamlin* made seven entries into Zone 1 in August. It used its active sonar on all visits.	September. The *Shark* used its active sonar and some hydrographic mapping equipment on all three visits. YUTA support ship *Gamlin* made two entries into Zone 2 in September. It used its active sonar both times.	*Shark* did not use its active sonar; presumably only passive sonar was used.
SEPT 2017	OSINT	State media have continued to point out the unfairness of the embargo, noting that the rebels have landline supply routes from hostile neighboring countries that do not respect the UN embargo on weapons to the conflict zone.		
SEPT 2017	SIGINT	Diverse communications between Sladivistian officials and YUTA indicate the mini-sub *Ghost* will be used for a delivery of a new ATM system. A conversation between John Tavish and UKN YUTA member indicates the *Ghost* has problems with navigating around fishing grounds. Tavish states the "advantages might outweigh disadvantages." Increasing levels of YUTA background communications noise observed in coast around Laurdal and Kipton.		
SEPT 2017	INTSUMs	***UNS Gartner:*** Conducted five patrols in Zone 1. Encountered *Shark* on two occasions apparently	***UNS Gartner:*** Conducted six patrols in Zone 2. NTR. Encountered *Shark* and	***UNS Gartner:*** Conducted seven patrols in Zone 3. NTR.

| | | practicing maneuvers to flood its launch bay. The maneuver takes about thirty minutes. They were aware we were watching. No mini-sub was launched.

UNS Pike: Conducted seven patrols in Zone 1. Encountered the *Shark* on three occasions. On all three occasions the *Shark* immediately began a launch bay flood maneuver. No mini-sub was launched.

Encountered *Gamlin* on one occasion sitting abnormally low in the water after a fuel stop in Bramaville. | *Gamlin* entering Laurdal Harbor for refueling.

UNS Pike: Conducted six patrols in Zone 2. Conducted covert observation on the *Shark* on four occasions. It appears the hydrographic equipment is no longer on board. | **UNS Pike:** Conducted five patrols in Zone 3. NTR. |
| SEPT 2017 | IMINT | **In response to AUG RFI 00:** *What are relative densities of fishing traps/nets in the three coastal zones?* Coast Zone A has the highest density of fish traps and nets. Coast Zone B has the second highest density of fish traps and nets. Coast Zone C has the lowest density of fish traps and nets. | | |

Guidance

1. Using the given channel tracker (see Table 15-2), identify abnormal congruences or incongruences.

2. List and discuss the merits of any deception hypotheses developed from the channel tracker.

3. Make a list of prioritized RFIs that could help confirm or deny any hypotheses developed.

BIBLIOGRAPHY

Ackroyd, David, and Julia Silverton, dir. *Wartime Deception*. History Channel (television network), 2001. Video recording.

Bell, J. Bowyer. "Toward a Theory of Deception." *International Journal of Intelligence and Counterintelligence* 16, no. 2 (2003): 244–79.

Bell, J. Bowyer, and Barton Whaley. *Cheating and Deception*. New Brunswick, NJ: Transaction Publishers, 1991.

Bennett, M., and E. Waltz. *Counterdeception: Principles and Applications for National Security*. Norwood, MA: Artech House, 2007.

Breuer, W. B. *Hoodwinking Hitler: The Normandy Deception*. Westport, CT: Praeger Press, 1993.

Central Intelligence Agency. *A Tradecraft Primer: Structured Analytic Techniques for Improving Intelligence Analysis* 2, no. 2 (2005): 14–15.

Cline, Lawrence. *Pseudo Operations and Counterinsurgency: Lessons from Other Countries*. Carlisle, PA: Strategic Studies Institute, 2005, http://www.strategic studiesinstitute.army.mil/pubs/download.cfm?q=607.

Cohen, F. "A Framework for Deception," in *National Security Issues in Science, Law, and Technology*, ed. T. A. Johnson. Boca Raton, FL: CRC Press, 2007.

Cook, Nick. "War of Extremes." *Jane's Defense Weekly*, July 7, 1999.

Daniel, Donald C., and Katherine Herbig, eds. *Strategic Military Deception*. New York: Pergamon, 1982.

Dewar, Michael. *The Art of Military Deception in Warfare*, 1st ed. Newton Abbot, UK: David & Charles, 1989.

Dunnigan, James F., and Albert A. Nofi. *Victory and Deceit: Dirty Tricks at War*. New York: William Morrow, 1995.

Godson, Roy, and James J. Wirtz. "Strategic Denial and Deception." *International Journal of Intelligence and Counterintelligence* 13, no. 4 (2000): 424–36.

———, eds. *Strategic Denial and Deception: A Twenty-First Century Challenge*. New Brunswick, NJ: Transaction Publishers, 2002.

Gooch, John, and Amos Perlmutter, eds. *Military Deception and Strategic Surprise*. New York: Frank Cass, 1982.

Grant, Rebecca. "True Blue: Behind the Kosovo Numbers Game." *Air Force Magazine* 83, no. 8 (August 2000): 74–78.

Gray, Douglas F. "Hacker Group: The Future of War Is Information." *Insurgency on the Internet,* CNN, December 30, 1999, http://www.cnn.com/1999/TECH/computing/12/30/info.war.idg/index.html.

Handel, Michael I. *Military Deception in Peace and War.* Jerusalem: Magnes Press, Hebrew University, 1985.

Heuer, R. J. "Strategic Deception and Counterdeception: A Cognitive Process Approach." *International Studies Quarterly* 25, no. 2 (1981): 294–327.

Holt, Thaddeus. *The Deceivers: Allied Military Deception in the Second World War.* New York: Skyhorse Publishing, 2007.

Jajko, Walter. "A Critical Commentary on the Department of Defense Authorities for Information Operations." *Comparative Strategy* 21, no. 2 (Apr–Jun 2002): 107–15.

Joint Military Intelligence College Foundation. "Denial, Deception, and Counterdeception." Entire issue, *Defense Intelligence Journal* 15, no. 2 (2006).

Joint Staff. *JP 3-13.4: Military Deception.* Washington, DC: US Department of Defense, 2006.

Kay, Martin. "Denial and Deception: The Lessons of Iraq," in *U.S. Intelligence at the Crossroads: Agendas for Reform*, ed. Roy Godson, Ernest R. May, and Gary Schmitt (pp. 109–27). Washington, DC: Brassey's, 1995.

Larsen, Henry S., III. *Operational Deception: U.S. Joint Doctrine and the Persian Gulf War* (monograph). Fort Leavenworth, KS: School of Advanced Military Studies, 1995.

Lasley, Jennifer. *Denial and Deception: A Serious Threat to Information Superiority?* Washington, DC: National War College, National Defense University, April 2000, http://www.ndu.edu/library/n2/n005605.pdf.

Latimer, Jon. *Deception in War.* Woodstock, NY: Overlook Press, 2001.

Marine Corps Intelligence Activity. *Information Operations/Information Warfare Reference Handbook* (MCIA-2700-001-03). Quantico, VA: Author, November 2002.

Mitnick, K. *The Art of Deception.* New York: Wiley, 2002.

Moore, D. T., and W. N. Reynolds. "So Many Ways to Lie: Complexity of Denial and Deception." *Defense Intelligence Journal* 15, no. 2 (2006): 95–116.

Perry, James. "Operation Allied Force: The View from Beijing." *Air & Space Chronicles* 22 (October 2000).

Plante, Chris, and Charles Bierbauer. "Pentagon's Supply of Favorite Weapons May Be Dwindling." *Focus on Kosovo.* CNN, March 20, 1999, http://www.cnn.com/US/9903/30/kosovo.pentagon/index.html.

Quinn, John T. *U.S. Marines in the Persian Gulf, 1990–1991. Marine Communications in Desert Shield and Desert Storm.* History and Museums Division, Headquarters, US Marine Corps. Washington, DC: US Government Printing Office, 1996.

Rowe, N. C. "Counterplanning Deceptions to Foil Cyber-Attack Plans." *Proceedings of the 2003 Workshop on Information Assurance.* West Point, NY.

Rowe, N. C., and H. C. Goh. "Thwarting Cyber-Attack Reconnaissance with Inconsistency and Deception." *Proceedings of the 2007 Workshop on Information Assurance.* West Point, NY.

Tiernan, R. K. "Hiding in Plain Sight." *Defense Intelligence Journal* 15, no. 2 (2006): 141–52.

Whaley, Barton. *Stratagem: Deception and Surprise in War.* Norwood, MA: Artech House, 2007.

————. "Toward a General Theory of Deception," in *Military Deception and Strategic Surprise,* ed. A. Perlmutter and J. Gooch (pp. 178–92). London: Frank Cass, 1982.

Yuill, J., D. Denning, and F. Feer. "Using Deception to Hide Things from Hackers: Processes, Principles, and Techniques." *Journal of Information Warfare* 5, no. 3 (2006): 26–40.

INDEX

Printed in the USA
CPSIA information can be obtained
at www.ICGtesting.com
JSHW011521111223
53420JS00011B/88

9 781506 375236